DATE DUE			

AN ACTOR'S WORKBOOK

An Actor's Workbook

**STANLEY
KAHAN**

California State College
at Long Beach

Harcourt, Brace & World, Inc.
New York / Chicago / San Francisco / Atlanta

Cover photograph by Jeff Smith

Library of Congress Catalog Card Number: 67-18542

Printed in the United States of America

For my father

PREFACE

*A*N ACTOR'S WORKBOOK is intended as a working source for the actor or director who wants a large collection of materials to use with his particular approach to acting. Many acting texts have been written, advocating a variety of approaches and—to use the word in its general sense—methods. My own text, *Introduction to Acting*, presents a generally eclectic approach. This workbook, however, advances no acting theory or technique; it is offered with the conviction that all such theories and techniques, to be useful, require materials to put them into practice. It may therefore be used with—or without—any acting textbook.

The book has two parts: exercises and scenes. The first, and much shorter, part contains physical exercises, improvisations, and vocal exercises, drawn from outside dramatic literature. These are provided to help the actor in the development of his basic expressive mechanisms: his body and his voice. The second part contains fifty scenes from successful and vital plays. For convenience, it is divided into four sections: "Serious Scenes," ranging from tragedy to melodrama and straight drama; "Comedy Scenes," including both sharp verbal wit and the broad physical aspects of farce; "Modern Verse Drama," a distinct and challenging vehicle for the actor; and "Scenes from Shakespeare," presenting matters of style not found in the other sections.

The scenes were chosen for variety in theme and style, and also for the opportunities they offer to different combinations of actors; they range from two-character dialogues to ensemble scenes. Equally important, however, is the quality of the material: no scene was included merely because it had the required number of characters or demonstrated a certain style. Each scene is a key scene from a memorable play.

The format of the book itself is intended to aid the actor as he works. The plastic comb binding allows the pages to lie flat or to be turned under; the margins give space for blocking notes, stage business, and interpretive comments. Printed aids at the end of each scene include a "Reference Key to Anthologies," which lists available sources of the complete play; "Further Reading," a selected reading list of critical and biographical materials on the play and its author; and "Recorded Performances," which lists selected recordings of the play.

A few words on these aids are in order. No dramatic scene can be effectively performed out of context; only in its relationship to the entire play does it assume its proper meaning. Therefore, while the headnote to each scene in the book briefly describes the situation, it is strongly recommended that the actor familiarize himself with the complete play before preparing the scene. The critical materials listed will further help the actor to understand the background of the play and the playwright's viewpoints. The recordings provide the actor with examples of the norm of professional competence in today's theatre. They should not, however, be used merely as models for imitation. While it is true that in every art form the apprentice learns from the established artist, the actor must understand that a recorded performance indicates only a single approach to a role and that he must create an interpretation consistent with his own attitudes and resources.

My reliance on the good judgment and patience of my wife Charlene during the preparation of the manuscript is a matter of private debt and public acknowledgment, for reasons of both fairness and domestic tranquility. A great debt is owed to my students, who have made me aware of the need to provide these materials. It is my earnest wish that the frayed, pencil-marked, and worn pages of this book will be the ultimate proof of its value for each actor.

S. K.

Long Beach, California

CONTENTS

ix

Part 1

EXERCISES

one _____

PHYSICAL EXERCISES

Pantomimes for developing the physical mechanism

Each of the following pantomimes requires the actor to dramatize specific actions, using various parts of his body. In some cases he will be required to deal with very detailed bits of stage business; in others he will utilize basic kinesthetic values. Certain pantomimes also require the use of imagination on the part of the actor. While some pantomimes are clearly defined, the actor needs to add to others his own pantomimic detail to complete the exercise. Exercise 6 is an example of the second type. Although the exercise seems to describe the action required in substantial detail, the alert actor will also ask himself: "How hungry am I?" and "How early in the morning is it and how tired am I?" Clearly, the manner in which these questions are answered will directly affect the pantomimic dramatization.

The actor must pay attention to all the details of these pantomimes to avoid the most common errors, such as confusing the sizes, weights, and locations of properties during the dramatization. The size, shape, texture, and temperature of these imaginary properties must be realized and *projected*. Carefully done, these exercises will help to develop the actor's physical expressiveness.

1. You cut two articles out of a large bound volume of newspapers and tape them into a large scrapbook. After finishing the job, you

notice that you have put the clippings on the wrong page and must remove them from the scrapbook without damaging them.

2. You are walking down the street and notice a ten-dollar bill that has fallen down a grate. You try to get the bill, although the grating is too small to admit your arm and the grate cannot be removed.

3. You come to a cave in which you have hidden a large amount of money. The entrance to the cave is blocked by a large boulder. You try to get into the cave.

4. You have found a large locked trunk, presumably filled with jewels; you must open the trunk. The only available tool is a screwdriver.

5. You are in a storage room looking for a lost parcel. You look throughout the room, lifting many large and heavy boxes, until you find the proper parcel.

6. You prepare a breakfast that includes scrambled eggs, toast and jam, and fresh coffee. Begin by taking out all the utensils and then prepare the food. You burn the toast.

7. You are in the boiler room of a large ship, trying to lower the steam pressure by turning a valve that is very stiff. The metal is becoming hotter and hotter.

8. You have been in a mine disaster. You try singlehandedly to pull away the debris (including rocks and timbers) covering a fellow miner.

9. You cross a narrow plank laid between the ledges of two buildings. The plank is about twenty feet long and six inches wide. The buildings are ten stories high, and the day is windy.

10. You are pulling the rope attached to a heavy bell in the belfry of a church.

11. You try to put on a rubberized skin-diving suit that is too small for you.

12. You try to put diapers on a baby who will not lie still but continues to roll over.

13. You try to cross an ice-skating rink without wearing skates.

14. You carry a large bucket completely filled with water across the stage, being careful not to spill any of the water.

15. You wrap a large, heavy package with wrapping paper and rope.

16. You iron a large shirt on an ironing board. You periodically test the iron to see if it is still hot.

17. You try to take a photograph of the profile of a baby who is crawling around on a lawn.

18. You have lost a cuff link (or earring) and crawl about a room, looking and reaching under all the furniture, trying to find it.

19. You wash and dry several dishes, pots, and pans and put them away in their proper places.

20. You find an exceedingly heavy knapsack, put it on and move across the stage, then take it off.

21. You are playing an exciting tennis match. You serve and play several points.

22. You chop down a medium-sized tree with an axe.

23. You have left your hat on a table on which there are several other hats, identical in style but of different sizes. You try on each hat until you find the right one.

24. You move along a very narrow ledge on the face of a cliff. The ledge is strewn with small rocks. Below the ledge is a drop of several hundred feet.

25. You are a custom tailor fitting a client for a dress suit.

26. You completely set a table for six, beginning with the tablecloth and adding napkins, flatware, dishes, water glasses, and centerpiece.

27. You use a hammer and several nails as you nail on the slats of a large crate. You must use a variety of sizes of nails, some too small, some too large to do the job properly.

28. During the hammering of the nails (see Exercise 27 above), you smash your thumb. You try to put a bandage on the wounded finger, using only one hand to manipulate the dressing.

29. You carry an awkward load of books a considerable distance from one bookcase to another. As you near your destination, the books begin to slip out of your grasp.

30. You try to type a letter on a typewriter on which the ribbon does not move. Consequently, you must make frequent adjustments, occasionally quite messy.

31. You shovel snow from a walkway that is exceedingly slippery.

32. You carve a turkey at a Thanksgiving dinner and serve the turkey to several guests. (Try this exercise twice, once with a sharp knife and once with a dull knife.)

33. You mow a lawn cluttered with small stones that hamper proper mowing.

34. You lay a fire in a fireplace, using all the necessary materials, including paper, kindling, logs, and starter fluid. You then light the fire and wait to make sure it is burning properly.

35. You are walking in the street when it suddenly begins to rain. You open your umbrella, and the wind blows it into an inverted shape. Fighting the wind and rain, you try several times to correct the shape of the umbrella but it is repeatedly blown out of shape. Finally it regains its shape, and you proceed on your way.

two _____

IMPROVISATIONS

Improvisations for one actor

Improvisation is an excellent test of the actor's creative imagination. Although the improvisations in this section are designed for one actor only, they contain all the necessary elements for a complete dramatic situation. The effectiveness and richness of the improvisation depends entirely on the actor himself.

For each improvisation the actor should choose one action, one character, and one location from the following lists. He may take the description of the action quite literally and add nothing of his own. Or he may choose to use the description as a basic scenario, containing only the bare bones of the action, and add his own creative gifts and imagination to the scene, much as the *commedia dell'arte* performer of the past improvised richly on a few traditional formulas.

Well over one thousand improvisations are possible by combining the items in the lists. In choosing an action, the actor must realize that within the context of that action many variables are present. It should be clear that different characters will react differently to the same stimulus. In addition, the environment in which a character operates and the action takes place may profoundly alter not only specific details, but the general texture and execution of the entire improvisation.

At first the actor may find the three elements of the improvisation too generalized. They may even seem to follow certain stereotypes. This, however, is to be expected from this type of improvisation. Yet, after some reflection, the actor will realize that not all bankers are the same, nor does every librarian resemble every other librarian. Within the context of the limited descriptions, the actor must add those elements of individuality that begin to bring a character and a scene to life. With this point of view, he will find that the number of improvisations is infinite.

Actions:

1. You are determined to secure evidence against a person who you believe has murdered your brother. You enter the premises to plant a tape recorder in an appropriate place. You examine the location carefully and then test the machine. As you are installing the device, you hear someone entering the premises. You hide, and after a short time the person leaves without seeing you. After the device has been properly planted, you leave.

2. You enter the premises to keep an appointment. After waiting briefly, you detect smoke and note that a short circuit (or similar mishap) has caused a fire to break out. Unable to get any help and due to the rapid spread of the fire, you are forced to put out the substantial blaze alone. After resting for a short time, you leave.

3. You enter the premises on a business call and find a one-year-old child alone, unhappy and wet. The child has his own ideas about what he wants to do. You try to quiet the child and keep him happy, as there is no one else in the vicinity. After a few minutes a telephone (or radiophone) call informs you that the child's parents are nearby and you are asked to take the child to them. You react to the request as you see fit.

4. You enter the premises intending to keep an appointment and sit in a chair. After starting to read a magazine or newspaper, you hear a strange sound and look up. Between you and the door is a large poisonous snake. You then react as your chosen character would under the circumstances.

5. You enter the premises to keep an appointment. You notice that the room is well stocked with fine old liqueurs and brandies. After some internal debating (the amount depending on the character you have chosen), you begin to sample the products and become progressively drunker. You finally react to your delayed appointment as dictated by your character and the number of samples tasted.

6. You enter the premises to keep an appointment with a friend you have not seen in several years. On a table you find a collection of

materials, such as letters and photographs, which remind you of your old friendship. You examine the mementoes. After a while a phone rings (telephone or radiophone). On answering it, you learn that your friend has been accidentally killed on his way to meet you. You react in character.

7. You enter the premises to keep an appointment. You look at your watch and realize you are an hour early. You decide to wait. While waiting, you notice a pile of papers and photographs on a table. You examine them and discover that they are documents and letters purporting to prove you guilty of murder. You then react and take whatever action is suitable to the character.

Characters: Male

1. An army colonel (*age:* mid-fifties)
2. A banker (*age:* mid-forties)
3. A hot-rod enthusiast (*age:* early twenties)
4. A butler (*age:* mid-forties)
5. A French fashion designer (*age:* mid-thirties)
6. An international playboy (*age:* your choice)
7. A medical missionary (*age:* mid-fifties)
8. A taxi driver (*age:* mid-forties)
9. A retired clerk (*age:* mid-eighties)
10. A professional pool shark (*age:* mid-twenties)
11. A European aristocrat (*age:* forty)
12. A young boy (*age:* twelve)
13. An escaped convict (*age:* thirty)
14. A ballet dancer (*age:* thirty-five)
15. A physical culture instructor (*age:* twenty-five)
16. An arthritic white-collar worker (*age:* mid-fifties)
17. A college student (*age:* nineteen)

Characters: Female

1. A maid (*age:* mid-forties)
2. A ballet dancer (*age:* mid-thirties)

3. A young girl (*age:* twelve)
4. A nearly blind seamstress (*age:* mid-fifties)
5. A European aristocrat (*age:* mid-forties)
6. An international film star (*age:* twenty-nine)
7. A college student (*age:* nineteen)
8. A registered nurse (*age:* mid-thirties)
9. A housewife (*age:* mid-forties)
10. A librarian (*age:* mid-thirties)
11. A burlesque dancer (*age:* thirty)
12. A fashion model (*age:* mid-twenties)
13. An arthritic clerk (*age:* mid-fifties)
14. A professional wrestler (*age:* mid-thirties)
15. A waitress (*age:* mid-twenties)
16. A retired white-collar worker (*age:* mid-eighties)
17. A business executive (*age:* thirty-five)

Locations:

1. The small cabin of a ship at sea during a heavy storm.
2. A business office late at night.
3. A farmhouse.
4. A dirty shack near an old mine in the mountains.
5. A small grocery store in a New England village.
6. A decrepit thatched hut in central Africa.
7. The deserted stage of an old theatre.
8. The kitchen of a famous restaurant.
9. The living room of a palatial mansion.
10. A stable.

Improvisations for two or more characters

The following improvisations make more complicated demands on the actor than did those for one character. The actor must now take into account the elements of reaction and interplay; he must also be prepared to maintain his character and intentions as actions unfold that are not completely under his control. These exercises are intended to make the actor determine the *reason* his character is operating in the scene and how the character wishes to see the problem resolved.

Each of the improvisations is a springboard for a large number of different actions. Let us examine the first improvisation. "A has come in response to an ad, placed in the newspaper by B, advertising a dog for sale." On the surface there seems to be little dramatic conflict suggested. However, on closer study we find that there are several possible purposes each character might have for participating in this situation.

It is possible that:

A wants a dog as a pet for a small child.

A wants a good watchdog.

A wants to make the acquaintance of the person selling the dog.

A wants a dog to give to someone else as a gift.

It is also possible that:

B wants to get rid of the dog at any price because it is vicious.

B loves the dog but is now impoverished and cannot afford to keep it.

B does not love the dog and needs a good deal of money.

B hopes to find a good home for the dog because B is leaving the country.

B is lonely and interested in making the acquaintance of anyone who might answer the ad.

Several other possibilities should also come to mind.

As each actor in turn chooses his central purpose and settles on specific character traits, the improvisation takes on a meaningful dramatic potential. It is also worth noting that one character in the improvisation need *not* know the purpose of the other character.

The possible purposes and motivations of the characters in each improvisation should be analyzed and chosen before the improvisation is played. The improvisations are deliberately made flexible enough to permit this choice by the actors.

1. A has come in response to an ad, placed in the newspaper by B, advertising a dog for sale.

2. A and B arrive at a bargain counter at the same moment. Each wants to buy the last remaining item on sale. C, who is the shop manager, is behind the counter at the time.

3. A and B are walking in opposite directions along the sidewalk. In the middle of the street is a twenty-dollar bill.

4. A is answering an advertisement by B requesting an experienced tutor for a sweet child.

5. A is applying for a position in a theatre repertory company managed by B.

6. A and B are dining at the same table in a restaurant. When C, the waiter, comes with the bills, A looks in his pocket and reports that his wallet is missing.

7. A and B are soldiers in a wartime army. They report to C, their commanding officer, who must send one soldier on a mission which he knows will probably cause the soldier's death.

8. A and B arrive at the home of C at the same time in response to an ad that C wishes to buy a two-year-old used Volkswagen automobile.

9. Student A is called into the office of teacher B who announces that A's term paper is identical to another paper turned in that semester.

10. A and B are former acquaintances in school. Now A is impoverished, B successful and wealthy. A calls on B in his office to request a loan.

three _____

VOCAL EXERCISES

Even as the actor must develop his physical mechanism in order to make it flexible and able to project the greatest possible range of physical expressiveness, so too must he make his voice adequate to the demands he will place on it in any given role. The purpose of the following selections is to provide practical exercises that will help develop a wide range of vocal expressiveness. The first group of exercises contains articulation problems frequently found in certain types of plays. The second group makes demands on a greater range of vocal resources, including variety, phrasing, emphasis, and dramatic pointing. Although many of the selections are not chosen from dramatic literature, all of them require the fullest competence in stage speech, if the actor is to realize their dramatic potential.

Articulation

Each of the following selections contains pitfalls for the actor with sloppy speech. Most of them are patter songs from the operettas of Gilbert and Sullivan. They require not only precise articulation, but facility in delivery and careful pointing. Merely getting through the selection without error should not be the goal of the actor here: *scintillating and seemingly effortless delivery* is necessary for the successful presentation of these exercises.

The Sorcerer's Song

W. S. GILBERT
The Sorcerer

Oh! my name is John Wellington Wells,
I'm a dealer in magic and spells,
    In blessings and curses
    And ever-filled purses,
In prophecies, witches, and knells.

If you want a proud foe to "make tracks"—
If you'd melt a rich uncle in wax—
    You've but to look in
    On our resident Djinn,
Number seventy, Simmery Axe!

We've a first-class assortment of magic;
    And for raising a posthumous shade
With effects that are comic or tragic,
    There's no cheaper house in the trade.
Love-philtre—we've quantities of it;
    And for knowledge if any one burns,
We keep an extremely small prophet, a prophet
    Who brings us unbounded returns:

        For he can prophesy
        With a wink *of* his eye,
        Peep with security
        Into futurity,
        Sum up your history,
        Clear up a mystery,
        Humour proclivity
        For a nativity—for a nativity;
        With mirrors so magical,
        Tetrapods tragical,
        Bogies spectacular,
        Answers oracular,
        Facts astronomical,
        Solemn or comical,
        And, if you want it, he
        Makes a reduction on taking a quantity!

Oh! If any one anything lacks,
He'll find it all ready in stacks,
If he'll only look in
On the resident Djinn,
Number seventy, Simmery Axe!

He can raise you hosts
Of ghosts,
And that without reflectors;
And creepy things
With wings,
And gaunt and grisly spectres.
He can fill you crowds
Of shrouds,
And horrify you vastly;
He can rack your brains
With chains,
And gibberings grim and ghastly!

Then, if you plan it, he
Changes organity,
With an urbanity,
Full of Satanity,
Vexes humanity
With an inanity
Fatal to vanity—
Driving your foes to the verge of insanity!

Barring tautology,
In demonology,
'Lectro-biology,
Mystic nosology,
Spirit philology,
High-class astrology,
Such is his knowledge, he
Isn't the man to require an apology!

Oh! my name is John Wellington Wells,
I'm a dealer in magic and spells,
In blessings and curses
And ever-filled purses,
In prophecies, witches, and knells.

If any one anything lacks,
He'll find it all ready in stacks,
   If he'll only look in
    On the resident Djinn,
Number seventy, Simmery Axe!

The Major-General's Song _____

W. S. GILBERT
The Pirates of Penzance

I am the very model of a modern Major-General,
I've information vegetable, animal, and mineral,
I know the kings of England, and I quote the fights historical,
From Marathon to Waterloo, in order categorical;
I'm very well acquainted too with matters mathematical,
I understand equations, both the simple and quadratical,
About binomial theorem I'm teeming with a lot o' news—
With many cheerful facts about the square of the hypotenuse.
I'm very good at integral and differential calculus,
I know the scientific names of beings animalculous;
In short, in matters vegetable, animal, and mineral,
I am the very model of a modern Major-General.

I know our mythic history, King Arthur's and Sir Caradoc's,
I answer hard acrostics, I've a pretty taste for paradox,
I quote in elegiacs all the crimes of Heliogabalus,
In conics I can floor peculiarities parabolous.
I can tell undoubted Raphaels from Gerard Dows and Zoffanies,
I know the croaking chorus from the *Frogs* of Aristophanes,
Then I can hum a fugue of which I've heard the music's din afore,

And whistle all the airs from that infernal nonsense *Pinafore*.
Then I can write a washing bill in Babylonic cuneiform,
And tell you every detail of Caractacus's uniform;
In short, in matters vegetable, animal, and mineral,
I am the very model of a modern Major-General.

In fact, when I know what is meant by "mamelon" and "ravelin,"
When I can tell at sight a chassepôt rifle from a javelin,
When such affairs as sorties and surprises I'm more wary at,
And when I know precisely what is meant by "commissariat,"
When I have learnt what progress has been made in modern gunnery,
When I know more of tactics than a novice in a nunnery:
In short, when I've a smattering of elemental strategy,
You'll say a better Major-Gener*al* has never *sat* a gee—
For my military knowledge, though I'm plucky and adventury,
Has only been brought down to the beginning of the century;
But still in matters vegetable, animal, and mineral,
I am the very model of a modern Major-General.

The Lord Chancellor's Nightmare ———————

W. S. GILBERT
Iolanthe

When you're lying awake with a dismal headache, and repose is tabooed
    by anxiety,
I conceive you may use any language you choose to indulge in without
    impropriety;
For your brain is on fire—the bedclothes conspire of usual slumber to
    plunder you:
First your counterpane goes and uncovers your toes, and your sheet slips
    demurely from under you;

Then the blanketing tickles—you feel like mixed pickles, so terribly sharp
is the pricking,
And you're hot and you're cross, and you tumble and toss till there's
nothing 'twixt you and the ticking;
Then your bedclothes all creep to the floor in a heap, and you pick 'em
all up in a tangle,
Next your pillow resigns and politely declines to remain at its usual angle.
Well, you get some repose in the form of a doze, with hot eyeballs and
head ever aching,
But your slumbering teems with such horrible dreams that you'd very
much better be waking;
For you dream you are crossing the Channel, and tossing about in a
steamer from Harwich—
Which is something between a large bathing machine and a very small
second-class carriage—
And you're giving a treat (penny ice and cold meat) to a party of friends
and relations—
They're a ravenous horde—and they all came on board at Sloan Square
and South Kensington Stations.
And bound on that journey you find your attorney (who started that
morning from Devon);
He's a bit undersized, and you don't feel surprised when he tells you
he's only eleven.
Well, you're driving like mad with this singular lad (by the by, the ship's
now a four-wheeler),
And you're playing round games, and he calls you bad names when you
tell him that "ties pay the dealer";
But this you can't stand, so you throw up your hand, and you find you're
as cold as an icicle,
In your shirt and your socks (the black silk with gold clocks), crossing
Salisbury Plain on a bicycle:
And he and the crew are on bicycles too—which they've somehow or
other invested in—
And he's telling the tars all the particulars of a company he's interested
in—
It's a scheme of devices, to get at low prices all goods from cough
mixtures to cables
(Which tickled the sailors), by treating retailers as though they were all
vegetables—
You get a good spadesman to plant a small tradesman (first take off his
boots with a boot-tree),
And his legs will take root, and his fingers will shoot, and they'll blossom
and bud like a fruit-tree—

From the greengrocer tree you get grapes and green pea, cauliflower, pineapple, and cranberries,
While the pastrycook plant cherry brandy will grant, apple puffs, and three-corners, and Banburys—
The shares are a penny, and ever so many are taken by Rothschild and Baring,
And just as a few are allotted to you, you awake with a shudder despairing—
You're a regular wreck, with a crick in your neck; and no wonder you snore for your head's on the floor, and you're needles and pins from your soles to your shins; and your flesh is a-creep, and your left leg's asleep; and you've cramps in your toes, and a fly on your nose, and some fluff in your lung, and a feverish tongue, and a thirst that's intense, and a general sense that you haven't been sleeping in clover;
But the darkness has passed, and it's daylight at last, and the night has been long—ditto, ditto, my song—and thank Goodness they're both of them over!

Rules and Regulations ────────────────────

Lewis Carroll

A *short* direction
To avoid dejection,
By variations
In occupations,
And prolongation
Of relaxation,
And combinations

Of recreations,
And disputation
On the state of the nation
In adaptation
To your station,
By invitations
To friends and relations,
By evitation
Of amputation,
By permutation
In conversation,
And deep reflection
You'll avoid dejection.

Learn well your grammar,
And never stammer,
Write well and neatly,
And sing most sweetly,
Be enterprising,
Love early rising,
Go walk of six miles,
Have ready quick smiles,
With lightsome laughter,
Soft flowing after.
Drink tea, not coffee;
Never eat toffy.
Eat bread with butter.
Once more, don't stutter.
Don't waste your money,
Abstain from honey.
Shut doors behind you,
(Don't slam them, mind you.)
Drink beer, not porter.
Don't enter the water
Till to swim you are able.
Sit close to the table.
Take care of a candle.
Shut a door by the handle,
Don't push with your shoulder
Until you are older.
Lose not a button.
Refuse cold mutton.

Starve your canaries.
Believe in fairies.
If you are able,
Don't have a stable
With any mangers.
Be rude to strangers.

Moral: Behave.

Giuseppe's Song

W. S. GILBERT
The Gondoliers

Rising early in the morning,
    We proceed to light the fire,
Then our Majesty adorning
    In its workaday attire,
        We embark without delay
        On the duties of the day.

First, we polish off some batches
Of political dispatches,
    And foreign politicians circumvent:
Then, if business isn't heavy,
We may hold a Royal *levée,*
    Or ratify some Acts of Parliament.
Then we probably review the household troops—
With the usual "Shalloo humps!" and "Shalloo hoops!"
Or receive with ceremonial and state

An interesting Eastern potentate.
    After that we generally
    Go and dress our private *valet*—
(It's a rather nervous duty—he's a touchy little man)—
    Write some letters literary
    For our private secretary—
He is shaky in his spelling, so we help him if we can.
    Then, in view of cravings inner,
    We go down and order dinner;
Then we polish the Regalia and the Coronation Plate—
    Spend an hour in titivating
    All our Gentlemen-in-Waiting;
Or we run on little errands for the Ministers of State.

    Oh, philosophers may sing
    Of the troubles of a King;
Yet the duties are delightful, and the privileges great;
    But the privilege and pleasure
    That we treasure beyond measure
Is to run on little errands for the Ministers of State.

After luncheon (making merry
On a bun and glass of sherry),
    If we've nothing in particular to do,
We may make a Proclamation,
Or receive a deputation—
    Then we possibly create a Peer or two.

    Oh, philosophers may sing
    Of the troubles of a King,
But of pleasures there are many and of worries there are none;
    And the culminating pleasure
    That we treasure beyond measure
Is the gratifying feeling that our duty has been done!

Then we help a fellow-creature on his path
With the Garter or the Thistle or the Bath
Or we dress and toddle off in semi-state
To a festival, a function, or a *fête*.
    Then we go and stand as sentry
    At the Palace (private entry),
Marching hither, marching thither, up and down and to and fro,

While the warrior on duty
Goes in search of beer and beauty
(And it generally happens that he hasn't far to go).
He relieves us, if he's able,
Just in time to lay the table,
Then we dine and serve the coffee, and at half-past twelve or one,
With a pleasure that's emphatic,
We retire to our attic
With the gratifying feeling that our duty has been done!

Point's Song

W. S. GILBERT
The Yeomen of the Guard

Oh! a private buffoon is a light-hearted loon,
If you listen to popular rumour;
From the morn to the night he's so joyous and bright,
And he bubbles with wit and good humour!
He's so quaint and so terse, both in prose and in verse;
Yet though people forgive his transgression,
There are one or two rules that all family fools
Must observe, if they love their profession.

There are one or two rules,
Half a dozen, may be,
That all family fools,
Of whatever degree,
Must observe, if they love their profession.

If you wish to succeed as a jester, you'll need
To consider each person's auricular:

What is all right for B would quite scandalise C
    (For C is so very particular);
And D may be dull, and E's very thick skull
    Is as empty of brains as a ladle;
While F is F sharp, and will cry with a carp
    That he's known your best joke from his cradle!

    When your humour they flout,
        You can't yet yourself go;
    And it *does* put you out
        When a person says, "Oh,
    I have known that old joke from my cradle!"

If your master is surly, from getting up early
    (And tempers are short in the morning),
An inopportune joke is enough to provoke
    Him to give you, at once, a month's warning.
Then if you refrain, he is at you again,
    For he likes to get value for money;
He'll ask then and there, with an insolent stare,
    "If you know that you're paid to be funny?"

    It adds to the tasks
        Of a merryman's place
    When your principal asks,
        With a scowl on his face,
    If you know that you're paid to be funny?

Comes a Bishop, maybe, or a solemn D.D.—
    Oh, beware of his anger provoking!
Better not pull his hair—don't stick pins in his chair;
    He don't understand practical joking.
If the jests that you crack have an orthodox smack,
    You may get a bland smile from these sages;
But should they, by chance, be imported from France,
    Half-a-crown is stopped out of your wages!

    It's a general rule,
        Though your zeal it may quench,
    If the family fool
        Tells a joke that's too French,
    Half-a-crown is stopped out of his wages!

Though your head it may rack with a bilious attack,
　　And your senses with toothache you're losing,
Don't be mopy and flat—they don't fine you for that,
　　If you're properly quaint and amusing!
Though your wife ran away with a soldier that day,
　　And took with her your trifle of money;
Bless your heart, they don't mind—they're exceedingly kind—
　　They don't blame you—as long as you're funny!

　　　　It's a comfort to feel,
　　　　　　If your partner should flit,
　　　　Though *you* suffer a deal,
　　　　　　They don't mind it a bit—
　　　　They don't blame you—so long as you're funny!

King Gama's Song

W. S. Gilbert
Princess Ida

If you give me your attention, I will tell you what I am:
I'm a genuine philanthropist—all other kinds are sham.
Each little fault of temper and each social defect
In my erring fellow-creatures I endeavour to correct.
To all their little weaknesses I open people's eyes;
And little plans to snub the self-sufficient I devise;
I love my fellow-creatures—I do all the good I can—
Yet everybody says I'm such a disagreeable man!
　　　　And I can't think why!

To compliments inflated I've a withering reply;
And vanity I always do my best to mortify;

A charitable action I can skilfully dissect;
And interested motives I'm delighted to detect;
I know everybody's income and what everybody earns;
And I carefully compare it with the income tax returns;
But to benefit humanity however much I plan,
Yet everybody says I'm such a disagreeable man!
   And I can't think why!

I'm sure I'm no ascetic; I'm as pleasant as can be;
You'll always find me ready with a crushing repartee,
I've an irritating chuckle, I've a celebrated sneer,
I've an entertaining snigger, I've a fascinating leer.
To everybody's prejudice I know a thing or two;
I can tell a woman's age in half a minute—and I do.
But although I try to make myself as pleasant as I can,
Yet everybody says I am a disagreeable man!
   And I can't think why!

The Colonel's Song

W. S. GILBERT
Patience

If you want a receipt for that popular mystery,
  Known to the world as a Heavy Dragoon,
Take all the remarkable people in history,
  Rattle them off to a popular tune.
The pluck of Lord Nelson on board of the *Victory*—
  Genius of Bismarck devising a plan—
The humour of Fielding (which sounds contradictory)—
  Coolness of Paget about to trepan—

The science of Jullien, the eminent musico—
 Wit of Macaulay, who wrote of Queen Anne—
The pathos of Paddy, as rendered by Boucicault—
 Style of the Bishop of Sodor and Man—
The dash of a D'Orsay, divested of quackery—
Narrative powers of Dickens and Thackeray—
Victor Emmanuel—peak-haunting Peveril—
Thomas Aquinas, and Doctor Sacheverell—
 Tupper and Tennyson—Daniel Defoe—
 Anthony Trollope and Mr. Guizot!
  Take of these elements all that is fusible,
  Melt them all down in a pipkin or crucible,
  Set them to simmer and take off the scum,
  And a Heavy Dragoon is the residuum!

If you want a receipt for this soldier-like paragon,
 Get at the wealth of the Czar (if you can)—
The family pride of a Spaniard from Aragon—
 Force of Mephisto pronouncing a ban—
A smack of Lord Waterford, reckless and rollicky—
 Swagger of Roderick, heading his clan—
The keen penetration of Paddington Pollaky—
 Grace of an Odalisque on a divan—
The genius strategic of Caesar or Hannibal—
Skill of Sir Garnet in thrashing a cannibal—
Flavour of Hamlet—the Stranger, a touch of him—
Little of Manfred (but not very much of him)—
 Beadle of Burlington—Richardson's show—
 Mr. Micawber and Madame Tussaud!
  Take of these elements all that is fusible,
  Melt them all down in a pipkin or crucible,
  Set them to simmer and take off the scum,
  And a Heavy Dragoon is the residuum!

The Duke of Plaza-Toro

W. S. GILBERT
The Gondoliers

In enterprise of martial kind,
When there was any fighting,
He led his regiment from behind—
He found it less exciting.
But when away his regiment ran,
His place was at the fore, O—
That celebrated,
Cultivated,
Underrated
Nobleman,
The Duke of Plaza-Toro!

In the first and foremost flight, ha, ha!
You always found that knight, ha, ha!
That celebrated,
Cultivated,
Underrated
Nobleman,
The Duke of Plaza-Toro!

When, to evade Destruction's hand,
To hide they all proceeded,
No soldier in that gallant band
Hid half as well as he did.
He lay concealed throughout the war,
And so preserved his gore, O!
That unaffected,
Undetected,
Well-connected
Warrior,
The Duke of Plaza-Toro!

In every doughty deed, ha, ha!
He always took the lead, ha, ha!
That unaffected,
Undetected,

Well-connected
Warrior,
The Duke of Plaza-Toro!

When told that they would all be shot
Unless they left the service,
That hero hesitated not,
So marvellous his nerve is.
He sent his resignation in,
The first of all his corps, O!
That very knowing,
Overflowing,
Easy-going
Paladin,
The Duke of Plaza-Toro!

To men of grosser clay, ha, ha!
He always showed the way, ha, ha!
That very knowing,
Overflowing,
Easy-going
Paladin,
The Duke of Plaza-Toro!

The Piper Pipes ──────────────────────

ROBERT BROWNING
The Pied Piper of Hamelin

Into the street the Piper stept,
Smiling first a little smile,
As if he knew what magic slept
In his quiet pipe the while;
Then, like a musical adept,

To blow the pipe his lips he wrinkled,
And green and blue his sharp eyes twinkled,
Like a candle-flame where salt is sprinkled;
And ere three shrill notes the pipe uttered,
You heard as if an army muttered;
And the muttering grew to a grumbling;
And the grumbling grew to a mighty rumbling;
And out of the houses the rats came tumbling.
Great rats, small rats, lean rats, brawny rats,
Brown rats, black rats, gray rats, tawny rats,
Grave old plodders, gay young friskers,
    Fathers, mothers, uncles, cousins,
Cocking tails and pricking whiskers,
    Families by tens and dozens,
Brothers, sisters, husbands, wives—
Followed the Piper for their lives.
From street to street he piped advancing,
And step for step they followed dancing,
Until they came to the river Weser,
    Wherein all plunged and perished!
—Save one who, stout as Julius Caesar,
Swam across and lived to carry
    (As he, the manuscript he cherished)
To Rat-land home his commentary:
Which was, "At the first shrill notes of the pipe,
I heard a sound as of scraping tripe,
And putting apples, wondrous ripe,
Into a cider-press's gripe:
And a moving away of pickle-tub-boards,
And a leaving ajar of conserve-cupboards,
And a drawing the corks of train-oil-flasks,
And a breaking the hoops of butter-casks:
And it seemed as if a voice
    (Sweeter far than bý harp or bý psaltery
Is breathed) called out, 'Oh rats, rejoice!
    The world is grown to one vast drysaltery!
So munch on, crunch on, take your nuncheon,
Breakfast, supper, dinner, luncheon!'
And just as a bulky sugar-puncheon,
All ready staved, like a great sun shone
Glorious scarce an inch before me,
Just as methought it said, 'Come, bore me!'
—I found the Weser rolling o'er me."

Bunthorne and Grosvenor's Duet _____

W. S. GILBERT
Patience

BUN.   When I go out of door,
　　　Of damozels a score
　　　　　(All sighing and burning,
　　　　　And clinging and yearning)
　　　Will follow me as before.
　　　I shall, with cultured taste,
　　　Distinguish gems from paste,
　　　　　And "High diddle diddle"
　　　　　Will rank as an idyll,
　　　If I pronounce it chaste!

BOTH   　　A most intense young man,
　　　　　A soulful-eyed young man,
　　　An ultra-poetical, super-aesthetical,
　　　　　Out-of-the-way young man!

GROS.   Conceive me, if you can,
　　　An every-day young man:
　　　　　A commonplace type,
　　　　　With a stick and a pipe,
　　　And a half-bred black-and-tan;
　　　　　Who thinks suburban "hops"
　　　　　More fun than "Monday Pops,"
　　　Who's fond of his dinner,
　　　And doesn't get thinner
　　　　　On bottled beer and chops.

BOTH   　　A commonplace young man,
　　　　　A matter-of-fact young man,
　　　A steady and stolid-y, jolly Bank-holiday
　　　　　Every-day young man!

BUN.   　　A Japanese young man,
　　　　　A blue-and-white young man,
　　　Francesca da Rimini, miminy, piminy,
　　　　　Je-ne-sais-quoi young man!

GROS.   A Chancery Lane young man,
A Somerset House young man,
A very delectable, highly respectable,
Threepenny-bus young man!

BUN.   A pallid and thin young man,
A haggard and lank young man,
A greenery-yallery, Grosvenor Gallery,
Foot-in-the-grave young man!

GROS.   A Sewell & Cross young man,
A Howell & James young man,
A pushing young particle—"What's the next article?"—
Waterloo-House young man!

ENSEMBLE

BUN.

Conceive me, if you can,
A crotchety, cracked young man,
An ultra-poetical, super-aesthetical,
Out-of-the-way young man!

GROS.

Conceive me, if you can,
A matter-of-fact young man,
An alphabetical, arithmetical,
Every-day young man!

Bunthorne's Song _____

W. S. GILBERT
Patience

If you're anxious for to shine in the high aesthetic line as a man of culture
    rare,
You must get up all the germs of the transcendental terms, and plant them
    everywhere.

You must lie upon the daisies and discourse in novel phrases of your
 complicated state of mind,
The meaning doesn't matter if it's only idle chatter of a transcendental
 kind.
>   And every one will say,
>   As you walk your mystic way,
"If this young man expresses himself in terms too deep for *me*,
Why, what a very singularly deep young man this deep young man must
 be!"

Be eloquent in praise of the very dull old days which have long since
 passed away,
And convince 'em, if you can, that the reign of good Queen Anne was
 Culture's palmiest day.
Of course you will pooh-pooh whatever's fresh and new, and declare it's
 crude and mean,
For Art stopped short in the cultivated court of the Empress Josephine.
>   And every one will say,
>   As you walk your mystic way,
"If that's not good enough for him which is good enough for *me*,
Why, what a very cultivated kind of youth this kind of youth must be!"

Then a sentimental passion of a vegetable fashion must excite your
 languid spleen,
An attachment *à la* Plato for a bashful young potato, or a not-too-French
 French bean!
Though the Philistines may jostle, you will rank as an apostle in the high
 aesthetic band,
If you walk down Piccadilly with a poppy or a lily in your medieval hand.
>   And every one will say,
>   As you walk your flowery way,
"If he's content with a vegetable love which would certainly not suit *me*,
Why, what a most particularly pure young man this pure young man must
 be!"

Vocal Variety

Many of these selections test the actor's ability to work with material of a highly descriptive nature. All of the resources of emphasis, phrasing, pause, and dramatic pointing should be called into play. Actual monologues from plays have not been widely used because characterization is not a basic concern in this section; the actor's attention should be devoted primarily to the development of vocal flexibility. Extensive work in making these isolated examples of prose and poetry exciting and dramatically effective will serve to extend the range of the actor's vocal expressiveness. Such exercises provide a means of preparing the actor to cope with the full vocal demands of a play.

On the Enslavement of Men

ABRAHAM LINCOLN
Debate with Stephen Douglas
Alton, Illinois, October 15, 1858

That is the issue that will continue in this country when these poor tongues of Judge Douglas and myself shall be silent. It is the eternal struggle between these two principles—right and wrong—throughout the world. They are the two principles that have stood face to face from the beginning of time; and will ever continue to struggle. The one is the common right of humanity, and the other the divine right of kings. It is the same principle in whatever shape it develops itself. It is the same spirit that says, "You toil and work and earn bread, and I'll eat it." No matter in what shape it comes, whether from the mouth of a king who seeks to bestride the people of his own nation and live by the fruit of their labor, or from one race of men as an apology for enslaving another race, it is the same tyrannical principle.

A True Sentence?

ABRAHAM LINCOLN
Address, September 30, 1859

It is said an Eastern monarch once charged his wise men to invent him a sentence to be ever in view, and which should be true and appropriate in all times and situations. They presented him the words: "And this, too, shall pass away." How much it expresses! How chastening in the hour of pride! How consoling in the depths of affliction! . . . And yet, let us hope, it is not quite true. Let us hope, rather, that by the best cultivation of the physical world beneath and around us, and the best intellectual and moral world within us, we shall secure an individual, social, and political prosperity and happiness, whose course shall be onward and upward, and which, while the earth endures, shall not pass away.

The Beating Heart

EDGAR ALLAN POE
The Tell-Tale Heart

When I had made an end of these labors, it was four o'clock—still dark as midnight. As the bell sounded the hour, there came a knocking at the street door. I went down to open it with a light heart,—for what had I *now* to fear? There entered three men, who introduced themselves, with perfect suavity, as officers of the police. A shriek had been heard by a neighbor during the night; suspicion of foul play had been aroused; information had been lodged at the police office, and they (the officers) had been deputed to search the premises.

I smiled,—for *what* had I to fear? I bade the gentlemen welcome. The shriek, I said, was my own in a dream. The old man, I mentioned, was absent in the country. I took my visitors all over the house. I bade them search—search *well*. I led them, at length, to *his* chamber. I showed them his treasures, secure, undisturbed. In the enthusiasm of my confidence, I brought chairs into the room, and desired them *here* to rest from their fatigues, while I myself, in the wild audacity of my perfect triumph, placed my own seat upon the very spot beneath which reposed the corpse of the victim.

The officers were satisfied. My *manner* had convinced them. I was singularly at ease. They sat, and while I answered cheerily, they chatted of familiar things. But, ere long, I felt myself getting pale and wished them gone. My head ached, and I fancied a ringing in my ears: but still they sat and still chatted. The ringing became more distinct:—it continued and became more distinct: I talked more freely to get rid of the feeling: but it continued and gained definitiveness—until, at length, I found that the noise was *not* within my ears.

No doubt I now grew *very* pale;—but I talked more fluently, and with a heightened voice. Yet the sound increased—and what could I do? It was *a low, dull, quick sound—much such a sound as a watch makes when enveloped in cotton.* I gasped for breath—and yet the officers heard it not. I talked more quickly—more vehemently; but the noise steadily increased. I arose and argued about trifles, in a high key and with violent gesticulations, but the noise steadily increased. Why *would* they not be gone? I paced the floor to and fro with heavy strides, as if excited to fury by the observation of the men—but the noise steadily increased. Oh God! what *could* I do? I foamed—I raved—I swore! I swung the chair upon which I had been sitting, and grated it upon the boards, but the noise arose over all and continually increased. It grew louder—louder—*louder!* And still the men chatted pleasantly, and smiled. Was it possible they heard not? Almighty God!—no, no! They heard!—they suspected!—they *knew!*—they were making a mockery of my horror!—this I thought, and this I think. But anything was better than this agony! Anything was more tolerable than this derision! I could bear those hypocritical smiles no longer! I felt that I must scream or die!—and now—again!—hark! louder! louder! louder! *louder!*—

"Villains!" I shrieked, "dissemble no more! I admit the deed!—tear up the planks!—here, here!—it is the beating of his hideous heart!"

Cassius' Speech _____

WILLIAM SHAKESPEARE
Julius Caesar

Why, man, he doth bestride the narrow world
Like a Colossus, and we petty men
Walk under his huge legs and peep about
To find ourselves dishonourable graves.
Men at some time are masters of their fates:
The fault, dear Brutus, is not in our stars,
But in ourselves, that we are underlings.
Brutus and Caesar: what should be in that Caesar?
Why should that name be sounded more than yours?
Write them together, yours is as fair a name;
Sound them, it doth become the mouth as well;
Weigh them, it is as heavy; conjure with 'em,
Brutus will start a spirit as soon as Caesar.
Now, in the names of all the gods at once,
Upon what meat doth this our Caesar feed,
That he is grown so great? Age, thou art shamed!
Rome, thou hast lost the breed of noble bloods!
When went there by an age, since the great flood,
But it was famed with more than with one man?
When could they say till now, that talk'd of Rome,
That her wide walls encompass'd but one man?
Now is it Rome indeed and room enough,
When there is in it but one only man.
O, you and I have heard our fathers say,
There was a Brutus once that would have brook'd
The eternal devil to keep his state in Rome
As easily as a king.

On the Declaration of Independence _____

DANIEL WEBSTER
Supposed Speech of John Adams

But whatever may be our fate, be assured that this Declaration will stand. It may cost treasure and it may cost blood; but it will stand, and it will richly compensate for both. Through the thick gloom of the present, I see the brightness of the future as the sun in heaven. We shall make this a glorious, an immortal day. When we are in our graves, our children will honor it. They will celebrate it with thanksgiving, with festivity, with bonfires, and illuminations. On its annual return, they will shed tears, copious, gushing tears, not of subjection and slavery, not of agony and distress, but of exultation, of gratitude, and of joy.

Sir, before God, I believe the hour is come. My judgment approves this measure, and my whole heart is in it. All that I have, and all that I am, and all that I hope in this life, I am now ready here to stake upon it; and I leave off as I began, that, live or die, survive or perish, I am for the Declaration. It is my living sentiment, and by the blessing of God it shall be my dying sentiment—Independence now, and INDEPENDENCE FOREVER!

The Best of Times _____

CHARLES DICKENS
A Tale of Two Cities

It was the best of times, it was the worst of times, it was the age of wisdom, it was the age of foolishness, it was the epoch of belief, it was the epoch of incredulity, it was the season of Light, it was the season of Darkness, it was the spring of hope, it was the winter of despair, we had everything before us, we had nothing before us, we were all going direct to Heaven, we were all going direct the other way—in short, the period was so far like the present period, that some of its noisiest authorities insisted on its being received, for good or for evil, in the superlative degree of comparison only.

There were a king with a large jaw and a queen with a plain face, on the throne of England; there were a king with a large jaw and a queen with a fair face, on the throne of France. In both countries it was clearer than crystal to the lords of the State preserves of loaves and fishes, that things in general were settled for ever.

The Wind _____

CHARLES DICKENS
Martin Chuzzlewit

Out upon the angry wind! how from sighing, it began to bluster round the merry forge, banging at the wicket, and grumbling in the chimney, as if it bullied the jolly bellows from doing anything to order. And what an impotent swaggerer it was, too, for all its poise; for if it had any influence on that hoarse companion, it was but to make him roar his cheerful song the louder, and by consequence to make the fire burn the brighter, and the sparks to dance more gayly yet; at length, they whizzed so madly round and round, that it was too much for such a surly wind to bear; so off it flew with a howl, giving the old sign before the alehouse door such a cuff as it went, that the Blue Dragon was more rampant than usual ever afterwards, and, indeed, before Christmas, reared clean out of his crazy frame.

It was small tyranny for a respectable wind to go wreaking its vengeance on such poor creatures as the fallen leaves, but this wind happening to come up with a great heap of them just after venting its humor on the insulted Dragon, did so disperse and scatter them that they fled away, pell-mell, some here, some there, rolling over each other, whirling round and round upon their thin edges, taking frantic flights into the air, and playing all manner of extraordinary gambols in the extremity of their distress. Nor was this enough for its malicious fury: for not content with driving them abroad, it charged small parties of them and hunted them into the wheel-wright's saw-pit, and below the planks and timbers in the yard, and scattering the sawdust in the air, it looked for them underneath, and when it did meet with any, whew, how it drove them on and followed at their heels!

The scared leaves only flew the faster for all this, and a giddy chase it was; for they got into unfrequented places, where there was no outlet, and where their pursuer kept them eddying round and round at his pleasure; and they crept under the eaves of the houses and clung tightly to the sides of hayricks, like bats; and tore in at open chamber windows, and cowered close to hedges; and, in short, went anywhere for safety. But the oddest feat they achieved was, to take advantage of the sudden opening of Mr. Pecksniff's front door, to dash wildly into his passage; whither the wind following close upon them, and finding the back door open, incontinently blew out the lighted candle held by Miss Pecksniff, and slammed the front door against Mr. Pecksniff who was at that moment entering, with such violence, that in the twinkling of an eye he lay on his back at the bottom of the steps. Being by this time weary of such trifling performances, the boisterous rover hurried away, rejoicing, roaring over moor and meadow, hill and flat, until it got out to sea, where it met with other winds similarly disposed, and made a night of it.

The Dead Whale _____

HERMAN MELVILLE
Moby Dick

The Pequod's whale being decapitated and the body stripped, the head was hoisted against the ship's side—about half way out of the sea, so that it might yet in great part be buoyed up by its native element. And there with the strained craft steeply leaning over it, by reason of the enormous downward drag from the lower mast-head, and every yard-arm on that side projecting like a crane over the waves; there, that blood-dripping head hung to the Pequod's waist like the giant Holofernes's from the girdle of Judith.

When this last task was accomplished it was noon, and the seamen went below to their dinner. Silence reigned over the before tumultuous but now deserted deck. An intense copper calm, like a universal yellow lotus, was more and more unfolding its noiseless measureless leaves upon the sea.

A short space elapsed, and up into this noiselessness came Ahab alone from his cabin. Taking a few turns on the quarter-deck, he paused to gaze over the side, then slowly getting into the main-chains he took Stubb's long spade—still remaining there after the whale's decapitation—and striking it into the lower part of the half-suspended mass, placed its other end crutch-wise under one arm, and so stood leaning over with eyes attentively fixed on this head.

It was a black and hooded head; and hanging there in the midst of so intense a calm, it seemed the Sphynx's in the desert. "Speak, thou vast and venerable head," muttered Ahab, "which, though ungarnished with a beard, yet here and there lookest hoary with mosses; speak, mighty head, and tell us the secret thing that is in thee. Of all divers, thou hast dived the deepest. That head upon which the upper sun now gleams, has moved amid this world's foundations. Where unrecorded names and navies rust, and untold hopes and anchors rot; where in her murderous hold this frigate earth is ballasted with bones of millions of the drowned; there, in that awful water-land, there was thy most familiar home. Thou hast been where bell or diver never went; hast slept by many a sailor's side, where sleepless mothers would give their lives to lay them down. Thou saw'st the locked lovers when leaping from their flaming ship; heart to heart they sank beneath the exulting wave; true to each other, when heaven seemed false to them. Thou saw'st the murdered mate when tossed by pirates from the midnight deck; for hours he fell into the deeper midnight of the insatiate maw; and his murderers still sailed on unharmed—while swift lightnings shivered the neighboring ship that would have borne a righteous husband to outstretched, longing arms. O head! thou hast seen enough to split the planets and make an infidel of Abraham, and not one syllable is thine!"

The Uninvited Guest _____

EDGAR ALLAN POE
The Masque of the Red Death

When the eyes of Prince Prospero fell upon this spectral image (which with a slow and solemn movement, as if more fully to sustain its role, stalked to and fro among the waltzers) he was seen to be convulsed in the first moment with a strong shudder either of terror or distaste; but in the next his brow reddened with rage.

"Who dares?" he demanded hoarsely of the courtiers who stood near him—"who dares insult us with this blasphemous mockery? Seize him and unmask him, that we may know whom we have to hang at sunrise from the battlements!"

It was the eastern or blue chamber in which stood the Prince Prospero as he uttered these words. They rang throughout the seven rooms loudly and clearly—for the prince was a bold and robust man, and the music had become hushed at the waving of his hand.

It was in the blue room where stood the prince, with a group of pale courtiers by his side. At first, as he spoke, there was a slight rushing movement of this group in the direction of the intruder, who at the moment was also near at hand, and now, with deliberate and stately step, made closer approach to the speaker. But, from a certain nameless awe with which the mad assumptions of the mummer had inspired the whole party, there were found none who put forth hand to seize him; so that unimpeded he passed within a yard of the prince's person; and while the vast assembly, as if with one impulse, shrank from the centres of the rooms to the walls, he made his way uninterruptedly, but with the same solemn and measured step which had distinguished him from the first, through the blue chamber to the purple—through the purple to the green—through the green to the orange—through this again to the white—and even thence to the violet, ere a decided movement had been made to arrest him. It was then, however, that the Prince Prospero, maddening with rage and shame of his own momentary cowardice, rushed hurriedly through the six chambers, while none followed him on account of a deadly terror that had seized upon all. He bore aloft a drawn dagger, and had approached in rapid impetuosity, to within three or four feet of the retreating figure, when the latter, having attained the extremity of the velvet apartment, turned suddenly and confronted his pursuer. There was a sharp cry—and the dagger dropped gleaming upon the sable carpet, upon which, instantly afterwards, fell prostrate in death the Prince Prospero. Then, summoning the wild courage of despair, a throng of the revellers at once threw themselves into the black apartment, and, seizing the mummer, whose tall figure stood erect and motionless within the shadow of the ebony clock, gasped in unutterable horror at finding the grave cerements and corpse-like mask which they handled with so violent a rudeness, untenanted by any tangible form.

And now was acknowledged the presence of the Red Death. He had come like a thief in the night. And one by one dropped the revellers in the blood-bedewed halls of their revel, and died each in the despairing posture of his fall. And the life of the ebony clock went out with that of the last of the gay. And the flames of the tripods expired. And Darkness and Decay and the Red Death held illimitable dominion over all.

Ichabod Crane

WASHINGTON IRVING
The Legend of Sleepy Hollow

He was, in fact, an odd mixture of small shrewdness and simple credulity. His appetite for the marvelous, and his powers of digesting it, were equally extraordinary; and both had been increased by his residence in this spell-bound region. No tale was too gross or monstrous for his capacious swallow. It was often his delight, after school was dismissed in the afternoon, to stretch himself on the rich bed of clover, bordering the little brook that whimpered by the schoolhouse, and there con over old Mather's direful tales, until the gathering dusk of the evening made the printed page a mere mist before his eyes. Then, as he wended his way by swamp, and stream and awful woodland, to the farmhouse where he happened to be quartered, every sound of nature at that witching hour, fluttered his excited imagination: the voice of the whippoorwill, that harbinger of storm; the dreary hooting of the screech-owl, or the sudden rustling in the thicket of birds frightened from their roost. The fireflies, too, which sparkled most vividly in the darkest places now and then startled him, as one of uncommon brightness would stream across his path, and if, by chance, a huge blockhead of a beetle came winging his blundering flight against him, the poor varlet was ready to give up the ghost, with the idea that he was struck with a witch's token. His only resource on such occasions, either to drown thought or drive away evil spirits, was to sing psalm tunes;—and the good people of Sleepy Hollow, as they sat by their doors of an evening, were often filled with awe, at hearing his nasal melody, "in linked sweetness long drawn out," floating from the distant hill or along the dusky road.

A Haunted Man

CHARLES DICKENS
*The Haunted Man and
the Ghost's Bargain*

Everybody said he looked like a haunted man. The extent of my present claim for everybody is, that they were so far right. He did.

Who could have seen his hollow cheek; his sunken brilliant eye; his black-attired figure, indefinably grim, although well-knit and well-proportioned; his grizzled hair hanging, like tangled sea-weed, about his face,—as if he had been, through his whole life, a lonely mark for the chafing and beating of the great deep of humanity,—but might have said he looked like a haunted man?

Who could have observed his manner, taciturn, thoughtful, gloomy, shadowed by habitual reserve, retiring always and jocund never, with a distraught air of reverting to a bygone place and time, or of listening to some old echoes in his mind, but might have said it was the manner of a haunted man?

Who could have heard his voice, slow-speaking, deep, and grave, with a natural fulness and melody in it which he seemed to set himself against and stop, but might have said it was the voice of a haunted man?

Who that had seen him in his inner chamber, part library and part laboratory,—for he was, as the world knew, far and wide, a learned man in chemistry, and a teacher on whose lips and hands a crowd of aspiring ears and eyes hung daily,—who that had seen him there, upon a winter night, alone, surrounded by his drugs and instruments and books; the shadow of his shaded lamp a monstrous beetle on the wall, motionless among a crowd of spectral shapes raised there by the flickering of the fire upon the quaint objects around him; some of these phantoms (the reflection of glass vessels that held liquids), trembling at heart like things that knew his power to uncombine them, and to give back their component parts to fire and vapour;—who that had seen him then, his work done, and he pondering in his chair before the rusted grate and red flame, moving his thin mouth as if in speech, but silent as the dead, would not have said that the man seemed haunted and the chamber too?

At the Tomb of Napoleon

ROBERT G. INGERSOLL
Selected Lectures

A little while ago, I stood by the grave of the old Napoleon—a magnificent tomb of gilt and gold, fit almost for a dead deity—and gazed upon the sarcophagus of black Egyptian marble, where rest at last the ashes of that restless man. I leaned over the balustrade and thought about the career of the greatest soldier of the modern world.

I saw him walking upon the banks of the Seine, contemplating suicide. I saw him at Toulon—I saw him putting down the mob in the streets of Paris—I saw him at the head of the army of Italy—I saw him crossing the bridge of Lodi with the tri-color in his hand—I saw him in Egypt in the shadow of the Pyramids—I saw him conquer the Alps and mingle the eagles of France with the eagles of the crags. I saw him at Marengo—at Ulm and Austerlitz. I saw him in Russia, where the infantry of the snow and the cavalry of the wild blast scattered his legions like winter's withered leaves. I saw him at Leipsic in defeat and disaster—driven by a million bayonets back upon Paris—clutched like a wild beast—banished to Elba. I saw him escape and retake an empire by the force of his genius. I saw him upon the frightful field of Waterloo, where Chance and Fate combined to wreck the fortunes of their former king. And I saw him at St. Helena, with his hands crossed behind him, gazing out upon the sad and solemn sea.

I thought of the orphans and widows he had made—of the tears that had been shed for his glory, and of the only woman who ever loved him, pushed from his heart by the cold hand of ambition. And I said I would rather have been a French peasant and worn wooden shoes. I would rather have lived in a hut with a vine growing over the door, and the grapes growing purple in the kisses of the autumn sun. I would rather have been that poor peasant with my loving wife by my side, knitting as the day died out of the sky—with my children upon my knees and their arms about me. I would rather have been that man and gone down to the tongueless silence of the dreamless dust than to have been that imperial impersonation of force and murder, known as Napoleon the Great.

My Last Duchess ——————————————————

ROBERT BROWNING

FERRARA

That's my last Duchess painted on the wall,
Looking as if she were alive. I call
That piece a wonder, now: Frà Pandolf's hands
Worked busily a day, and there she stands.
Will 't please you sit and look at her? I said
"Frà Pandolf" by design, for never read
Strangers like you that pictured countenance,
The depth and passion of its earnest glance,
But to myself they turned (since none puts by
The curtain I have drawn for you, but I)
And seemed as they would ask me, if they durst,
How such a glance came there; so, not the first
Are you to turn and ask thus. Sir, 'twas not
Her husband's presence only, called that spot
Of joy into the Duchess' cheek: perhaps
Frà Pandolf chanced to say, "Her mantle laps
Over my lady's wrist too much," or "Paint
Must never hope to reproduce the faint
Half-flush that dies along her throat:" such stuff
Was courtesy, she thought, and cause enough
For calling up that spot of joy. She had
A heart—how shall I say?—too soon made glad,
Too easily impressed: she liked whate'er
She looked on, and her looks went everywhere.
Sir, 'twas all one! My favor at her breast,
The dropping of the daylight in the West,
The bough of cherries some officious fool
Broke in the orchard for her, the white mule
She rode with round the terrace—all and each
Would draw from her alike the approving speech,
Or blush, at least. She thanked men,—good! but thanked
Somehow—I know not how—as if she ranked
My gift of a nine-hundred-years-old name
With anybody's gift. Who'd stoop to blame

This sort of trifling? Even had you skill
In speech—(which I have not)—to make your will
Quite clear to such an one, and say, "Just this
Or that in you disgusts me; here you miss,
Or there exceed the mark"—and if she let
Herself be lessoned so, nor plainly set
Her wits to yours, forsooth, and made excuse,
—E'en then would be some stooping; and I choose
Never to stoop. Oh, sir, she smiled, no doubt,
Whene'er I passed her; but who passed without
Much the same smile? This grew; I gave commands;
Then all smiles stopped together. There she stands
As if alive. Will 't please you rise? We'll meet
The company below, then. I repeat,
The Count your master's known munificence
Is ample warrant that no just pretence
Of mine for dowry will be disallowed;
Though his fair daughter's self, as I avowed
At starting, is my object, Nay, we'll go
Together down, sir. Notice Neptune, though,
Taming a sea-horse, thought a rarity,
Which Claus of Innsbruck cast in bronze for me!

Catiline's Defiance

BEN JONSON
Catiline

"Traitor!" I go; but, I return! This—trial!
Here I devote your Senate! I've had wrongs
To stir a fever in the blood of age,
Or make the infant's sinews strong as steel.

This day's the birth of sorrow; this hour's work
Will breed proscriptions! Look to your hearths, my Lords!
For there, henceforth, shall sit, for household gods,
Shapes hot from Tartarus; all shames and crimes;
Wan Treachery, with his thirsty dagger drawn;
Suspicion, poisoning his brother's cup;
Naked Rebellion, with the torch and axe,
Making his wild sport of your blazing thrones;
Till Anarchy comes down on you like night,
And Massacre seals Rome's eternal grave.

Part 2

SCENES

one _____

SERIOUS SCENES

THIS group of scenes comprises a cross section of material from modern plays, both American and European. They represent no one distinct approach in playwriting style or attitude. Their serious themes distinguish them from scenes that may be classified in the genre of comedy. We find in this section plays that might be classified as *tragedy, melodrama, serious drama,* and even *comedy-drama.* Occasionally, humorous elements may be found in certain of these scenes, as in portions of *Tea and Sympathy, Marty, Saint Joan,* and others. However, the basic attitude and view of the playwrights, no matter how varied their technique, decidedly is not humorous.

Some scenes are situations subtly revealing character qualities and relationships; some are direct and angry confrontations of tormented individuals. Within the range of these scenes, the actor should find stimulating and exciting drama, with more than enough potential to challenge both the beginner and the advanced student.

The Visit, Friedrich Dürrenmatt, adapted by Maurice Valency:
 scene for one man, one woman, page 52.
Tea and Sympathy, Robert Anderson:
 scene for one man, one woman, page 56.

50

The Visit _____

Friedrich Dürrenmatt (1956)
adapted by Maurice Valency
From Act III

SCENE:	For one man, one woman
CHARACTERS:	Claire Zachanassian Anton Schill
SETTING:	A forest on the outskirts of the little town of Güllen, somewhere in Europe.
TIME:	The present.
SITUATION:	*The Visit* is a strange tale of revenge. Forced to leave the village of Güllen as a young woman, Claire Zachanassian has returned to revenge herself on Anton Schill, the man who caused her misery many years before. Ill and pregnant with Schill's child, Claire roamed the streets of Europe, sinking into degradation until by a sudden stroke of fortune she married one of Europe's richest men. Now fabulously wealthy, she has offered the town of Güllen one billion marks for the life of Anton Schill. At first righteously indignant at the offer, the villagers slowly turn against Schill and start to spend money in anticipation of his death. As these bizarre events unfold, however, there seems to be no real antagonism between Claire and Schill. This scene depicts their last meeting. Both know that very soon Schill's body will be delivered to Claire, and yet there is an almost tender quality in their meeting that seems to make it something of a strange love scene. Schill is alone on a bench in the forest as the scene begins.

CLAIRE   (*comes in. She gazes slowly up at the trees, kicks at some leaves. Then she walks slowly* D.C. *She stops before a tree, glances up the trunk.*) Bark-borers. The old tree is dying.

[*She catches sight of* SCHILL.]

SCHILL   Clara.

CLAIRE   How pleasant to see you here. I was visiting my forest. May I sit by you?

SCHILL   Oh, yes. Please do. (*She sits next to him.*) I've just been saying good-bye to my family. They've gone to the cinema. Karl has bought himself a car.

CLAIRE   How nice.

SCHILL   Ottilie is taking French lessons. And a course in English literature.

CLAIRE   You see? They're beginning to take an interest in higher things.

SCHILL   Listen. A finch. You hear?

CLAIRE   Yes. It's a finch. And a cuckoo in the distance. Would you like some music?

SCHILL   Oh, yes. That would be very nice.

CLAIRE   Anything special?

SCHILL   "Deep in the Forest."

CLAIRE   Your favorite song. They know it.

[*She raises her hand. Offstage, the mandolin and guitar play the tune softly.*]

SCHILL   We had a child?

CLAIRE   Yes.

SCHILL   Boy or girl?

CLAIRE   Girl.

SCHILL   What name did you give her?

CLAIRE   I called her Genevieve.

SCHILL   That's a very pretty name.

CLAIRE   Yes.

SCHILL   What was she like?

CLAIRE   I saw her only once. When she was born. Then they took her away from me.

SCHILL   Her eyes?

CLAIRE   They weren't open yet.

SCHILL   And her hair?

CLAIRE   Black, I think. It's usually black at first.

SCHILL   Yes, of course. Where did she die, Clara?

CLAIRE   In some family. I've forgotten their name. Meningitis, they said. The officials wrote me a letter.

SCHILL   Oh, I'm so very sorry, Clara.

CLAIRE   I've told you about our child. Now tell me about myself.

SCHILL   About yourself?

CLAIRE   Yes. How I was when I was seventeen in the days when you loved me.

SCHILL   I remember one day you waited for me in the great barn. I had to look all over the place for you. At last I found you lying in the hay-cart with nothing on and a long straw between your lips . . .

CLAIRE   Yes. I was pretty in those days.

SCHILL   You were beautiful, Clara.

CLAIRE   You were strong. The time you fought with those two railway men who were following me, I wiped the blood from your face with my red petticoat. (*The music ends.*) They've stopped.

SCHILL   Tell them to play "Thoughts of Home."

CLAIRE   They know that too.

[*The music plays.*]

SCHILL   Here we are, Clara, sitting together in our forest for the last time. The town council meets tonight. They will condemn me to death, and one of them will kill me. I don't know who and I don't know where. Clara, I only know that in a little while a useless life will come to an end.

[*He bows his head on her bosom. She takes him in her arms.*]

CLAIRE   (*tenderly*) I shall take you in your coffin to Capri. You will have your tomb in the park of my villa, where I can see you from my bedroom window. White marble and onyx in a grove of green cypress. With a beautiful view of the Mediterranean.

SCHILL   I've always wanted to see it.

CLAIRE   Your love for me died years ago, Anton. But my love for you would not die. It turned into something strong, like the hidden roots of the forest; something evil, like white mushrooms that grow unseen in the darkness. And slowly it reached out for your life. Now I have you. You are mine. Alone. At last, and forever, a peaceful ghost in a silent house.

[*The music ends.*]

SCHILL   The song is over.

CLAIRE   Adieu, Anton.

[CLAIRE *kisses* ANTON, *a long kiss. Then she rises.*]

SCHILL   Adieu.

[*She goes.* SCHILL *remains sitting on the bench.*]

Reference Key to Plays in Anthologies

Copies of the complete play may be found in the following selected volumes:
Numbers 9, 46.
See also *Theatre Arts*, December, 1959.

Further Reading on Dürrenmatt and *The Visit*

Askew, Melvin W. "Dürrenmatt's *The Visit of the Old Lady*." *Tulane Drama Review*, Vol. 5, No. 4 (Summer, 1961), pp. 89–105.

Klarmann, Adolf. "Friedrich Dürrenmatt and the Tragic Sense of Comedy." *Tulane Drama Review*, Vol. 4, No. 4 (May, 1960), pp. 77–104.

Rogoff, Gordon. "Mr. Dürrenmatt Buys New Shoes." *Tulane Drama Review*, Vol. 3, No. 1 (Autumn, 1958), pp. 27–34.

Valency, Maurice. "*The Visit*–A Modern Tragedy." *Theatre Arts*, Vol. 42, No. 5 (May, 1958), pp. 17, 90–91.

Tea and Sympathy ————————————————

ROBERT ANDERSON (1953)
From Act II

SCENE:	For one man, one woman
CHARACTERS:	Laura, wife of the housemaster Al, a teenage boy living in the house
SETTING:	The living room of a small old colonial house now used as a dormitory in a boy's school in New England.
TIME:	A day in the spring. The present time.
SITUATION:	Laura, the wife of a housemaster of a boy's school, has taken a particular interest in the problems of Al's roommate, Tom Lee. Tom is suspected by his classmates of being a homosexual. Al's friends have advised Al to move to another room for the next school year if he wants to be captain of the baseball team. Just before this scene begins, Al has talked to his father by phone. His father has also urged Al to move out of his present room. Al has just knocked on the door to the housemaster's living room to inform him and his wife of his decision.

LAURA *(comes from inside the house and opens the door)* Oh, hello, Al.
AL   Is Mr. Reynolds in?
LAURA   Why, no, he isn't. Can I do something?
AL   I guess I better drop down when he's in.
LAURA   All right. I don't really expect him home till after supper tonight.
AL   *(thinks for a moment)* Well . . . well, you might tell him just so he'll know and can make other plans . . . I won't be rooming in this house next year. This is the last day for changing, and I want him to know that.
LAURA   *(moves into the room to get a cigarette)* I see. Well, I know he'll be sorry to hear that, Al.

AL I'm going across the street to Harmon House.

LAURA Both you and Tom going over?

AL No.

LAURA Oh.

AL Just me.

LAURA I see. Does Tom know this?

AL No. I haven't told him.

LAURA You'll have to tell him, won't you, so he'll be able to make other plans.

AL Yes, I suppose so.

LAURA Al, won't you sit down for a moment, please? (AL *hesitates, but comes in and sits down. Offers* AL *a cigarette*) Cigarette?

AL (*reaches for one automatically, then stops*) No, thanks. I'm in training. (*He slips a pack of cigarettes from his shirt pocket to his trousers pocket.*)

LAURA That's right. I'm going to watch you play Saturday afternoon. (AL *smiles at her.*)You're not looking forward to telling Tom, are you, Al? (AL *shakes his head "No."*) I suppose I can guess why you're not rooming with him next year. (AL *shrugs his shoulders.*) I wonder if you know how much it has meant for him to room with you this year. It's done a lot for him too. It's given him a confidence to know he was rooming with one of the big men of the school.

AL (*embarrassed*) Oh . . .

LAURA You wouldn't understand what it means to be befriended. You're one of the strong people. I'm surprised, Al.

AL (*blurting it out*) My father's called me three times. How he ever found out about Harris and Tom, I don't know. But he did. And some guy called him and asked him, "Isn't that the boy your son is rooming with?" . . . and he wants me to change for next year.

LAURA What did you tell your father?

AL I told him Tom wasn't so bad, and . . . I'd better wait and see Mr. Reynolds.

LAURA Al, you've lived with Tom. You know him better than anyone else knows him. If you do this, it's as good as finishing him so far as this school is concerned, and maybe farther.

AL (*almost whispering it*) Well, he *does* act sort of queer, Mrs. Reynolds. He . . .

LAURA You never said this before. You never paid any attention before. What do you mean, "queer?"

AL Well, like the fellows say, he sort of walks lightly, if you know what I mean. Sometimes the way he moves . . . the things he talks about . . . long hair music all the time.

LAURA All right. He wants to be a singer. So he talks about it.

AL   He's never had a girl up for any of the dances.

LAURA   Al, there are good explanations for all these things you're saying. They're silly . . . and prejudiced . . . and arguments all dug up to suit a point of view. They're all after the fact.

AL   I'd better speak to Mr. Reynolds.

[*He starts for the door.*]

LAURA   Al, look at me. (*She holds his eyes for a long time, wondering whether to say what she wants to say.*)

AL   Yes?

LAURA   (*She decides to do it.*) Al, what if I were to start the rumor to-morrow that you were . . . well, queer, as you put it.

AL   No one would believe it.

LAURA   Why not?

AL   Well, because . . .

LAURA   Because you're big and brawny and an athlete. What they call a top guy and a hard hitter?

AL   Well, yes.

LAURA   You've got some things to learn, Al. I've been around a little, and I've met men, just like you—same setup—who weren't men, some of them married and with children.

AL   Mrs. Reynolds, you wouldn't do a thing like that.

LAURA   No, Al, I probably wouldn't. But I could, and I almost would to show you how easy it is to smear a person, and once I got them be-lieving it, you'd be surprised how quickly your . . . manly virtues would be changed into suspicious characteristics.

AL   (*has been standing with his hands on his hips.* LAURA *looks pointedly at this stance.* AL *thrusts his hands down to his side, and then behind his back.*) Mrs. Reynolds, I got a chance to be captain of the baseball team next year.

LAURA   I know. And I have no right to ask you to give up that chance. But I wish somehow or other you could figure out a way . . . so it wouldn't hurt Tom.

[TOM *comes in the hall and goes up the stairs. He's pretty broken up, and mad. After a few moments he appears in his room, shuts the door, and sits on the bed, trying to figure something out.*]

AL   (*as* TOM *enters house*) Well . . .

LAURA   That's Tom now. (AL *looks at her, wondering how she knows.*) I know all your footsteps. He's coming in for tea. (AL *starts to move to door.*) Well, Al? (AL *makes a helpless motion.*) You still want me to tell Mr. Reynolds about your moving next year?

AL   (*after a moment*) No.

LAURA   Good.

AL   I mean, I'll tell him when I see him.

LAURA   Oh.

AL   *(turns on her)* What can I do?

LAURA   I don't know.

AL   Excuse me for saying so, but it's easy for you to talk the way you have. You're not involved. You're just a bystander. You're not going to be hurt. Nothing's going to happen to you one way or the other. I'm sorry.

LAURA   That's a fair criticism, Al. I'm sorry I asked you . . . As you say, I'm not involved.

AL   I'm sorry. I think you're swell, Mrs. Reynolds. You're the nicest housemaster's wife I've ever ran into . . . I mean . . . Well, you know what I mean. It's only that . . . *(He is flustered. He opens the door.)* I'm sorry.

LAURA   I'm sorry too, Al.

Reference Key to Plays in Anthologies

Copies of the complete play may be found in the following selected volumes: Numbers 39, 62, 70.

See also *Theatre Arts,* September, 1954.

Further Reading on Anderson and *Tea and Sympathy*

Anderson, Robert. "Walk a Ways with Me." *Theatre Arts,* Vol. 38, No. 1 (January, 1954), pp. 30–31.

Bentley, Eric. "Folklore on Forty-seventh Street." *The Dramatic Event.* Boston: Beacon, 1956, pp. 149–53.

"Fame Taps a Playwright." *New York Times,* November 8, 1953, sec. 2, p. 3.

"Tea and Sympathy." *Theatre Arts,* Vol. 37, No. 12 (December, 1953), pp. 18–19.

Marty _____

PADDY CHAYEFSKY (1953)
From Act I
(of the television play)

SCENE: For two men, two women

CHARACTERS: Mother
Marty, her son
Thomas, her nephew
Virginia, Thomas' wife

SETTING: Marty's home in the Bronx, New York City.

TIME: Dinner time, Saturday night. The present.

SITUATION: The scenes from *Marty* are a somewhat different form of acting exercise, since they come from a television play. This sequence occurs early in the teleplay. It is Saturday night, and Marty, a lonely bachelor, again does not have a date.

As this scene begins, Marty's cousin and his wife are seated at the table in the dining room with Marty's mother. They have just shared some bad news.

See also the following scene from *Marty* (p. 67), which occurs later in the play.

MOTHER   (*after a pause*) Well, Thomas, I knew sooner or later this was gonna happen. I told Marty, I said: "Marty, you watch. There's gonna be real trouble over there in your cousin Thomas' house." Because your mother was here, Thomas, you know?

THOMAS   When was this, Aunt Theresa?

MOTHER   This was one, two, three days ago. Wednesday. Because I went to the fruit shop on Wednesday, and I came home. And I come arounna back, and there's your mother sitting onna steps onna porch. And I said: "Catherine, my sister, wadda you doing here?" And she look uppa me, and she beganna cry.

THOMAS   (*to his wife*) Wednesday. That was the day you threw the milk bottle.

FROM *Marty* by Paddy Chayefsky. Copyright © 1954 by Paddy Chayefsky. Reprinted by permission of Simon and Schuster, Inc.

MOTHER   That's right. Because I said to her: "Catherine, watsa matter?"
And she said to me: "Theresa, my daughter-in-law, Virginia, she just
threw the milk bottle at me."

VIRGINIA   Well, you see what happen, Aunt Theresa . . .

MOTHER   I know, I know . . .

VIRGINIA   She comes inna kitchen, and she begins poking her head over
my shoulder here and poking her head over my shoulder there . . .

MOTHER   I know, I know . . .

VIRGINIA   And she begins complaining about this, and she begins complaining about that. And she got me so nervous, I spilled some milk I
was making for the baby. You see, I was making some food for the
baby, and . . .

MOTHER   So I said to her, "Catherine . . ."

VIRGINIA   So, she got me so nervous I spilled some milk. So she said:
"You're spilling the milk." She says: "Milk costs twenty-four cents a
bottle. Wadda you, a banker?" So I said: "Mama, leave me alone,
please. You're making me nervous. Go on in the other room and turn
on the television set." So then she began telling me how I waste money,
and how I can't cook, and how I'm raising my baby all wrong, and she
kept talking about these couple of drops of milk I spilt, and I got so
mad, I said: "Mama, you wanna see me really spill some milk?" So I
took the bottle and threw it against the door. I didn't throw it at her.
That's just something she made up. I didn't throw it anywheres near
her. Well, of course, alla milk went all over the floor. The whole
twenty-four cents. Well, I was sorry right away, you know, but she ran
outta the house.

[pause]

MOTHER   Well, I don't know what you want me to do, Virginia. If you
want me, I'll go talk to her tonight.

[THOMAS and VIRGINIA suddenly frown and look down at their hands
as if of one mind.]

THOMAS   Well, I'll tell you, Aunt Theresa . . .

VIRGINIA   Lemme tell it, Tommy.

THOMAS   Okay.

VIRGINIA   (leaning forward to the MOTHER) We want you to do a very big
favor for us, Aunt Theresa.

MOTHER   Sure.

VIRGINIA   Aunt Theresa, you got this big house here. You got four bedrooms upstairs. I mean, you got this big house just for you and Marty.
All your other kids are married and got their own homes. And I
thought maybe Tommy's mother could come here and live with you
and Marty.

MOTHER   Well . . .

VIRGINIA   She's miserable living with Tommy and me, and you're the only one that gets along with her. Because I called up Tommy's brother, Joe, and I said: "Joe, she's driving me crazy. Why don't you take her for a couple of years?" And he said: "Oh, no!" I know I sound like a terrible woman . . .

MOTHER   No, Virginia, I know how you feel. My husband, may God bless his memory, his mother, she lived with us for a long time, and I know how you feel.

VIRGINIA   (*practically on the verge of tears*) I just can't stand it no more! Every minute of the day! Do this! Do that! I don't have ten minutes alone with my husband! We can't even have a fight! We don't have no privacy! Everybody's miserable in our house!

THOMAS   All right, Ginnie, don't get so excited.

MOTHER   She's right. She's right. Young husband and wife, they should have their own home. And my sister, Catherine, she's my sister, but I gotta admit, she's an old goat. And plenny-a times in my life I feel like throwing the milk bottle at her myself. And I tell you now, as far as I'm concerned, if Catherine wantsa come live here with me and Marty, it's all right with me.

[VIRGINIA *promptly bursts into tears.*]

THOMAS   (*not far from tears himself, lowers his face*) That's very nice-a you, Aunt Theresa.

MOTHER   We gotta ask Marty, of course, because this is his house too. But he's gonna come home any minute now.

VIRGINIA   (*having mastered her tears*) That's very nice-a you, Aunt Theresa.

MOTHER   (*rising*) Now, you just sit here. I'm just gonna turn onna small fire under the food.

[*She exits into the kitchen.*]

VIRGINIA   (*calling after her*) We gotta go right away because I promised the baby sitter we'd be home by six, and it's after six now . . .

[*She kind of fades out. A moment of silence.* THOMAS *takes out a cigarette and lights it.*]

THOMAS   (*calling to his aunt in the kitchen*) How's Marty been lately, Aunt Theresa?

MOTHER   (*off in kitchen*) Oh, he's fine. You know a nice girl he can marry? (*She comes back into the dining room, wiping her hands on a kitchen towel.*) I'm worried about him, you know? He's thirty-six years old, gonna be thirty-seven in January.

THOMAS   Oh, he'll get married, don't worry, Aunt Theresa.

MOTHER (*sitting down again*) Well, I don't know. You know a place where he can go where he can find a bride?

THOMAS The Waverly Ballroom. That's a good place to meet girls, Aunt Theresa. That's a kind of big dance hall, Aunt Theresa. Every Saturday night, it's just loaded with girls. It's a nice place to go. You pay seventy-seven cents. It used to be seventy-seven cents. It must be about a buck and a half now. And you go in and you ask some girl to dance. That's how I met Virginia. Nice, respectable place to meet girls. You tell Marty, Aunt Theresa, you tell him: "Go to the Waverly Ballroom. It's loaded with tomatoes."

MOTHER (*committing the line to memory*) The Waverly Ballroom. It's loaded with tomatoes.

THOMAS Right.

VIRGINIA You tell him, go to the Waverly Ballroom.

[*There is the sound of a door being unlatched off through the kitchen. The* MOTHER *promptly rises.*]

MOTHER He's here.

[*She hurries into the kitchen. At the porch entrance to the kitchen,* MARTY *has just come in. He is closing the door behind him. He carries his butcher's apron in a bundle under his arm.*]

MARTY Hello, Ma.

[*She comes up to him, lowers her voice to a whisper.*]

MOTHER (*whispers*) Marty, Thomas and Virginia are here. They had another big fight with your Aunt Catherine. So they ask me, would it be all right if Catherine come to live with us. So I said, all right with me, but we have to ask you. Marty, she's a lonely old lady. Nobody wants her. Everybody's throwing her outta their house. . . .

MARTY Sure, Ma, it's okay with me.

[*The* MOTHER's *face breaks into a fond smile. She reaches up and pats his cheek with genuine affection.*]

MOTHER You gotta good heart. (*turning and leading the way back to the dining room.* THOMAS *has risen.*) He says okay, it's all right Catherine comes here.

THOMAS Oh, Marty, thanks a lot. That really takes a load offa my mind.

MARTY Oh, we got plenny-a room here.

MOTHER Sure! Sure! It's gonna be nice! It's gonna be nice! I'll come over tonight to your house, and I talk to Catherine, and you see, everything is gonna work out all right.

THOMAS I just wanna thank you people again because the situation was just becoming impossible.

MOTHER   Siddown, Thomas, siddown. All right, Marty, siddown. . . .

(She exits into the kitchen.)

[MARTY *has taken his seat at the head of the table and is waiting to be served.* THOMAS *takes a seat around the corner of the table from him and leans across to him.*]

THOMAS   You see, Marty, the kinda thing that's been happening in our house is Virginia was inna kitchen making some food for the baby. Well, my mother comes in, and she gets Virginia so nervous, she spills a couple-a drops . . .

VIRGINIA   *(tugging at her husband)* Tommy, we gotta go. I promise the baby sitter six o'clock.

THOMAS   *(rising without interrupting his narrative)* So she starts yelling at Virginia, waddaya spilling the milk for. So Virginia gets mad . . . *(His wife is slowly pulling him to the kitchen door.)* She says, "You wanna really see me spill milk?" So Virginia takes the bottle and she throws it against the wall. She's got a real Italian temper, my wife, you know that . . . *(He has been tugged to the kitchen door by now.)*

VIRGINIA   Marty, I don't have to tell you how much we appreciate what your mother and you are doing for us.

THOMAS   All right, Marty, I'll see you some other time . . . I'll tell you all about it.

MARTY   I'll see you, Tommy.

[THOMAS *disappears into the kitchen after his wife.*]

VIRGINIA   *(off, calling)* Good-by, Marty!

[*close in on* MARTY, *sitting at table*]

MARTY   Good-by, Virginia! See you soon! *(He folds his hands on the table before him and waits to be served.)*

[*The* MOTHER *enters from the kitchen. She sets the meat plate down in front of him and herself takes a chair around the corner of the table from him.* MARTY *without a word takes up his knife and fork and attacks the mountain of food in front of him. His mother sits quietly, her hands a little nervous on the table before her, watching him eat. Then . . .*]

MOTHER   So what are you gonna do tonight, Marty?

MARTY   I don't know, Ma. I'm all knocked out. I may just hang arounna house.

[*The* MOTHER *nods a couple of times. There is a moment of silence. Then . . .*]

MOTHER   Why don't you go to the Waverly Ballroom?

[*This gives* MARTY *pause. He looks up.*]

MARTY   What?

MOTHER   I say, why don't you go to the Waverly Ballroom? It's loaded with tomatoes.

[MARTY *regards his mother for a moment.*]

MARTY   It's loaded with what?

MOTHER   Tomatoes.

MARTY   (*snorts*) Ha! Who told you about the Waverly Ballroom?

MOTHER   Thomas, he told me it was a very nice place.

MARTY   Oh, Thomas. Ma, it's just a big dance hall, and that's all it is. I been there a hundred times. Loaded with tomatoes. Boy, you're funny, Ma.

MOTHER   Marty, I don't want you hang arounna house tonight. I want you to go take a shave and go out and dance.

MARTY   Ma, when are you gonna give up? You gotta bachelor on your hands. I ain't never gonna get married.

MOTHER   You gonna get married.

MARTY   Sooner or later, there comes a point in a man's life when he gotta face some facts, and one fact I gotta face is that whatever it is that women like, I ain't got it. I chased enough girls in my life. I went to enough dances. I got hurt enough. I don't wanna get hurt no more. I just called a girl this afternoon, and I got a real brush-off, boy. I figured I was past the point of being hurt, but that hurt. Some stupid woman who I didn't even wanna call up. She gave me the brush. That's the history of my life. I don't wanna go to the Waverly Ballroom because all that ever happened to me there was girls made me feel like I was a bug. I got feelings, you know. I had enough pain. No, thank you.

MOTHER   Marty . . .

MARTY   Ma, I'm gonna stay home and watch Sid Caesar.

MOTHER   You gonna die without a son.

MARTY   So I'll die without a son.

MOTHER   Put on your blue suit . . .

MARTY   Blue suit, gray suit, I'm still a fat little man. A fat little ugly man.

MOTHER   You not ugly.

MARTY   (*his voice rising*) I'm ugly . . . I'm ugly! . . . I'm UGLY!

MOTHER   Marty . . .

MARTY   (*crying aloud, more in anguish than in anger*) Ma! Leave me alone! . . . (*He stands abruptly, his face pained and drawn. He makes half-formed gestures to his mother, but he can't find words at the moment. He turns and marches a few paces away, turns to his mother again.*) Ma, waddaya want from me?! Waddaya want from me?! I'm miserable enough as it is! Leave me alone! I'll go to the Waverly Ballroom! I'll put onna blue suit and I'll go! And you know what I'm gonna get for my trouble? Heartache! A big night of heart-ache! (*He sullenly marches back to his seat, sits down, picks up his fork, plunges it into the lasagna, and stuffs a mouthful into his mouth; he chews vigorously for a moment. It is impossible to remain angry for long. After a while he is shaking his head and muttering*) Loaded with tomatoes . . . boy, that's rich . . .

Reference Key to Plays in Anthologies

Copies of the complete play may be found in the following selected volumes: Numbers 8, 9, 56.

Further Reading on Chayefsky and *Marty*

Gassner, John. *Theatre at the Crossroads: Plays and Playwrights of the Mid-Century American Stage*. New York: Holt, Rinehart and Winston, 1960, pp. 309–10.

Sayre, Nora and Robert B. Silvers. "An Interview with Paddy Chayefsky." *Horizon*, Vol. 3, No. 1 (September, 1960), pp. 49–56.

Wadsworth, Frank. "The TV Plays of Paddy Chayefsky." *Quarterly of Film, Radio, and Television*, Vol. 10, No. 2 (Winter, 1955), pp. 109–24.

Marty

PADDY CHAYEFSKY (1953)
From Act II
(of the television play)

SCENE: For one man, two women

CHARACTERS: Marty
Girl (Clara)
Mother

SETTING: Marty's home in the Bronx, New York City.

TIME: Late Saturday evening. The present.

SITUATION: See the preceding scene from *Marty* (p. 60), which occurs earlier in the play.

This scene is a sequence from the television play *Marty*, later adapted by Chayefsky into the award-winning film of the same name. Marty, a lonely bachelor, has gone alone to the Waverly Ballroom. There he met a plain young woman who had been jilted by her blind date. Marty, despite his unattractive, awkward appearance, is a man of great sensitivity. He tells the girl honestly, "You get kicked around long enough, you get to be a real professor of pain. I know exactly how you feel."

The scene begins as Marty and the Girl appear in the doorway of the rear porch leading to the kitchen in Marty's house.

MARTY Wait a minute. Lemme find the light.

[*He finds the light. The kitchen is suddenly brightly lit. The two of them stand squinting to adjust to the sudden glare.*]

MARTY I guess my mother ain't home yet. I figure my cousin Thomas and Virginia musta gone to the movies, so they won't get back till one o'clock, at least.

[*The* GIRL *has advanced into the kitchen, a little ill at ease, and is looking around.* MARTY *closes the porch door.*]

MARTY   This is the kitchen.

GIRL   Yes, I know.

[MARTY *leads the way into the dining room.*]

MARTY   Come on inna dining room. (*He turns on the light in there as he goes. The* GIRL *follows him in.*) Siddown, take off your coat. You want something to eat? We gotta whole halfa chicken left over from yesterday.

GIRL   (*perching tentatively on the edge of a chair*) No, thank you. I don't think I should stay very long.

MARTY   Sure. Just take off your coat a minute.

[*He helps her off with her coat and stands for a moment behind her, looking down at her. Conscious of his scrutiny, she sits uncomfortably, her breasts rising and falling unevenly.* MARTY *takes her coat into the dark living room. The* GIRL *sits patiently, nervously.* MARTY *comes back, sits down on another chair. Awkward silence*]

MARTY   So I was telling you, my kid brother Nickie got married last Sunday . . . That was a very nice affair. And they had this statue of some woman, and they had whisky spouting outta her mouth. I never saw anything so grand in my life. (*The silence falls between them again.*) And watta meal. I'm a butcher, so I know a good hunka steak when I see one. That was choice filet, right off the toppa the chuck. A buck-eighty a pound. Of course, if you wanna cheaper cut, get rib steak. That gotta lotta waste on it, but it comes to about a buck and a quarter a pound, if it's trimmed. Listen, Clara, make yourself comfortable. You're all tense.

GIRL   Oh, I'm fine.

MARTY   You want me to take you home, I'll take you home.

GIRL   Maybe that would be a good idea.

[*She stands. He stands, frowning, a little angry—turns sullenly and goes back into the living room for her coat. She stands unhappily. He comes back and wordlessly starts to help her into her coat. He stands behind her, his hands on her shoulders. He suddenly seizes her, begins kissing her on the neck. Camera comes up quickly to intensely intimate close-up, nothing but the heads. The dialogue drops to quick, hushed whispers.*]

GIRL   No, Marty, please . . .

MARTY   I like you, I like you, I been telling you all night I like you . . .

GIRL   Marty . . .

MARTY   I just wanna kiss, that's all . . .

[*He tries to turn her face to him. She resists.*]

GIRL No . . .

MARTY Please . . .

GIRL No . . .

MARTY Please . . .

GIRL Marty . . .

[*He suddenly releases her, turns away violently.*]

MARTY (*crying out*) All right! I'll take you home! All right! (*He marches a few angry paces away, deeply disturbed. Turns to her*) All I wanted was a lousy kiss! What am I, a leper or something?!

[*He turns and goes off into the living room to hide the flush of hot tears threatening to fill his eyes. The* GIRL *stands, herself on the verge of tears.*]

GIRL (*mutters, more to herself than to him*) I just didn't feel like it, that's all.

[*She moves slowly to the archway leading to the living room.* MARTY *is sitting on the couch, hands in his lap, looking straight ahead. The room is dark except for the overcast of the dining-room light reaching in. The* GIRL *goes to the couch, perches on the edge beside him. He doesn't look at her.*)

MARTY Well, that's the history of my life. I'm a little, short, fat, ugly guy. Comes New Year's Eve, everybody starts arranging parties. I'm the guy they gotta dig up a date for. I'm old enough to know better. Let me get a packa cigarettes, and I'll take you home.

[*He starts to rise, but doesn't . . . sinks back onto the couch, looking straight ahead. The* GIRL *looks at him, her face peculiarly soft and compassionate.*]

GIRL I'd like to see you again, very much. The reason I didn't let you kiss me was because I just didn't know how to handle the situation. You're the kindest man I ever met. The reason I tell you this is because I want to see you again very much. Maybe, I'm just so desperate to fall in love that I'm trying too hard. But I know that when you take me home, I'm going to just lie on my bed and think about you. I want very much to see you again.

[MARTY *stares down at his hands in his lap.*]

MARTY (*without looking at her*) Waddaya doing tomorrow night?

GIRL Nothing.

MARTY I'll call you up tomorrow morning. Maybe we'll go see a movie.

GIRL I'd like that very much.

MARTY The reason I can't be definite about it now is my Aunt Catherine is probably coming over tomorrow, and I may have to help out.

GIRL   I'll wait for your call.

MARTY   We better get started to your house because the buses only run about one an hour now.

GIRL   All right.

[*She stands.*]

MARTY   I'll just get a packa cigarettes.

[*He goes into his bedroom. We can see him through the doorway, opening his bureau drawer and extracting a pack of cigarettes. He comes out again and looks at the girl for the first time. They start to walk to the dining room. In the archway,* MARTY *pauses, turns to the* GIRL.]

MARTY   Waddaya doing New Year's Eve?

GIRL   Nothing.

[*They quietly slip into each other's arms and kiss. Slowly their faces part, and* MARTY's *head sinks down upon her shoulder. He is crying. His shoulders shake slightly. The* GIRL *presses her cheek against the back of his head. They stand . . . there is the sound of the rear porch door being unlatched. They both start from their embrace. A moment later the* MOTHER's *voice is heard off in the kitchen.*]

MOTHER   Hallo! Hallo, Marty? (*She comes into the dining room, stops at the sight of the* GIRL.) Hallo, Marty, when you come home?

MARTY   We just got here about fifteen minutes ago, Ma. Ma, I want you to meet Miss Clara Davis. She's a graduate of New York University. She teaches history in Benjamin Franklin High School.

[*This seems to impress the* MOTHER.]

MOTHER   Siddown, siddown. You want some chicken? We got some chicken in the icebox.

GIRL   No, Mrs. Pilletti, we were just going home. Thank you very much anyway.

MOTHER   Well, siddown a minute. I just come inna house. I'll take off my coat. Siddown a minute.

[*She pulls her coat off.*]

MARTY   How'd you come home, Ma? Thomas give you a ride?

[*The* MOTHER *nods.*]

MOTHER   Oh, it's a sad business, a sad business.

[*She sits down on a dining-room chair, holding her coat in her lap. She turns to the* GIRL, *who likewise sits.*]

MOTHER   My sister Catherine, she doesn't get along with her daughter-in-law, so she's gonna come live with us.

MARTY Oh, she's coming, eh, Ma?

MOTHER Oh, sure. (*to the* GIRL) It's a very sad thing. A woman, fifty-six years old, all her life, she had her own home. Now, she's just an old lady, sleeping on her daughter-in-law's couch. It's a curse to be a mother, I tell you. Your children grow up and then what is left for you to do? What is a mother's life but her children? It is a very cruel thing when your son has no place for you in his home.

GIRL Couldn't she find some sort of hobby to fill out her time?

MOTHER Hobby! What can she do? She cooks and she cleans. You gotta have a house to clean. You gotta have children to cook for. These are the terrible years for a woman, the terrible years.

GIRL You musn't feel too harshly against her daughter-in-law. She also wants to have a house to clean and a family to cook for.

[*The* MOTHER *darts a quick, sharp look at the* GIRL—*then looks back to her hands, which are beginning to twist nervously.*]

MOTHER You don't think my sister Catherine should live in her daughter-in-law's house?

GIRL Well, I don't know the people, of course, but, as a rule, I don't think a mother-in-law should live with a young couple.

MOTHER Where do you think a mother-in-law should go?

GIRL I don't think a mother should depend so much upon her children for her rewards in life.

MOTHER That's what it says in the book in New York University. You wait till you are a mother. It don't work out that way.

GIRL Well, it's silly for me to argue about it. I don't know the people involved.

MARTY Ma, I'm going to take her home now. It's getting late, and the buses only run about one an hour.

MOTHER (*standing*) Sure.

[*The* GIRL *stands.*]

GIRL It was very nice meeting you, Mrs. Pilletti. I hope I'll see you again.

MOTHER Sure.

[MARTY *and the* GIRL *move to the kitchen.*]

MARTY All right, Ma. I'll be back in about an hour.

MOTHER Sure.

GIRL Good night, Mrs. Pilletti.

MOTHER Good night.

[MARTY *and the* GIRL *exit into the kitchen. The* MOTHER *stands, expressionless, by her chair watching them go. She remains standing rigidly even after the porch door can be heard being opened and shut. The camera moves up to a close-up of the MOTHER. Her eyes are wide. She is staring straight ahead. There is fear in her eyes.*]

For anthologies containing the complete text and for a list of suggested readings, see the preceding scene from *Marty* (p. 66).

Billy Budd

Louis O. Coxe and
Robert Chapman (1951)
From Act I, Scene 2

SCENE:	For two men
CHARACTERS:	Billy Budd, Foretopman John Claggart, Master-at-arms
SETTING:	The maindeck of the H. M. S. *Indomitable* at sea.
TIME:	Early evening. August, 1798, the year following the naval mutinies at Spithead and the Nore.
SITUATION:	The play *Billy Budd* is based on Herman Melville's short story of the same title.

Billy Budd has been impressed into service aboard the British warship H. M. S. *Indomitable*. Billy shows no ill will toward his officers; rather he seems to be the personification of everything that is honest and decent—an ideal sailor. His only flaw is a slight speech impediment: strong emotion causes him to stutter. Billy's integrity and sincerity have made him a favorite of the crew. Claggart, on the other hand, is obsessed with the basic evil in man's nature and has done everything he can to torment the crew. All the sailors except Billy hate Claggart for his cruelty. Billy cannot or will not see the cruelty in Claggart, choosing instead to look for the kindness and humanity he senses Claggart must possess. Billy does not realize that precisely because of Billy's essential innocent goodness that refuses to let him see evil in men, Claggart hates Billy even more than the other sailors.

See also the following scene from *Billy Budd* (p. 77), which occurs later in the play.

BILLY Good evening, sir.

CLAGGART (*startled, then subtly sarcastic*) Good evening.

BILLY Will it be all right if I stay topside a bit to watch the water?

CLAGGART I suppose the Handsome Sailor may do many things forbidden to his messmates.

BILLY Yes, sir. The sea's calm tonight, isn't it? Calm and peaceful.

CLAGGART The sea's deceitful, boy; calm above, and underneath, a world of gliding monsters preying on their fellows. Murderers, all of them. Only the sharpest teeth survive.

BILLY I'd like to know about such things, as you do, sir.

CLAGGART You're an ingenuous sailor, Billy Budd. Is there, behind that youthful face, the wisdom pretty virtue has need of? Even the gods must know their rivals, boy; and Christ had first to recognize the ills before he cured 'em.

BILLY What, sir?

CLAGGART Never mind. But tell me this: how have you stomach to stand here and talk to me? Are you so innocent and ignorant of what I am? You know my reputation. Jenkins and the rest are witnesses, and certainly you've heard them talking to me. Half of them would knife me in the back some night and do it gladly; Jenkins is thinking of it. Doubtless he'll try one day. How do you dare, then? Have you not intelligence enough to be afraid of me? To hate me as all the others do?

BILLY Why should I be afraid of you, sir? You speak to me friendly when we meet. I know some of the men . . . are fearful of you, sir, but I can't believe they're right about it.

CLAGGART You're a fool, fellow. In time, you'll learn to fear me like the rest. Young you are, and scarcely used to the fit of your man's flesh.

BILLY I know they're wrong, sir. You aren't like they say. Nobody could be so.

CLAGGART So . . . ? So what, boy? Vicious, did you mean to say, or brutal? But they aren't wrong, and you would see it, but for those blue eyes that light so kindly on your fellow men.

BILLY Oh, I've got no education, I know that. There must be a lot of things a man misses when he's ignorant. But learning's hard. Must be sort of lonely, too.

CLAGGART What are you prating of, half-man, half-child? Your messmates crowd around, admire your yellow hair and your blue eyes, do tricks and favors for you out of love, and you talk about loneliness!

BILLY I just noticed the way you were looking off to leeward as I came up, sir. Kind of sad, you were looking.

CLAGGART Not sadness, boy. Another feeling, more like . . . pleasure. That's it. I can feel it now, looking at you. A certain . . . pleasure.

BILLY (*flattered*) Thank you, sir.

CLAGGART (*annoyed at* BILLY's *incomprehension*) Pah.

BILLY Just talking with you, sir, I can tell they're wrong about you. They're ignorant, like me.

CLAGGART Compliment for compliment, eh, boy? Have you no heart for terror, fellow? You've seen this stick in use. Have you not got sense and spleen and liver to be scared, even to be cowardly?

BILLY No, sir, I guess not. I like talking to you, sir. But please, tell me something.

CLAGGART I wonder if I can. Well, ask it.

BILLY Why do you want us to believe you're cruel, and not really like everybody else?

CLAGGART I think you are the only child alive who wouldn't understand if I explained; or else you'd not believe it.

BILLY Oh, I'd believe you, sir. There's much I could learn from you: I never knew a man like you before.

CLAGGART (slowly) Do you—like me, Billy Budd?

BILLY You've always been most pleasant with me, sir.

CLAGGART Have I?

BILLY Yes, sir. In the mess, the day I came aboard? And almost every day you have a pleasant word.

CLAGGART And what I have said tonight, are these pleasant words?

BILLY Yes, sir. I was wondering . . . could I talk to you between watches, when you've nothing else to do?

CLAGGART You're a plausible boy, Billy. Aye, the nights are long, and talking serves to pass them.

BILLY Thank you, sir. That would mean a lot to me.

CLAGGART Perhaps to me as well. (*drops his rattan.* BILLY *picks it up and hands it back to him.* CLAGGART *stares at it a moment, then at* BILLY.) No, No! Charm me, too, would you! Get away!

BILLY (*surprised and puzzled*) Aye, sir.

[*He exits down the hatchway.*]

Reference Key to Plays in Anthologies

Copies of the complete play may be found in the following selected volumes:
Numbers 38, 52.
See also *Theatre Arts*, February, 1952.

Further Reading on *Billy Budd*

Brown, John Mason. "Hanged From the Yardarm." *As They Appear.* New York: McGraw-Hill, 1952, pp. 186–92.

Gassner, John. "Entropy in the Drama." *Theatre Arts*, Vol. 35, No. 9 (September, 1951), pp. 16–17, 73. (See particularly p. 73 for Gassner's assessment of the play's potential as tragedy.)

Nathan, George Jean. "*Billy Budd.*" *Theatre Book of the Year, 1950–51.* New York: Knopf, 1951, pp. 219–21.

Billy Budd

LOUIS O. COXE AND
ROBERT CHAPMAN (1951)
From Act III, Scene 1

SCENE: For four men

CHARACTERS: Edward Fairfax Vere, Captain, Royal Navy
Philip Michael Seymour, First Officer
John Ratcliffe, First Lieutenant
Bordman Wyatt, Sailing Officer

SETTING: Captain Vere's cabin aboard H. M. S. *Indomitable*, at sea.

TIME: An evening in August, 1798.

SITUATION: See the preceding scene from *Billy Budd* (p. 73), which occurs earlier in the play.

The confrontation between good and evil, symbolized by Billy Budd and Claggart, has ended in Claggart's death. Accused by Claggart of mutiny, Billy Budd was unable to speak to defend himself because of a speech impediment and in anguish struck Claggart and killed him.

Captain Vere convenes the ship's officers to try Billy for murder. First Officer Seymour presides. He has taken statements from Captain Vere, who witnessed the incident, and from Billy and other sailors. When this scene begins, the evidence gathered so far clearly points to justifiable homicide.

SEYMOUR   Have you anything to say, Ratcliffe?

RATCLIFFE   Yes, sir. Claggart was killed because Budd couldn't speak. In that sense, that he stammers, he's a cripple. You don't hang a man for that, for speaking the only way he could.

WYATT   If you condemn him, it's the same thing as condoning the apparent lie the Master-at-Arms clearly told. I'd have struck him, too. The boy is clearly innocent, struck him in self-defense.

RATCLIFFE Aye. I'm ready to acquit him now.

SEYMOUR Good. Then we can reach a verdict at once.

VERE Hitherto I have been a witness at this trial, no more. And I hesitate to interfere, except that at this clear crisis you ignore one fact we cannot close our eyes to.

SEYMOUR With your pardon, sir, as Senior Member of this court, I must ask if you speak now as our commanding officer or as a private man.

VERE As convening authority, Seymour. I summoned this court, and I must review its findings and approve them before passing them on to the Admiralty.

SEYMOUR Aye, sir, that is your right.

VERE No right. Which of us here has rights? It is my duty, and I must perform it. Budd has killed a man—his superior officer.

SEYMOUR We have found a verdict, sir.

VERE I know that, Seymour. Your verdict sets him free, and so would I wish to do. But are we free to choose as we would do if we were private citizens? The Admiralty has its code. Do you suppose it cares who Budd is? Who you and I are?

SEYMOUR We don't forget that, sir. But surely Claggart's tales were simply lies. We've established that.

VERE Aye. But the Nore and Spithead were brute facts, and must not come again. The men were starved out before, but if they should think we are afraid . . .

RATCLIFFE Captain, how could they? They certainly know Budd is no mutineer.

WYATT Of course not. Since he came on board, he's done more to keep the crew in hand than any of us.

SEYMOUR That's true. The men took naturally to him.

VERE As officers we are concerned to keep this ship effective as a weapon. And the law says what we must do in such a case as this. Come now, you know the facts, and the Mutiny Act's provisions. At sea, in time of war, an impressed man strikes his superior officer, and the blow is fatal. The mere blow alone would hang him, at least according to the Act. Well then, the men on board know that as well as you and I. And we acquit him. They have sense, they know the proper penalty to follow, and yet it does not follow.

SEYMOUR But they know Budd, sir, and Claggart too, I daresay. Would they not applaud the decision that frees Budd? They would thank us.

WYATT String him to a yard, and they'll turn round and rescue him, and string us up instead!

RATCLIFFE Aye, that's a point. It's twice as dangerous to hang the boy as it would be to let him go. If there's a mutinous temper in the crew, condemning Budd would surely set it off.

VERE   That is possible. Whatever step we take, the risk is great; but it is ours. That is what makes us officers. Yet if in fear of what our office demands we shirk our duty, we only play at war, at being men. If by our lawful rigor mutiny comes, there is no blame for us. But if in fear, miscalled a kind of mercy, we pardon Budd against specific order, and then the crew revolts, how culpable and weak our verdict would appear! The men on board know what our case is, how we are haunted by the Spithead risings. Have they forgotten how the panic spread through England? No. Your clemency would be accounted fear, and they would say we flinch from practising a lawful rigor lest new outbreaks be provoked. What shame to us! And what a deadly blow to discipline!

RATCLIFFE   I concede that, sir. But this case is exceptional, and pity, if we are men, is bound to move us, Captain.

VERE   So am I moved. Yet we cannot have warm hearts betraying heads that should be cool. In such a case ashore, an upright judge does not allow the pleading tears of women to touch his nature. Here at sea, the heart, the female in a man, weeps like a woman. She must be ruled out, hard though it be. (*pause*) Still silent? Very well, I see that something in all your downcast faces seems to urge that not alone the heart moves hesitancy. Conscience, perhaps. The private conscience moves you.

WYATT   Aye, that's it, sir. How can we condemn this man and live at peace again within ourselves? We have our standards; ethics, if you like.

VERE   Challenge your scruples! They move as in a dusk. Come, do they import something like this: if we are bound to judge, regardless of palliating circumstances, the death of Claggart as the prisoner's deed, then does that deed appear a capital crime whereof the penalty is mortal? But can we adjudge to summary and shameful death a fellow creature innocent before God, and whom we feel to be so? Does that state the case rightly?

SEYMOUR   That is my feeling, sir.

VERE   You all feel, I am sure, that the boy in effect is innocent; that what he did was from an unhappy stricture of speech that made him speak with blows. And I believe that, too; believe as you do, that he struck his man down, tempted beyond endurance. Acquit him, then, you say, as innocent?

RATCLIFFE   Exactly! Oh I know the Articles prescribe death for what Budd has done, but that . . .

WYATT   Oh, stow the Articles! They don't account for such a case as this. You yourself say Budd is innocent.

VERE   In intent, Wyatt, in intent.

WYATT Does that count for nothing? His whole attitude, his motive, count for nothing? If his intent . . .

VERE The intent or non-intent of Budd is nothing to the purpose. In a court more merciful than martial it would extenuate, and shall, at the last Assizes, set him free. But here we have these alternatives only: condemn or let go.

SEYMOUR But it seems to me we've got to consider the problem as a moral one, sir, despite the fact that we're not moralists. When Claggart told you his lie, the case immediately went beyond the scope of military justice.

VERE I, too, feel that. But do these gold stripes across our arms attest that our allegiance is to Nature?

RATCLIFFE To our country, sir.

VERE Aye, Ratcliffe; to the King. And though the sea, which is inviolate Nature primeval, though it be the element whereon we move and have our being as sailors, is our official duty hence to Nature? No. So little is that true that we resign our freedom when we put this on. And when war is declared, are we, the fighters commissioned to destroy, consulted first?

WYATT Does that deny us the right to act like men? We're not trying a murderer, a dock-side cut-throat!

VERE The gold we wear shows that we serve the King, the Law. What does it matter that our acts are fatal to our manhood, if we serve as we are forced to serve? What bitter salt leagues move between our code and God's own judgments! We are conscripts, every one, upright in this uniform of flesh. There is no truce to war born in the womb. We fight at command.

WYATT All I know is that I can't sit by and see Budd hanged!

VERE I say we fight by order, by command of our superiors. And if our judgments approve the war, it is only coincidence. And so it is with all our acts. So now, would it be so much we ourselves who speak as judges here, as it would be martial law operating through us? For that law, and for its rigor, we are not responsible. Our duty lies in this: that we are servants only.

RATCLIFFE The Admiralty doesn't want service like that. What good would it do? Who'd profit by Budd's death?

WYATT You want to make us murderers!

SEYMOUR Wyatt! Control yourself!

VERE What is this vessel that you serve in, Wyatt, an ark of peace? Go count her guns; then tell your conscience to lie quiet, if you can.

RATCLIFFE But that is war. This would be downright killing!

SEYMOUR It's all war, Ratcliffe; war to the death, for all of us.

VERE You see that, Seymour? That this war began before our time?

SEYMOUR   And will end long after it.

VERE   Here we have the Mutiny Act for justice. No child can own a closer tie to parent than can that Act to what it stems from: War. This is a wartime cruise and in this ship are Englishmen who fight against their wills, perhaps against their conscience, 'pressed by war into the service of the King. Though we as fellow creatures understand their lot, what does it matter to the officer, or to the enemy? The French will cut down conscripts in the same swath with volunteers, and we will do as much for them. War has no business with anything but surfaces. War's child, the Mutiny Act, is featured like the father.

RATCLIFFE   Couldn't we mitigate the penalty if we convict him?

VERE   No, Ratcliffe. The penalty is prescribed.

RATCLIFFE   I'd like to think it over, Captain. I'm not sure.

VERE   I repeat, then, that while we ponder and you hesitate over anxieties I confess to sharing, the enemy comes nearer. We must act, and quickly. The French close in on us; the crew will find out shortly what has happened. Our consciences are private matters, Ratcliffe. But we are public men, controlling life and death within this world at sea. Tell me whether or not in our positions we dare let our consciences take precedence of the code that makes us officers and calls this case to trial.

RATCLIFFE   (after a pause; quietly) No, sir.

WYATT   Can you stand Budd's murder on your conscience?

SEYMOUR   Wyatt! Hold your tongue!

WYATT   (jumping up) I say let him go!

SEYMOUR   Sit down, sir!

VERE   Let him speak.

WYATT   I won't bear a hand to hang a man I know is innocent! My blood's not cold enough. I can't give the kind of judgment you want to force on us! I ask to be excused from sitting upon this court.

SEYMOUR   Do you know what you're saying? Sit down and hold your tongue, man!

VERE   The kind of judgment I ask of you is only this, Wyatt: that you recognize your function in this ship. I believe you know it quite as well as we, yet you rebel. Can't you see that you must first strip off the uniform you wear, and after that your flesh, before you can escape the case at issue here? Decide you must, Wyatt. Oh you may be excused and wash your hands of it, but someone must decide. We are the law; law orders us to act, and shows us how. Do you imagine Seymour, or Ratcliffe here, or I, would not save this boy if we could see a way consistent with our duties? Acquit Budd if you can. God knows I wish I could. If in your mind as well as in your heart, you can say freely that his life is not forfeit to the law we serve, reason with us!

Show us how to save him without putting aside our function. Or if you can't do that, teach us to put by our responsibility and not betray ourselves. Can you do this? Speak, man, speak! Show us how! Save him, Wyatt, and you save us all. (WYATT *slowly sits down.*) You recognize the logic of the choice I force upon you. But do not think me pitiless in thus demanding sentence on a luckless boy. I feel as you do for him. But even more, I think there is a grace of soul within him that shall forgive the law we bind him with, and pity us, stretched on the cross of choice. (*turns away*)

SEYMOUR   Well, gentlemen. Will you decide. (*Officers write their verdicts on paper before them, and hand them to* SEYMOUR, *who rises, draws his dirk and places it on the table, pointing forward.*) He is condemned, sir. Shall we appoint the dawn?

For anthologies containing the complete text and for a list of suggested readings, see the preceding scene from *Billy Budd* (pp. 75–76).

The Glass Menagerie _____

TENNESSEE WILLIAMS (1945)
From Scene II

SCENE: For two women

CHARACTERS: Amanda Wingfield
Laura Wingfield, her daughter

SETTING: The Wingfield apartment at the rear of a building facing an alley. St. Louis, Missouri.

TIME: Afternoon, the 1930's.

SITUATION: After her husband abandoned her, Amanda Wingfield reared her children, Tom and Laura. Amanda has great dreams for her children, now grown, far outstripping their potential or their wishes. Laura is an exceedingly shy, introverted young woman. Her personality has been affected by a deformed foot which causes her to limp. She has retreated to the world of her glass menagerie, a collection of small glass animals. Amanda has been paying for typing lessons for Laura so that she might be employable as a secretary.

As the scene begins, Laura has been polishing her glass collection when she hears Amanda. She thrusts the ornaments away and sits stiffly before a typewriter diagram on the wall. Amanda slowly lets herself in.

LAURA   Hello, Mother, I was—

[*She makes a nervous gesture toward the chart on the wall.* AMANDA *leans against the shut door and stares at* LAURA *with a martyred look.*]

AMANDA   Deception? Deception?

[*She slowly removes her hat and gloves, continuing the sweet suffering stare. She lets the hat and gloves fall on the floor—a bit of acting.*]

LAURA   (*shakily*) How was the D.A.R. meeting? (AMANDA *slowly opens her purse and removes a dainty white handkerchief which she shakes out delicately and delicately touches to her lips and nostrils.)* Didn't you go to the D.A.R. meeting, Mother?

AMANDA *(faintly, almost inaudibly)*—No.—No. *(then more forcibly)* I did not have the strength—to go to the D.A.R. In fact, I did not have the courage! I wanted to find a hole in the ground and hide myself in it forever!

[*She crosses slowly to the wall and removes the diagram of the typewriter keyboard. She holds it in front of her for a second, staring at it sweetly and sorrowfully—then bites her lips and tears it in two pieces.*]

LAURA *(faintly)* Why did you do that, Mother? (AMANDA *repeats the same procedure with the chart of the Gregg Alphabet.*) Why are you—

AMANDA Why? Why? How old are you, Laura?

LAURA Mother, you know my age.

AMANDA I thought that you were an adult; it seems that I was mistaken.

[*She crosses slowly to the sofa and sinks down and stares at* LAURA.]

LAURA Please don't stare at me, Mother.

[AMANDA *closes her eyes and lowers her head. Count ten.*]

AMANDA What are we going to do, what is going to become of us, what is the future?

[*Count ten.*]

LAURA Has something happened, Mother? (AMANDA *draws a long breath and takes out the handkerchief again. Dabbing process*) Mother, has —something happened?

AMANDA I'll be all right in a minute, I'm just bewildered—(*Count five.*)— by life. . . .

LAURA Mother, I wish that you would tell me what's happened!

AMANDA As you know, I was supposed to be inducted into my office at the D.A.R. this afternoon. But I stopped off at Rubicam's Business College to speak to your teachers about your having a cold and ask them what progress they thought you were making down there.

LAURA Oh. . . .

AMANDA I went to the typing instructor and introduced myself as your mother. She didn't know who you were. Wingfield, she said. We don't have any such student enrolled at the school!

I assured her she did, that you have been going to classes since early in January.

"I wonder," she said, "if you could be talking about that terribly shy little girl who dropped out of school after only a few days' attendance?"

"No," I said, "Laura, my daughter, has been going to school every day for the past six weeks!"

"Excuse me," she said. She took the attendance book out and there was your name, unmistakably printed, and all the dates you were absent until they decided that you had dropped out of school.

I still said, "No, there must have been some mistake! There must have been some mix-up in the records!"

And she said, "No—I remember her perfectly now. Her hands shook so that she couldn't hit the right keys! The first time we gave a speed-test, she broke down completely—was sick at the stomach and almost had to be carried into the wash-room! After that morning she never showed up any more. We phoned the house but never got any answer" —while I was working at Famous and Barr, I suppose, demonstrating those—Oh!

I felt so weak I could barely keep on my feet!

I had to sit down while they got me a glass of water!

Fifty dollars' tuition, all of our plans—my hopes and ambitions for you—just gone up the spout, just gone up the spout like that. (LAURA *draws a long breath and gets awkwardly to her feet. She crosses to the victrola and winds it up.*) What are you doing?

LAURA   Oh! (*She releases the handle and returns to her seat.*)

AMANDA   Laura, where have you been going when you've gone out pretending that you were going to business college?

LAURA   I've just been going out walking.

AMANDA   That's not true.

LAURA   It is. I just went walking.

AMANDA   Walking? Walking? In winter? Deliberately courting pneumonia in that light coat? Where did you walk to, Laura?

LAURA   All sorts of places—mostly in the park.

AMANDA   Even after you'd started catching that cold?

LAURA   It was the lesser of two evils, Mother. I couldn't go back up. I— threw up—on the floor!

AMANDA   From half past seven till after five every day you mean to tell me you walked around in the park, because you wanted to make me think that you were still going to Rubicam's Business College?

LAURA   It wasn't as bad as it sounds. I went inside places to get warmed up.

AMANDA   Inside where?

LAURA   I went in the art museum and the birdhouses at the Zoo. I visited the penguins every day! Sometimes I did without lunch and went to the movies. Lately I've been spending most of my afternoons in the Jewel-box, that big glass house where they raise the tropical flowers.

AMANDA   You did all this to deceive me, just for deception? (LAURA *looks down.*) Why?

LAURA Mother, when you're disappointed, you get that awful suffering look on your face, like the picture of Jesus' mother in the museum!

AMANDA Hush!

LAURA I couldn't face it.

[*Pause. A whisper of strings*]

AMANDA (*hopelessly fingering the huge pocketbook*) So what are we going to do the rest of our lives? Stay home and watch the parades go by? Amuse ourselves with the glass menagerie, darling? Eternally play those worn-out phonograph records your father left as a painful reminder of him?

We won't have a business career—we've given that up because it gave us nervous indigestion! (*laughs wearily*) What is there left but dependency all our lives? I know so well what becomes of unmarried women who aren't prepared to occupy a position. I've seen such pitiful cases in the South—barely tolerated spinsters living upon the grudging patronage of sister's husband or brother's wife!—stuck away in some little mouse-trap of a room—encouraged by one in-law to visit another —little birdlike women without any nest—eating the crust of humility all their life!

Is that the future that we've mapped out for ourselves?

I swear it's the only alternative I can think of!

It isn't a very pleasant alternative, is it?

Of course—some girls *do marry*. (LAURA *twists her hands nervously.*) Haven't you ever liked some boy?

LAURA Yes. I liked one once. (*rises*) I came across his picture a while ago.

AMANDA (*with some interest*) He gave you his picture?

LAURA No, it's in the year-book.

AMANDA (*disappointed*) Oh—a high-school boy.

LAURA Yes. His name was Jim. (LAURA *lifts the heavy annual from the claw-foot table.*) Here he is in *The Pirates of Penzance*.

AMANDA (*absently*) The what?

LAURA The operetta the senior class put on. He had a wonderful voice and we sat across the aisle from each other Mondays, Wednesdays and Fridays in the Aud. Here he is with the silver cup for debating! See his grin?

AMANDA (*absently*) He must have had a jolly disposition.

LAURA He used to call me—Blue Roses.

AMANDA Why did he call you such a name as that?

LAURA When I had that attack of pleurosis—he asked me what was the matter when I came back. I said pleurosis—he thought that I said Blue Roses! So that's what he always called me after that. Whenever he saw me, he'd holler, "Hello, Blue Roses!" I didn't care for the girl that he went out with. Emily Meisenbach. Emily was the best-dressed girl at Soldan. She never struck me, though, as being sincere . . . . It says in the Personal Section—they're engaged. That's—six years ago! They must be married by now.

AMANDA Girls that aren't cut out for business careers usually wind up married to some nice man. (*gets up with a spark of revival*) Sister, that's what you'll do!

[LAURA *utters a startled, doubtful laugh. She reaches quickly for a piece of glass.*]

LAURA But, Mother—

AMANDA Yes? (*crossing to photograph*)

LAURA (*in a tone of frightened apology*) I'm—crippled!

AMANDA Nonsense! Laura, I've told you never, never to use that word. Why, you're not crippled, you just have a little defect—hardly noticeable, even! When people have some slight disadvantage like that, they cultivate other things to make up for it—develop charm—and vivacity—and—*charm!* That's all you have to do! (*She turns again to the photograph.*) One thing your father had *plenty of*—was *charm!*

Reference Key to Plays in Anthologies

Copies of the complete play may be found in the following selected volumes: Numbers 9, 26, 30, 31, 37, 45, 47, 50, 64, 66, 67, 69.

Further Reading on Williams and *The Glass Menagerie*

Funke, Lewis and John E. Booth. "Williams on Williams." *Theatre Arts*, Vol. 46, No. 1 (January, 1962), pp. 16–19, 72–73.

Gassner, John. "Tennessee Williams: Dramatist of Frustration." *College English*, Vol. 10, No. 1 (October, 1948), pp. 1–7.

Moor, Paul. "A Mississippian Named Tennessee." *Harper's*, Vol. 198, No. 1178 (July, 1948), pp. 63–71.

Nelson, Benjamin. *Tennessee Williams, His Life and Work*. New York: Obolensky, 1962.

Williams, Edwina Dakin. *Remember Me to Tom*. New York: Putnam, 1963. (Tennessee Williams' mother discusses the factors which shaped his life and works.)

Young, Stark. *"The Glass Menagerie." The New Republic,* Vol. 112, No. 16 (April 16, 1945), pp. 505–06. (An excellent summary of the performances given in 1945 by the original creators of the roles.)

For still additional sources regarding the work of Williams, see the data following the scene from *A Streetcar Named Desire* (p. 137).

Recorded Performances

Complete performance: Jessica Tandy as Amanda, Julie Harris as Laura, Montgomery Clift as Tom, and David Wayne as the Gentleman Caller, Caedmon 301 (stereo S-301), two records.

Saint Joan

GEORGE BERNARD SHAW (1923)

From Scene 2

SCENE: For one man, one woman

CHARACTERS: Joan
Charles, the Dauphin

SETTING: The throne room of the Dauphin of France at Chinon, in Touraine.

TIME: Late afternoon, March, 1429.

SITUATION: Joan, the maid, has come to the court of the Dauphin to persuade him to give her arms so that she may lead the disconsolate French armies to victory against the English. Shaw has developed an interesting portrait of Joan, creating a character imbued with common sense, determination, and idealism. Charles is twenty-six years old, physically weak and of an ungainly appearance, but with a good sense of humor. Despite his age he has not matured sufficiently to exercise real control over his court. At the opening of this scene, the court has left, and Joan is alone with Charles for the first time. A product of Shaw's irreverent wit, this scene contains more humor than any excerpt in this section.

The next scene in this book, taken from *The Lark* by Jean Anouilh, concerns the same time in Joan's life. In that scene, Anouilh takes a different approach to the maid. Comparing and performing the two Joans should provide a most distinctive challenge to the actress.

JOAN (*to the* DAUPHIN) Who be old Gruff-and-Grum?
CHARLES He is the Duke de la Trémouille.
JOAN What be his job?
CHARLES He pretends to command the army. And whenever I find a friend I can care for, he kills him.

FROM *Saint Joan* by George Bernard Shaw. Reprinted by permission of The Public Trustee and The Society of Authors.

JOAN Why dost let him?

CHARLES (*petulantly moving to the throne side of the room to escape from her magnetic field*) How can I prevent him? He bullies me. They all bully me.

JOAN Art afraid?

CHARLES Yes: I am afraid. It's no use preaching to me about it. It's all very well for these big men with their armor that is too heavy for me, and their swords that I can hardly lift, and their muscle and their shouting and their bad tempers. They like fighting: most of them are making fools of themselves all the time they are not fighting; but I am quiet and sensible; and I dont want to kill people: I only want to be left alone to enjoy myself in my own way. I never asked to be a king: it was pushed on me. So if you are going to say "Son of St. Louis: gird on the sword of your ancestors, and lead us to victory" you may spare your breath to cool your porridge; for I cannot do it. I am not built that way; and there is an end of it.

JOAN (*trenchant and masterful*) Blethers! We are all like that to begin with. I shall put courage into thee.

CHARLES But I dont want to have courage put into me. I want to sleep in a comfortable bed, and not live in continual terror of being killed or wounded. Put courage into the others, and let them have their bellyful of fighting; but let me alone.

JOAN It's no use, Charlie: thou must face what God puts on thee. If thou fail to make thyself king, thoult be a beggar: what else art fit for? Come! Let me see thee sitting on the throne. I have looked forward to that.

CHARLES What is the good of sitting on the throne when the other fellows give all the orders? However! (*He sits enthroned, a piteous figure.*) here is the king for you! Look your fill at the poor devil.

JOAN Thourt not king yet, lad: thourt but Dauphin. Be not led away by them around thee. Dressing up dont fill empty noddle. I know the people: the real people that make thy bread for thee; and I tell thee they count no man king of France until the holy oil has been poured on his hair, and himself consecrated and crowned in Rheims Cathedral. And thou needs new clothes, Charlie. Why does not Queen look after thee properly?

CHARLES We're too poor. She wants all the money we can spare to put on her own back. Besides, I like to see her beautifully dressed; and I dont care what I wear myself: I should look ugly anyhow.

JOAN There is some good in thee, Charlie; but it is not yet a king's good.

CHARLES We shall see. I am not such a fool as I look. I have my eyes open; and I can tell you that one good treaty is worth ten good fights. These fighting fellows lose all on the treaties that they gain on the fights. If we can only have a treaty, the English are sure to have the worst of it, because they are better at fighting than at thinking.

JOAN If the English win, it is they that will make the treaty: and then God help poor France! Thou must fight, Charlie, whether thou will or no. I will go first to hearten thee. We must take our courage in both hands: aye, and pray for it with both hands too.

CHARLES (*descending from his throne and again crossing the room to escape from her dominating urgency*) Oh do stop talking about God and praying. I cant bear people who are always praying. Isnt it bad enough to have to do it at the proper times?

JOAN (*pitying him*) Thou poor child, thou hast never prayed in thy life. I must teach thee from the beginning.

CHARLES I am not a child: I am a grown man and a father; and I will not be taught any more.

JOAN Aye, you have a little son. He that will be Louis the Eleventh when you die. Would you not fight for him?

CHARLES No: a horrid boy. He hates me. He hates everybody, selfish little beast! I dont want to be bothered with children. I dont want to be a father; and I dont want to be a son: especially a son of St Louis. I dont want to be any of these fine things you all have your heads full of: I want to be just what I am. Why cant you mind your own business, and let me mind mine?

JOAN (*again contemptuous*) Minding your own business is like minding your own body: it's the shortest way to make yourself sick. What is my business? Helping mother at home. What is thine? Petting lapdogs and sucking sugarsticks: I call that muck. I tell thee it is God's business we are here to do: not our own. I have a message to thee from God; and thou must listen to it, though thy heart break with the terror of it.

CHARLES I dont want a message; but can you tell me any secrets? Can you do any cures? Can you turn lead into gold, or anything of that sort?

JOAN I can turn thee into a king, in Rheims Cathedral; and that is a miracle that will take some doing, it seems.

CHARLES If we go to Rheims, and have a coronation, Anne will want new dresses. We cant afford them. I am all right as I am.

JOAN As you are! And what is that? Less than my father's poorest shepherd. Thourt not lawful owner of thy own land of France till thou be consecrated.

CHARLES But I shall not be lawful owner of my own land anyhow. Will the consecration pay off my mortgages? I have pledged my last acre to the Archbishop and that fat bully. I owe money even to Bluebeard.

JOAN (*earnestly*) Charlie: I come from the land, and have gotten my strength working on the land; and I tell thee that the land is thine to rule righteously and keep God's peace in, and not to pledge at the pawnshop as a drunken woman pledges her children's clothes. And I come from God to tell thee to kneel in the cathedral and solemnly give thy kingdom to Him for ever and ever, and become the greatest king in the world as His steward and His bailiff, His soldier and His servant. The very clay of France will become holy; her soldiers will be the soldiers of God: the rebel dukes will be rebels against God: the English will fall on their knees and beg thee let them return to their lawful homes in peace. Wilt be a poor little Judas, and betray me and Him that sent me?

CHARLES (*tempted at last*) Oh, if I only dare!

JOAN I shall dare, dare, and dare again, in God's name! Art for or against me?

CHARLES (*excited*) I'll risk it, I warn you I shant be able to keep it up; but I'll risk it. You shall see. (*running to the main door and shouting*) Hallo! Come back, everybody. (*to* JOAN, *as he runs back to the arch opposite*) Mind you stand by and dont let me be bullied. (*through the arch*) Come along, will you: the whole Court. (*He sits down in the royal chair as they all hurry in to their former places, chattering and wondering.*) Now I'm in for it; but no matter: here goes! (*to the* PAGE) Call for silence, you little beast, will you?

Reference Key to Plays in Anthologies

A copy of the complete play may be found in the following volume:
Number 71.
See also Shaw, Bernard. *Complete Plays with Prefaces.* New York: Dodd, Mead, 1963. 6 vols., Vol. 2.

Further Reading on Shaw and *Saint Joan*

Colbourne, Maurice. *The Real Bernard Shaw.* London: J. M. Dent, 1949.
Ervine, St. John. *Bernard Shaw.* New York: Morrow, 1956.
Gassner, John. "Bernard Shaw and the British Compromise." *Masters of the Drama.* 3rd ed. New York: Dover, 1954, pp. 575–628.

Henderson, Archibald. *George Bernard Shaw: Man of the Century*. New York: Appleton-Century-Crofts, 1956. (Probably the best all-around study of Shaw, his ideas, and the development of his plays, by Shaw's official biographer.)

Pearson, Hesketh. *George Bernard Shaw: His Life and Personality*. New York: Atheneum, 1963.

Purdom, C. B. *A Guide to the Plays of Bernard Shaw*. London: Methuen, 1963.

Recorded Performances

Complete performances:

Siobhan McKenna as Joan, Caedmon 311 (stereo S-311), three records.
Siobhan McKenna as Joan, Victor LOC-6133, three records.

The Lark _____

JEAN ANOUILH (1955)
adapted by LILLIAN HELLMAN
From Act I

SCENE: For one man, one woman

CHARACTERS: Joan
Charles, the Dauphin

SETTING: The throne room of the Dauphin of France at Chinon, in Touraine.

TIME: Late afternoon, March, 1429.

SITUATION: The situation in this scene is identical to that found in the preceding scene from *Saint Joan* by Shaw. Shaw and Anouilh have, however, given their Joans distinctive qualities that reveal their different views of the girl.

As in the previous version, Joan has found Charles a weak and indecisive Dauphin. The scene begins as Charles, somewhat uncertainly, has dismissed the court in order to speak to the young lady.

CHARLES   (*He holds his noble pose for an instant, then bursts into laughter.*) And they went. It's the first time they ever obeyed me. (*very worried*) You haven't come here to kill me? (*She smiles.*) No. No, of course not. You have an honest face. I've lived so long with those pirates that I've almost forgotten what an honest face looks like. Are there other people who have honest faces?

JOAN   (*gravely*) Many, sire.

CHARLES   I never see them. Brutes and whores, that's all I ever see. And the little Queen. She's nice, but she's stupid. And Agnes. She's not stupid—and she's not nice. (*He climbs on his throne, hangs his feet over one of the arms and sighs.*) All right. Start boring me. Tell me that I ought to be a great King.

JOAN   (*softly*) Yes, Charles.

CHARLES   Listen. If you want to make an impression on the Archbishop and the council, we'll have to stay in this room for at least an hour. If you talk to me of God and the Kingdom of France, I'll never live through the hour. Let's do something else. Do you know how to play at cards?

JOAN   I don't know what it is.

CHARLES   It is a nice game invented to amuse my Papa when he was ill. I'll teach you. (*He begins to hunt for the cards.*) I hope they haven't stolen them. They steal everything from me around here and cards are expensive. Only the wealthiest princes can have them. I got mine from Papa. I'll never have the price of another pack. If those pigs have stolen them—No. Here they are. (*He finds them in his pocket.*) My Papa was crazy. Went crazy young—in his thirties. Did you know that? Sometimes I am glad I am a bastard. At least I don't have to be so frightened of going crazy. Then sometimes I wish I were his son and knew that I was meant to be a king. It's confusing.

JOAN   Of the two, which would you prefer?

CHARLES   Well, on the days when I have a little courage, I'd risk going crazy. But on the days when I haven't any courage—that's from Sunday to Saturday—I would rather let everything go to hell and live in peace in some foreign land on whatever little money I have left.

JOAN   Today, Charles, is this one of the days when you have courage?

CHARLES   Today? (*He thinks a minute.*) Yes, it seems to me I have a little bit today. Not much, but a little bit. I was sharp with the Archbishop, and—

JOAN   You will have courage every day. Beginning now.

CHARLES   You have a charm in a bottle or a basket?

JOAN   I have a charm.

CHARLES   You are a witch? You can tell me, you know, because I don't care. I swear to you that I won't repeat it. I have a horror of people being tortured. A long time ago, they made me witness the burning of a heretic at the stake. I vomited all night long.

JOAN   I am not a witch. But I have a charm.

CHARLES   Sell it to me without telling the others.

JOAN   I will give it to you, Charles. For nothing.

CHARLES   Then I don't want it. What you get free costs too much. (*He shuffles the cards.*) I act like a fool so that people will let me alone. My Papa was so crazy they think I am, too. He was very crazy, did all kinds of strange things, some of them very funny. One day he thought it would be nice to have a great funeral, but nobody happened to die just then so he decided to bury a man who'd been dead four years. It cost a fortune to dig him out and put him back, but it was fun. (*He laughs merrily, catches himself, stares at* JOAN.) But don't think you can catch me too easily. I know a little about the world.

JOAN You know too much. You are too smart.

CHARLES Yes. Because I must defend myself against these cutthroats. They've got large bones, I've got puny sticks. But my head's harder than theirs and I've clung to my throne by using it.

JOAN (*gently*) I would like to defend you against them, Charles. I would give my life to do it.

CHARLES Do you mean that?

JOAN Yes. And I'm not afraid of anything.

CHARLES You're lucky. Or you're a liar. Sit down and I'll teach you to play.

JOAN All right. You teach me this game and I'll teach you another game.

CHARLES What game do you know?

JOAN How not to be too smart. (*softly*) And how not to be afraid.

CHARLES (*laughs*) You'll be here a lifetime, my girl. Now. See these cards? They have pictures painted on them. Kings, queens and knaves, just as in real life. Now which would you say was the most powerful, which one could take all the rest?

JOAN The king.

CHARLES Well, you're wrong. This large heart can take the king. It can put him to rout, break his heart, win all his money. This card is called—

JOAN I know. It is called God. Because God is more powerful than kings.

CHARLES Oh, leave God alone for a minute. It's called the ace. Are you running this game? God this and God that. You talk as if you dined with Him last night. Didn't anybody tell you that the English also say their prayers to God? Every man thinks God is on his side. The rich and powerful know He is. But we're not rich and powerful, you and I —and France.

JOAN That isn't what God cares about. He is angry with us because we have no courage left. God doesn't like frightened people.

CHARLES Then He certainly doesn't like me. And if He doesn't like me, why should I like Him? He could have given me courage. I wanted it.

JOAN (*sharply*) Is God your nurse? Couldn't you have tried to do a little better? God gave you sense. And what do you do with it? Play cards. Bounce a ball in the air. Play baby tricks with the Archbishop and act the fool for all to see. You have a son. But what have you made for him? Nothing. And when he's grown he, too, will have a right to say, "God didn't like me, so why should I like Him?" But when he says God he will mean you because every son thinks his father is God. And when he's old enough to know that, he will hate you for what you didn't give him.

CHARLES Give him? What can I give him? I'm glad to be alive. I've told you the truth: I am afraid. I've always been and I always will be.

JOAN And now I'll tell you the truth: I am also afraid. (*with force*) And why not? Only the stupid are not afraid. What is the matter with you? Don't you understand that it was far more dangerous for me to get here than it is for you to build a kingdom? I've been in danger every minute of the way, and every minute of the way I was frightened. I don't want to be beaten, I don't want pain, I don't want to die. I am scared.

CHARLES (softly) What do you do when you get scared?

JOAN Act as if I wasn't. It's that simple. Try it. Say to yourself, yes, I am afraid. But it's nobody else's business, so go on, go on. And you do go on.

CHARLES (softly) Where do you go?

JOAN (slowly, carefully) To the English, outside Orleans. And when you get there and see the cannon and the archers, and you know you are outnumbered, you will say to yourself, all right, they are stronger than I am, and that frightens me, as well it should. But I'll march right through because I had sense enough to get frightened first.

CHARLES March through a stronger army? That can't be done.

JOAN Yes it can. If you have sense and courage. Do you want to know what happened in my village last year? They tell the story as a miracle now but it wasn't. The Bouchon boy went hunting. He's the best poacher in our village, and this day he was poaching on the master's grounds. The master kept a famous dog, trained to kill, and the dog found the Bouchon boy. The boy was caught and death faced him. So he threw a stone and the dog turned his head. That was sense. And while the dog turned his head the boy decided the only way was to stand and fight. That was courage. He strangled the dog. That was victory. See?

CHARLES Didn't the dog bite him?

JOAN (as if to a stupid child) You're like the old people in the village— you really believe in miracles. Of course the dog bit him. But I told you the boy had sense, and sense saved his life. God gave man an inside to his head, and He naturally doesn't want to see it wasted. (smiles) See? That's my secret. The witches' secret. What will you pay me for it now?

CHARLES What do you want?

JOAN The army of France. Believe in God and give me the army.

CHARLES (moves away from her) Tomorrow. I'll have time to get ready—

JOAN (moves after him) No, right now. You are ready. Come on, Charlie.

CHARLES Perhaps I am. Perhaps I've been waiting for you and didn't know—(laughs nervously) Shall we send for the Archbishop and La Tremouille and tell them that I have decided to give the army to you? It would be fun to see their faces.

JOAN Call them.

CHARLES (*in a panic*) No. I am frightened.

JOAN Are you as afraid as you ever can be, ever were or will be, then, now and in the future? Are you sick?

CHARLES (*holding his stomach*) I think so.

JOAN Good. Good. Then the worst is over. By the time they get scared, you'll be all over yours. Now, if you're as sick as you can get, I'll call them. (*She runs upstage and calls out.*) Monseigneur the Archbishop. Monseigneur de la Tremouille. Please come to the Dauphin.

CHARLES (*almost happy*) I am very sick.

JOAN (*moves him gently to the throne and arranges his hands and feet*) God is smiling. He is saying to Himself, "Look at that little Charles. He is sicker than he's ever been in his life. But he has called in his enemies and will face them. My, such a thing is wonderful." (*with great force*) Hang on, Charles. We'll be in Orleans. We'll march right up.

Reference Key to Plays in Anthologies

A copy of the complete play may be found in the following volume:
Number 43.
See also *Theatre Arts*, March, 1957.

Further Reading on Anouilh and *The Lark*

Champigny, Robert. "Theatre in a Mirror: Anouilh." *Yale French Studies*, Vol. 45, No. 14 (1955), pp. 57–64.

Chiari, Joseph. *The Contemporary French Theatre*. New York: Macmillan, 1959. (See particularly pp. 170–204.)

Gassner, John. "European Drama in the American Theatre: *The Lark*." *Twenty Best European Plays on the American Stage*. New York: Crown, 1957, pp. 29–32.

Hewitt, Alan. "*The Lark*: Theatrical Bird of Passage." *Theatre Arts*, Vol. 40, No. 3 (March, 1956), pp. 63–64, 96.

Marsh, Edward. *Jean Anouilh, Poet of Pierrot and Pantaloon*. London: W. H. Allen, 1953.

Pronko, Leonard Cabell. *The World of Jean Anouilh*. Berkeley: Univ. of Calif. Press, 1961.

Valency, Maurice. "The World of Jean Anouilh." *Theatre Arts*, Vol. 41, No. 7 (July, 1957), pp. 31–32, 92–93.

Death of a Salesman

ARTHUR MILLER (1949)

From Act I

SCENE: For three men, one woman

CHARACTERS: Willy Loman
Linda Loman, his wife
Biff Loman, his older son
Happy Loman, his younger son

SETTING: The kitchen and bedroom of a small, middle-class frame house in Brooklyn. It is surrounded by the towering walls of apartment houses.

TIME: A spring evening in the late 1940's. The year, however, might just as well be the present one.

SITUATION: Willy Loman, a salesman, is old and exhausted. His wife Linda has just finished berating Biff for his lack of consideration for his father and his refusal to stay at home. As the scene opens, Biff is contrite. When Willy enters, however, another angry conflict ensues. Yet between Willy and Biff there is a strong bond of affection.

See also the following scene from *Death of a Salesman* (p. 106), which occurs later in the play.

BIFF *(kissing her)* All right, pal, all right. It's all settled now. I've been remiss. I know that, Mom. But now I'll stay, and I swear to you, I'll apply myself. *(kneeling in front of her, in a fever of self-reproach)* It's just—you see, Mom, I don't fit in business. Not that I won't try. I'll try, and I'll make good.

HAPPY Sure you will. The trouble with you in business was you never tried to please people.

BIFF I know, I—

HAPPY Like when you worked for Harrison's. Bob Harrison said you

Death of a Salesman 99

were tops, and then you go and do some damn fool thing like whistling whole songs in the elevator like a comedian.

BIFF (*against* HAPPY) So what? I like to whistle sometimes.

HAPPY You don't raise a guy to a responsible job who whistles in the elevator!

LINDA Well, don't argue about it now.

HAPPY Like when you'd go off and swim in the middle of the day instead of taking the line around.

BIFF (*his resentment rising*) Well, don't you run off? You take off sometimes, don't you? On a nice summer day?

HAPPY Yeah, but I cover myself!

LINDA Boys!

HAPPY If I'm going to take a fade the boss can call any number where I'm supposed to be and they'll swear to him that I just left. I'll tell you something that I hate to say, Biff, but in the business world some of them think you're crazy.

BIFF (*angered*) Screw the business world!

HAPPY All right, screw it! Great, but cover yourself!

LINDA Hap, Hap!

BIFF I don't care what they think! They've laughed at Dad for years, and you know why? Because we don't belong in this nuthouse of a city! We should be mixing cement on some open plain, or—or carpenters. A carpenter is allowed to whistle!

[WILLY *walks in from the entrance of the house, at left.*]

WILLY Even your grandfather was better than a carpenter. (*pause. They watch him.*) You never grew up. Bernard does not whistle in the elevator, I assure you.

BIFF (*as though to laugh* WILLY *out of it*) Yeah, but you do, Pop.

WILLY I never in my life whistled in an elevator! And who in the business world thinks I'm crazy?

BIFF I didn't mean it like that, Pop. Now don't make a whole thing out of it, will ya?

WILLY Go back to the West! Be a carpenter, a cowboy, enjoy yourself!

LINDA Willy, he was just saying—

WILLY I heard what he said!

HAPPY (*trying to quiet* WILLY) Hey, Pop, come on now . . .

WILLY (*continuing over* HAPPY's *line*) They laugh at me, heh? Go to Filene's, go to the Hub, go to Slattery's, Boston. Call out the name Willy Loman and see what happens! Big shot!

BIFF All right, Pop.

WILLY Big!

BIFF All right!

WILLY   Why do you always insult me?

BIFF   I didn't say a word. (to LINDA) Did I say a word?

LINDA   He didn't say anything, Willy.

WILLY   (going to the doorway of the living room) All right, good night, good night.

LINDA   Willy, dear, he just decided . . .

WILLY   (to BIFF) If you get tired hanging around tomorrow, paint the ceiling I put up in the living room.

BIFF   I'm leaving early tomorrow.

HAPPY   He's going to see Bill Oliver, Pop.

WILLY   (interestedly) Oliver? For what?

BIFF   (with reserve, but trying, trying) He always said he'd stake me. I'd like to go into business, so maybe I can take him up on it.

LINDA   Isn't that wonderful?

WILLY   Don't interrupt. What's wonderful about it? There's fifty men in the City of New York who'd stake him. (to BIFF) Sporting goods?

BIFF   I guess so. I know something about it and—

WILLY   He knows something about it! You know sporting goods better than Spalding, for God's sake! How much is he giving you?

BIFF   I don't know, I didn't even see him yet, but—

WILLY   Then what're you talkin' about?

BIFF   (getting angry) Well, all I said was I'm gonna see him, that's all!

WILLY   (turning away) Ah, you're counting your chickens again.

BIFF   (starting left for the stairs) Oh, Jesus, I'm going to sleep!

WILLY   (calling after him) Don't curse in this house!

BIFF   (turning) Since when did you get so clean?

HAPPY   (trying to stop them) Wait a . . .

WILLY   Don't use that language to me! I won't have it!

HAPPY   (grabbing BIFF, shouts) Wait a minute! I got an idea. I got a feasible idea. Come here, Biff, let's talk this over now, let's talk some sense here. When I was down in Florida last time, I thought of a great idea to sell sporting goods. It just came back to me. You and I, Biff—we have a line, the Loman Line. We train a couple of weeks, and put on a couple of exhibitions, see?

WILLY   That's an idea!

HAPPY   Wait! We form two basketball teams, see? Two water-polo teams. We play each other. It's a million dollars' worth of publicity. Two brothers, see? The Loman Brothers. Displays in the Royal Palms—all the hotels. And banners over the ring and the basketball court: "Loman Brothers." Baby, we could sell sporting goods!

WILLY   That is a one-million-dollar idea!

LINDA   Marvelous!

Death of a Salesman   101

BIFF   I'm in great shape as far as that's concerned.

HAPPY   And the beauty of it is, Biff, it wouldn't be like a business. We'd be out playin' ball again . . .

BIFF   (*filled with enthusiasm*) Yeah, that's . . .

WILLY   Million-dollar . . .

HAPPY   And you wouldn't get fed up with it, Biff. It'd be the family again. There'd be the old honor, and comradeship, and if you wanted to go off for a swim or somethin'—well, you'd do it! Without some smart cooky gettin' up ahead of you!

WILLY   Lick the world! You guys together could absolutely lick the civilized world.

BIFF   I'll see Oliver tomorrow. Hap, if we could work that out . . .

LINDA   Maybe things are beginning to—

WILLY   (*wildly enthusiastic, to* LINDA) Stop interrupting! (*to* BIFF) But don't wear sport jacket and slacks when you see Oliver.

BIFF   No, I'll—

WILLY   A business suit, and talk as little as possible, and don't crack any jokes.

BIFF   He did like me. Always liked me.

LINDA   He loved you!

WILLY   (*to* LINDA) Will you stop! (*to* BIFF) Walk in very serious. You are not applying for a boy's job. Money is to pass. Be quiet, fine, and serious. Everybody likes a kidder, but nobody lends him money.

HAPPY   I'll try to get some myself, Biff. I'm sure I can.

WILLY   I see great things for you kids, I think your troubles are over. But remember, start big and you'll end big. Ask for fifteen. How much you gonna ask for?

BIFF   Gee, I don't know—

WILLY   And don't say "Gee." "Gee" is a boy's word. A man walking in for fifteen thousand dollars does not say "Gee!"

BIFF   Ten, I think, would be top though.

WILLY   Don't be so modest. You always started too low. Walk in with a big laugh. Don't look worried. Start off with a couple of your good stories to lighten things up. It's not what you say, it's how you say it—because personality always wins the day.

LINDA   Oliver always thought the highest of him—

WILLY   Will you let me talk?

BIFF   Don't yell at her, Pop, will ya?

WILLY   (*angrily*) I was talking, wasn't I?

BIFF   I don't like you yelling at her all the time, and I'm tellin' you, that's all.

WILLY   What're you, takin' over this house?

LINDA   Willy—

WILLY (*turning on her*) Don't take his side all the time, god-dammit!

BIFF (*furiously*) Stop yelling at her!

WILLY (*suddenly pulling on his cheek, beaten down, guilt ridden*) Give my best to Bill Oliver—he may remember me. (*He exits through the living-room doorway.*)

LINDA (*her voice subdued*) What'd you have to start that for? (BIFF *turns away.*) You see how sweet he was as soon as you talked hopefully? (*She goes over to* BIFF.) Come up and say good night to him. Don't let him go to bed that way.

HAPPY Come on, Biff, let's buck him up.

LINDA Please, dear. Just say good night. It takes so little to make him happy. Come. (*She goes through the living-room doorway, calling up-stairs from within the living room.*) Your pajamas are hanging in the bathroom, Willy!

HAPPY (*looking toward where* LINDA *went out*) What a woman! They broke the mold when they made her. You know that, Biff?

BIFF He's off salary. My God, working on commission!

HAPPY Well, let's face it: he's no hot-shot selling man. Except that some-times, you have to admit, he's a sweet personality.

BIFF (*deciding*) Lend me ten bucks, will ya? I want to buy some new ties.

HAPPY I'll take you to a place I know. Beautiful stuff. Wear one of my striped shirts tomorrow.

BIFF She got gray. Mom got awful old. Gee, I'm gonna go in to Oliver to-morrow and knock him for a—

HAPPY Come on up. Tell that to Dad. Let's give him a whirl. Come on.

BIFF (*steamed up*) You know, with ten thousand bucks, boy!

HAPPY (*as they go into the living room*) That's the talk, Biff, that's the first time I've heard the old confidence out of you! (*from within the living room, fading off*) You're gonna live with me, kid, and any babe you want just say the word . . .

[*The last lines are hardly heard. They are mounting the stairs to their parents' bedroom.*]

LINDA (*entering her bedroom and addressing* WILLY, *who is in the bath-room. She is straightening the bed for him.*) Can you do anything about the shower? It drips.

WILLY (*from the bathroom*) All of a sudden everything falls to pieces! Goddam plumbing, oughta be sued, those people. I hardly finished putting it in and the thing . . .

[*His words rumble off.*]

LINDA I'm just wondering if Oliver will remember him. You think he might?

WILLY (*coming out of the bathroom in his pajamas*) Remember him?

What's the matter with you, you crazy? If he'd've stayed with Oliver he'd be on top by now! Wait'll Oliver gets a look at him. You don't know the average caliber any more. The average young man today— (*He is getting into bed.*)—is got a caliber of zero. Greatest thing in the world for him was to bum around.

[BIFF *and* HAPPY *enter the bedroom. Slight pause*]

WILLY (*stops short, looking at* BIFF) Glad to hear it, boy.

HAPPY We wanted to say good night to you, sport.

WILLY (*to* BIFF) Yeah. Knock him dead, boy. What'd you want to tell me?

BIFF Just take it easy, Pop. Good night. (*He turns to go.*)

WILLY (*unable to resist*) And if anything falls off the desk while you're talking to him—like a package or something—don't you pick it up. They have office boys for that.

LINDA I'll make a big breakfast—

WILLY Will you let me finish? (*to* BIFF) Tell him you were in the business in the West. Not farm work.

BIFF All right, Dad.

LINDA I think everything—

WILLY (*going right through her speech*) And don't undersell yourself. No less than fifteen thousand dollars.

BIFF (*unable to bear him*) Okay. Good night, Mom. (*He starts moving.*)

WILLY Because you got a greatness in you, Biff, remember that. You got all kinds a greatness. . . .

[*He lies back, exhausted.* BIFF *walks out.*]

LINDA (*calling after* BIFF) Sleep well, darling!

HAPPY I'm gonna get married, Mom. I wanted to tell you.

LINDA Go to sleep, dear.

HAPPY (*going*) I just wanted to tell you.

WILLY Keep up the good work. (HAPPY *exits.*) God . . . remember that Ebbets Field game? The championship of the city?

LINDA Just rest. Should I sing to you?

WILLY Yeah. Sing to me. (LINDA *hums a soft lullaby.*) When that team came out—he was the tallest, remember?

LINDA Oh, yes. And in gold.

[BIFF *enters the darkened kitchen, takes a cigarette, and leaves the house. He comes downstage into a golden pool of light. He smokes, staring at the night.*]

WILLY Like a young god. Hercules—something like that. And the sun, the sun all around him. Remember how he waved to me? Right up from the field, with the representatives of three colleges standing by?

And the buyers I brought, and the cheers when he came out—Loman, Loman, Loman! God Almighty, he'll be great yet. A star like that, magnificent, can never really fade away!

Reference Key to Plays in Anthologies

Copies of the complete play may be found in the following selected volumes: Numbers 5, 7, 9, 38, 42, 47, 62, 69, 74, 77, 79.
See also *Theatre Arts*, March, 1951.

Further Reading on Miller and *Death of a Salesman*

Atkinson, Brooks, et al. "Reviews." in Eric Bentley, ed., *The Play: A Critical Anthology*. New York: Prentice-Hall, 1951, pp. 729–47. (A well-rounded collection of reviews of the original production of *Death of a Salesman*.)

Couchman, Gordon W. "Arthur Miller's Tragedy of Babbitt." *Educational Theatre Journal*, Vol. 7, No. 3 (October, 1955), pp. 206–11.

Gassner, John. *The Theatre in Our Times*. New York: Crown, 1954, pp. 364–73.

Hitchens, Gordon. *Attention Must Be Paid: A Study of Social Values in Four Plays by Arthur Miller*. Privately published, 1962.

Hurrell, John D. *Two Modern American Tragedies*. New York: Scribner's, 1961, pp. 54–88. (Includes a collection of reviews and criticisms of the play.)

Miller, Arthur. "The Family in Modern Drama." *Atlantic*, Vol. 197, No. 4 (April, 1956), pp. 35–41.

———. "Tragedy and the Common Man." *Theatre Arts*, Vol. 35, No. 3 (March, 1951), pp. 48 ff. (Miller's proposition of the validity of creating tragedy in modern society.)

Welland, Dennis. *Arthur Miller*. New York: Evergreen, 1961.

Recorded Performances

Complete performance:

Lee J. Cobb (the creator of the role) as Willy, Caedmon 310 (stereo S-310), three records.

Slightly abridged performance:

Original Broadway cast, but with Thomas Mitchell as Willy, Decca DX-102, two records.

Death of a Salesman ——————————

ARTHUR MILLER (1949)

From Act II

SCENE:	For two men
CHARACTERS:	Willy Loman, a salesman Howard, his boss
SETTING:	Howard's office
TIME:	A morning in the late 1940's. The year, however, might just as well be the present one.
SITUATION:	See the preceding scene from *Death of a Salesman* (p. 99), which occurs earlier in the play.

Arthur Miller's perceptive drama of the slow erosion and self-destruction of the little man is often placed among the few great American plays of our time. Willy Loman, a travelling salesman, finds that at sixty-three he is unable to earn enough money on a straight commission basis to support his family. He escapes from reality by daydreaming and has even considered suicide.

Hoping to change his job on the road for a position at the home office, Willy comes to Howard's office to request a transfer. Howard seems preoccupied.

WILLY   Pst! Pst!

HOWARD   Hello, Willy, come in.

WILLY   Like to have a little talk with you, Howard.

HOWARD   Sorry to keep you waiting. I'll be with you in a minute.

WILLY   What's that, Howard?

HOWARD   Didn't you ever see one of these? Wire recorder.

WILLY   Oh. Can we talk a minute?

HOWARD   Records things. Just got delivery yesterday. Been driving me crazy, the most terrific machine I ever saw in my life. I was up all night with it.

WILLY   What do you do with it?

HOWARD   I bought it for dictation, but you can do anything with it. Listen to this. I had it home last night. Listen to what I picked up. The first one is my daughter. Get this. (*He flicks the switch and "Roll out the Barrel!" is heard being whistled.*) Listen to that kid whistle.

WILLY   That is lifelike, isn't it?

HOWARD   Seven years old. Get that tone.

WILLY   Ts, ts. Like to ask a little favor of you . . .

[*The whistling breaks off, and the voice of* HOWARD's *daughter is heard.*]

HIS DAUGHTER   "Now you, Daddy."

HOWARD   She's crazy for me! (*Again the same song is whistled.*) That's me! Ha! (*He winks.*)

WILLY   You're very good!

[*The whistling breaks off again. The machine runs silent for a moment.*]

HOWARD   Sh! Get this now, this is my son.

HIS SON   "The capital of Alabama is Montgomery; the capital of Arizona is Phoenix; the capital of Arkansas is Little Rock; the capital of California is Sacramento . . ." (*and on, and on*)

HOWARD   (*holding up five fingers*) Five years old, Willy.

WILLY   He'll make an announcer some day!

HIS SON   (*continuing*) "The capital . . ."

HOWARD   Get that—alphabetical order! (*The machine breaks off suddenly.*) Wait a minute. The maid kicked the plug out.

WILLY   It certainly is a—

HOWARD   Sh, for God's sake.

HIS SON   "It's nine o'clock, Bulova watch time. So I have to go to sleep."

WILLY   That really is—

HOWARD   Wait a minute! The next is my wife.

[*They wait.*]

HOWARD'S VOICE   "Go on, say something." (*pause*) "Well, you gonna talk?"

HIS WIFE   "I can't think of anything."

HOWARD'S VOICE   "Well, talk—it's turning."

HIS WIFE   (*shyly, beaten*) "Hello." (*silence*) "Oh, Howard, I can't talk into this . . ."

HOWARD   (*snapping the machine off*) That was my wife.

WILLY   That is a wonderful machine. Can we—

HOWARD   I tell you, Willy, I'm gonna take my camera, and my bandsaw, and all my hobbies, and out they go. This is the most fascinating relaxation I ever found.

WILLY   I think I'll get one myself.

HOWARD   Sure, they're only a hundred and a half. You can't do without it. Supposing you wanna hear Jack Benny, see? But you can't be at home at that hour. So you tell the maid to turn the radio on when Jack Benny comes on, and this automatically goes on with the radio . . .

WILLY   And when you come home you . . .

HOWARD   You can come home twelve o'clock, one o'clock, any time you like, and you get yourself a Coke and sit yourself down, throw the switch, and there's Jack Benny's program in the middle of the night!

WILLY   I'm definitely going to get one. Because lots of time I'm on the road, and I think to myself, what I must be missing on the radio!

HOWARD   Don't you have a radio in the car?

WILLY   Well, yeah, but who ever thinks of turning it on?

HOWARD   Say, aren't you supposed to be in Boston?

WILLY   That's what I want to talk to you about, Howard. You got a minute? (*He draws a chair in from the wing.*)

HOWARD   What happened? What're you doing here?

WILLY   Well . . .

HOWARD   You didn't crack up again, did you?

WILLY   Oh, no. No . . .

HOWARD   Geez, you had me worried there for a minute. What's the trouble?

WILLY   Well, tell you the truth, Howard. I've come to the decision that I'd rather not travel any more.

HOWARD   Not travel! Well, what'll you do?

WILLY   Remember, Christmas time, when you had the party here? You said you'd try to think of some spot for me here in town.

HOWARD   With us?

WILLY   Well, sure.

HOWARD   Oh, yeah, yeah. I remember. Well, I couldn't think of anything for you, Willy.

WILLY   I tell ya, Howard. The kids are all grown up, y'know. I don't need much any more. If I could take home—well, sixty-five dollars a week, I could swing it.

HOWARD   Yeah, but Willy, see I—

WILLY   I tell ya why, Howard. Speaking frankly and between the two of us, y'know—I'm just a little tired.

HOWARD   Oh, I could understand that, Willy. But you're a road man, Willy, and we do a road business. We've only got a half-dozen salesmen on the floor here.

WILLY   God knows, Howard, I never asked a favor of any man. But I was with the firm when your father used to carry you in here in his arms.

HOWARD   I know that, Willy, but—

WILLY Your father came to me the day you were born and asked me what I thought of the name of Howard, may he rest in peace.

HOWARD I appreciate that, Willy, but there just is no spot here for you. If I had a spot I'd slam you right in, but I just don't have a single solitary spot.

[*He looks for his lighter.* WILLY *has picked it up and gives it to him. Pause.*]

WILLY (*with increasing anger*) Howard, all I need to set my table is fifty dollars a week.

HOWARD But where am I going to put you, kid?

WILLY Look, it isn't a question of whether I can sell merchandise, is it?

HOWARD No, but it's a business, kid, and everybody's gotta pull his own weight.

WILLY (*desperately*) Just let me tell you a story, Howard—

HOWARD 'Cause you gotta admit, business is business.

WILLY (*angrily*) Business is definitely business, but just listen for a minute. You don't understand this. When I was a boy—eighteen, nineteen—I was already on the road. And there was a question in my mind as to whether selling had a future for me. Because in those days I had a yearning to go to Alaska. See, there were three gold strikes in one month in Alaska, and I felt like going out. Just for the ride, you might say.

HOWARD (*barely interested*) Don't say.

WILLY Oh, yeah, my father lived many years in Alaska. He was an adventurous man. We've got quite a little streak of self-reliance in our family. I thought I'd go out with my older brother and try to locate him, and maybe settle in the North with the old man. And I was almost decided to go, when I met a salesman in the Parker House. His name was Dave Singleman. And he was eighty-four years old, and he drummed merchandise in thirty-one states. And old Dave, he'd go up to his room, y'understand, put on his green velvet slippers—I'll never forget—and pick up his phone and call the buyers, and without ever leaving his room, at the age of eighty-four, he made his living. And when I saw that, I realized that selling was the greatest career a man could want. 'Cause what could be more satisfying than to be able to go, at the age of eighty-four, into twenty or thirty different cities, and pick up a phone, and be remembered and loved and helped by so many different people? Do you know? when he died—and by the way he died the death of a salesman, in his green velvet slippers in the smoker of the New York, New Haven and Hartford, going into Boston —when he died, hundreds of salesmen and buyers were at his funeral. Things were sad on a lotta trains for months after that. (*He stands up.*

HOWARD *has not looked at him.*) In those days there was personality in it, Howard. There was respect, and comradeship, and gratitude in it. Today, it's all cut and dried, and there's no chance for bringing friendship to bear—or personality. You see what I mean? They don't know me any more.

HOWARD (*moving away, to the right*) That's just the thing, Willy.

WILLY If I had forty dollars a week—that's all I'd need. Forty dollars, Howard.

HOWARD Kid, I can't take blood from a stone, I—

WILLY (*Desperation is on him now.*) Howard, the year Al Smith was nominated, your father came to me and—

HOWARD (*starting to go off*) I've got to see some people, kid.

WILLY (*stopping him*) I'm talking about your father! There were promises made across this desk! You mustn't tell me you've got people to see —I put thirty-four years into this firm, Howard, and now I can't pay my insurance! You can't eat the orange and throw the peel away—a man is not a piece of fruit! (*after a pause*) Now pay attention. Your father—in 1928 I had a big year. I averaged a hundred and seventy dollars a week in commissions.

HOWARD (*impatiently*) Now, Willy, you never averaged—

WILLY (*banging his hand on the desk*) I averaged a hundred and seventy dollars a week in the year of 1928! And your father came to me—or rather, I was in the office here—it was right over this desk—and he put his hand on my shoulder—

HOWARD (*getting up*) You'll have to excuse me, Willy, I gotta see some people. Pull yourself together. (*going out*) I'll be back in a little while.

[*On* HOWARD's *exit, the light on his chair grows very bright and strange.*]

WILLY Pull myself together! What the hell did I say to him? My God, I was yelling at him! How could I! (WILLY *breaks off, staring at the light, which occupies the chair, animating it. He approaches this chair, standing across the desk from it.*) Frank, Frank, don't you remember what you told me that time? How you put your hand on my shoulder, and Frank . . . (*He leans on the desk and as he speaks the dead man's name he accidentally switches on the recorder, and instantly*)

HOWARD'S SON ". . . of New York is Albany. The capital of Ohio is Cincinnati, the capital of Rhode Island is . . ." (*The recitation continues.*)

WILLY (*leaping away with fright, shouting*) Ha! Howard! Howard! Howard!

HOWARD (*rushing in*) What happened?

WILLY (*pointing at the machine, which continues nasally, childishly, with the capital cities*) Shut it off! Shut it off!

HOWARD   (*pulling the plug out*) Look, Willy . . .

WILLY   (*pressing his hands to his eyes*) I gotta get myself some coffee. I'll get some coffee . . .

[WILLY *starts to walk out.* HOWARD *stops him.*]

HOWARD   (*rolling up the cord*) Willy, look . . .

WILLY   I'll go to Boston.

HOWARD   Willy, you can't go to Boston for us.

WILLY   Why can't I go?

HOWARD   I don't want you to represent us. I've been meaning to tell you for a long time now.

WILLY   Howard, are you firing me?

HOWARD   I think you need a good long rest, Willy.

WILLY   Howard—

HOWARD   And when you feel better, come back, and we'll see if we can work something out.

WILLY   But I gotta earn money, Howard. I'm in no position to—

HOWARD   Where are your sons? Why don't your sons give you a hand?

WILLY   They're working on a very big deal.

HOWARD   This is no time for false pride, Willy. You go to your sons and you tell them that you're tired. You've got two great boys, haven't you?

WILLY   Oh, no question, no question, but in the meantime . . .

HOWARD   Then that's that, heh?

WILLY   All right, I'll go to Boston tomorrow.

HOWARD   No, no.

WILLY   I can't throw myself on my sons. I'm not a cripple!

HOWARD   Look, kid, I'm busy this morning.

WILLY   (*grasping* HOWARD's *arm*) Howard, you've got to let me go to Boston!

HOWARD   (*hard, keeping himself under control*) I've got a line of people to see this morning. Sit down, take five minutes, and pull yourself together, and then go home, will ya? I need the office, Willy. (*He starts to go, turns, remembering the recorder, starts to push off the table holding the recorder.*) Oh, yeah. Whenever you can this week, stop by and drop off the samples. You'll feel better, Willy, and then come back and we'll talk. Pull yourself together, kid, there's people outside.

[HOWARD *exits, pushing the table off left.* WILLY *stares into space, exhausted.*]

For anthologies containing the complete text and for a list of suggested readings, see the preceding scene from *Death of a Salesman* (p. 105).

The Country Girl

CLIFFORD ODETS (1950)

From Act II, Scene 1

SCENE: For one man, one woman

CHARACTERS: Bernie Dodd, a theatre director
Georgie Elgin, the wife of a drunken actor

SETTING: A dressing room in a Boston theatre.

TIME: Sometime after midnight. The present.

SITUATION: Bernie Dodd, the dynamic young director of a new play in the midst of its out-of-town tryout, has been nursing along a broken-down actor, Frank Elgin. Elgin was at one time a talented and successful actor. Since his decline he has begun drinking heavily, and Bernie believes Elgin's wife Georgie is partly responsible. Actually Georgie has been trying to help her husband, and she is upset when she sees that despite his promises, Frank has begun to drink again. It is early morning following a long session with the photographers.

[GEORGIE *remains standing at the mirror; she takes off her glasses and looks at herself. Something poignant reaches out from image to reality. The radio has begun playing a waltz.* GEORGIE *begins to sway to its rhythm, and in another moment she is waltzing alone, almost as if it were possible to waltz herself back to a better time. What she is murmuring to herself we cannot hear. Then she stops abruptly. A sardonic* BERNIE *stands in the doorway.*]

BERNIE Excuse me, the both of you. (*He steps into the room.*)

GEORGIE (*crossing to the make-up shelf*) Some aspirin . . . a headache.

BERNIE (*extends an aspirin tin taken from his pocket*) It's the Age of Aspirin, they say.

[*She puts on her glasses, gets some water, and swallows. Finally she turns.*]

GEORGIE   A splitting headache . . . too much stuffy dressing room . . .

BERNIE   Where's Frank?

GEORGIE   Onstage. (*As he starts out she stops him, now in control.*) His cold is getting worse, Mr. Dodd. He shouldn't be kept up this late. It's more than flesh and blood can stand.

BERNIE   Them's melodramatic words. We need production pictures, don't we? How's his spirit?

GEORGIE   Low.

BERNIE   The show's in fair shape—why?

GEORGIE   Ask the Boston critics. Everyone doesn't have your confidence.

BERNIE   (*promptly*) That's true.

GEORGIE   And while I'm on the subject, that confidence makes you push. That makes you a bit of a bully.

BERNIE   (*even more promptly*) That's true, too.

GEORGIE   Don't minimize what I say by agreeing with me—it's REALLY true.

[*Tired, he looks at her with the typical curl of a smile and sits, almost as if to bait her, a way of releasing his own tension.*]

BERNIE   What else is bothering friend Frank?

GEORGIE   You didn't come back after the show tonight. Neither did Mr. Cook.

BERNIE   This last month I've spent from ten to fifteen hours a day with Frank. Nothing ever bothers him except through your mouth. Why?

GEORGIE   We've been through all of that before . . . (*She closes the door and stops the radio.*) He thinks it's a crime to lack a sense of humor. He doesn't want to be disliked. He hides when he's nervous. Either he jigs and jabbers away, or he sits in silence and rots away inside. But either way, for your edification, he's headed for a bender!

BERNIE   (*mockingly*) Women always think they understand their men, don't they?

GEORGIE   (*deliberately dimming her electricity*) I won't fight with you, Mr. Dodd. He expected you backstage tonight. Your absence was a reprimand. If you care at all for his sense of security—

BERNIE   Follow your advice?

GEORGIE   (*looks at him as one wrestler looks at another*) Do you know anything about drinkers?

BERNIE   Something.

GEORGIE   If you're not careful, you'll have him full of whisky before he goes to bed tonight. He's got a bad cold. That's a respectable surface reason for any drinker to jump down the well.

BERNIE   Why work so hard at this marriage? Why not take a rest? You wear your husband down! You make him tense, uneasy. You don't stop "handling" him. You try to "handle" me, too.

GEORGIE (*in a flash of temper*) And don't think I can't, after handling a cunning drunkard for ten years!

BERNIE (*quickly up on his feet*) Who the hell do you think you are? Secretary of State?

GEORGIE (*defiantly*) I am a drunkard's wife.

BERNIE (*snorting*) Girlie, I have to give you credit, but—

GEORGIE (*quickly*) No compliments, Mr. Dodd!

BERNIE But I'm going to fight you as hard as I can for this man!

GEORGIE (*smiling faintly*) Not too hard. I may let you have him.

BERNIE No, you want him wholly dependent! Now let's not waste words. I—

GEORGIE Oh, it's much too late for that.

BERNIE I was married to one like you. Roughly half my weight—ninety-seven pounds. It took her two years—she sewed me up!

GEORGIE (*dryly*) Love is hell . . .

BERNIE We'll leave it at that—joke ending. (*He goes to the door and turns.*) What a bitter pity you don't realize the size of your husband's talent!

GEORGIE What have *you* given up for that talent?

BERNIE (*coming back*) Then why do you stay?

GEORGIE Because he's helpless!

BERNIE I'll help him!

GEORGIE *You!* You wouldn't know where to begin. Life with him is three-quarters the avoidance of painful scenes. He's taught me to be a fish, to swim in any direction, including up, down, and sideways. Now, disregarding facts, you happen to think I wheedle his life away. You're very—

BERNIE (*unable to contain himself*) Look, look, look! Half the world's shamed by sentiment. Say "mother" or "babe," "sacrifice," and they drip like axle grease. But you have ruined this man—don't explain it away by sentiment!

GEORGIE (*incredulously*) How did I so overrate your intellect? You're a boy!

BERNIE Man or boy, I'm putting on a show—it has to work! We can discuss universals some other day! To be frank, you are slightly grotesque to me, Mrs. Elgin!

GEORGIE (*bitterly*) And what about yourself? Look at you, fearful of failure, effective and hard-hitting—a machine, without manners or style—self-driven, curt, wary, and worried—pretending to a humanity you never practice!

BERNIE (*contemptuously*) You called your own husband a cunning drunkard?

GEORGIE (*flatly*) It is necessary for you to know it!

[*A pause. They are murdering each other with their eyes.*]

GEORGIE This is getting stupid. Now tell me, in God's name, exactly what you want me to do for Frank. (*She sits down at the make-up shelf.*)

BERNIE (*pointing a finger at her*) That's fair! I'll believe everything you say. Prove it!

GEORGIE How?

BERNIE Get out of town! (*He pauses.*) I've just had a bad fight in the box office with Cook. He's got a first-class replacement for Frank and seventy thousand dollars to protect! Frank will improve every day—I think he will, Cook thinks he won't. Well, he won't, unless *you get out of town!*

[GEORGIE *thinks, stops, looks, and listens.*]

GEORGIE Umm . . . I'll do it. I'll go back to New York. (*She stops him from leaving.*) But only on one condition: let *me* carefully tell Frank, in my own way, at my own time.

BERNIE As long as you're on the train by tomorrow night, understand?

GEORGIE (*nodding*) Life is earnest, life is real, and so are investments— I understand. But you may be sorry.

BERNIE You're as phony to me as an opera soprano!

[GEORGIE *abruptly slashes him across the face with her open hand.*]

GEORGIE (*fiercely*) Did I forget to tell you I'm proud? Someone has to stop you from calling me any name that pops into your little head!

BERNIE (*frigidly*) Maybe I deserved that. Maybe not. Time alone will tell.

GEORGIE It brings all things, they say. (*holding back tears*) Thank God for *that* inevitability.

Reference Key to Plays in Anthologies

A copy of the complete play may be found in the following volume:
Number 24.
See also *Theatre Arts*, May, 1952.

Further Reading on Odets and *The Country Girl*

Clurman, Harold. *The Fervent Years: The Story of the Group Theatre and the Thirties.* New York: Hill and Wang, 1957. (Thorough treatment of Odets' early playwriting career.)

Gassner, John. *The Theatre in Our Times.* New York: Crown, 1954, pp. 303–10.

Hyams, Barry. "Twenty Years on a Tightrope." *Theatre Arts,* Vol. 39, No. 4 (April, 1955), pp. 68–70, 86.

Mersand, Joseph. "Clifford Odets, Dramatist of Young America." *The American Drama Since 1930.* New York: Modern Chapbooks, 1951, pp. 66–90.

Shuman, R. Baird. *Clifford Odets.* New York: Twayne, 1962.

The Rainmaker _____

N. Richard Nash (1954)

From Act II

SCENE:	For one man, one woman
CHARACTERS:	Bill Starbuck, an itinerant rainmaker Lizzie Curry, a young woman
SETTING:	A tack room adjacent to the Curry ranch house.
TIME:	A summer evening in the 1920's.
SITUATION:	During a period of extreme drought in the plains states, an adventuresome young man who calls himself Bill Starbuck has promised to bring rain—for a slight fee, of course. While boarding with the Curry family, he notices Lizzie Curry's loneliness and her family's fear that since she is already twenty-seven years old and still unmarried, she may become an old maid.

As the scene begins, Starbuck is lying on his cot in the bunkroom after an argument with members of the Curry family, one of whom has called Lizzie plain. He is humming a lonely song when he hears a sound and suddenly sits up.

STARBUCK   Who's that? (*He rises tautly.*)

[LIZZIE *stands in the doorway, trying not to look into the room. She is carrying the bed linens. She knocks on the door frame.*]

LIZZIE   (*trying to sound calm*) It's me—Lizzie.

[STARBUCK *starts to put on his shirt. An awkward moment. Then* LIZZIE, *without entering the room, hands the bedding across the threshold.*]

LIZZIE   Here.

STARBUCK   What's that?

LIZZIE   Bed linens—take them.

STARBUCK   Is that what you came out for?

LIZZIE (*after a painful moment*) No . . . I came out because . . . (*She finds it too difficult to continue.*)

STARBUCK (*gently*) Go on, Lizzie.

LIZZIE I came out to thank you for what you said to Noah.

STARBUCK I meant every word of it.

LIZZIE What you said about Jim—I'm sure you meant that.

STARBUCK What I said about you.

LIZZIE I don't believe you.

STARBUCK Then what are you thankin' me for? What's the matter, Lizzie? You afraid that if you stop bein' sore at me you'll like me a little?

LIZZIE No . . . (*and she starts to go.*)

STARBUCK (*stopping her*) Then stay and talk to me! (*as she hesitates*) It's lonely out here and I don't think I'll sleep much—not in a strange place.

LIZZIE Then I guess you never sleep. Running from one strange place to another.

STARBUCK (*with a smile*) Not runnin'—travelin'.

LIZZIE Well, if that's the kind of life you like . . .

STARBUCK Oh, it's not what a man likes—it's what he's got to do. Now what would a fella in my business be doin' stayin' in the same place? Rain's nice—but it ain't nice all the time.

LIZZIE (*relaxing a bit*) No, I guess not.

STARBUCK People got no use for me—except maybe once in a lifetime. And when my work's done, they're glad to see me go.

LIZZIE (*caught by the loneliness in his voice*) I never thought of it that way.

STARBUCK Why would you? You never thought of me as a real rain-maker—not until just now.

LIZZIE I still don't think it!

[*Now she starts to go more determinedly than before.* STARBUCK *stops her physically this time.*]

STARBUCK Lizzie—wait! Why don't you let yourself think of me the way you *want* to?

LIZZIE (*unnerved*) What do you mean?

STARBUCK Think like Lizzie, not like Noah.

LIZZIE I don't know what you're talking about.

STARBUCK What are you scared of?

LIZZIE You! I don't trust you!

STARBUCK Why? What don't you trust about me?

LIZZIE Everything! The way you talk, the way you brag—why, even your name.

STARBUCK   What's wrong with my name?

LIZZIE   It sounds fake! It sounds like you made it up!

STARBUCK   You're darn right! I did make it up.

LIZZIE   There! Of course!

STARBUCK   Why not? You know what name I was born with? Smith! Smith, for the love of Mike, *Smith!* Now what kind of handle is that for a fella like me? I needed a name that had the whole sky in it! And the power of a man! Star-buck! Now there's a name—and it's mine.

LIZZIE   No, it's not. You were born Smith—and that's your name.

STARBUCK   You're wrong, Lizzie. The name you choose for yourself is more your own than the name you were born with. And if I was you I'd choose another name than Lizzie.

LIZZIE   Thank you—I'm very pleased with it.

STARBUCK   Oh, no you ain't. You ain't pleased with anything about yourself. And I'm sure you ain't pleased with "Lizzie."

LIZZIE   I don't ask *you* to be pleased with it, Starbuck. I *am.*

STARBUCK   Lizzie? Why, it don't *stand* for anything.

LIZZIE   It stands for me! *Me!* I'm not the Queen of Sheba—I'm not Lady Godiva—I'm not Cinderella at the Ball.

STARBUCK   Would you like to be?

LIZZIE   Starbuck, you're ridiculous!

STARBUCK   What's ridiculous about it? Dream you're somebody—*be* somebody! But Lizzie? That's nobody! So many millions of wonderful women with wonderful names! (*in an orgy of delight*) Leonora, Desdemona, Carolina, Paulina! Annabella, Florinda, Natasha, Diane! (*then, with a pathetic little lift of his shoulders*) Lizzie.

LIZZIE   Good night, Starbuck!

STARBUCK   (*with a sudden inspiration*) Just a minute, Lizzie—just one little half of a minute. I got the greatest name for you—the greatest name—just listen. (*then, like a love lyric*) Melisande.

LIZZIE   (*flatly*) I don't like it.

STARBUCK   That's because you don't know anything about her. But when I tell you who she was—lady, when I tell you who she was!

LIZZIE   Who?

STARBUCK   (*improvising*) She was the most beautiful . . . ! She was the beautiful wife of King Hamlet! Ever hear of him?

LIZZIE   (*giving him the rope*) Go on! Go on!

STARBUCK   He was the fella who sailed across the ocean and brought back the Golden Fleece! And you know why he did that? Because Melisande begged him for it! I tell you, that Melisande—she was so beautiful and her hair was so long and curly—every time he looked at her he just fell right down and died. And this King Hamlet, he'd do anything for her—anything she wanted. So when she said: "Hamlet, I got a terrible hankerin' for a soft Golden Fleece," he just naturally sailed right off to find it. And when he came back—all bleedin' and torn—he went and laid that Fleece of Gold right down at her pretty white feet. And she took that fur piece and wrapped it around her pink naked shoulders and she said: "I got the Golden Fleece—and I'll never be cold no more." . . . Melisande! What a woman! What a *name!*

LIZZIE (*quietly*) Starbuck, you silly jackass. You take a lot of stories— that I've read in a hundred different places—and you roll them up into one big fat ridiculous lie!

STARBUCK (*angry, hurt*) I wasn't lyin'—I was dreamin'!

LIZZIE It's the same thing!

STARBUCK (*with growing anger*) If you think it's the same thing then I take it back about your name! Lizzie—it's just right for you. I'll tell you another name that would suit you—Noah! Because you and your brother—you've got no dream.

LIZZIE (*with an outcry*) You think all dreams have to be your kind! Golden Fleece and thunder on the mountain! But there are other dreams, Starbuck! Little quiet ones that come to a woman when she's shining the silverware and putting moth flakes in the closet.

STARBUCK Like what?

LIZZIE (*crying*) Like a man's voice saying: "Lizzie, is my blue suit pressed?" And the same man saying: "Scratch between my shoulder blades." And kids laughing and teasing and setting up a racket. And how it feels to say the word "Husband!" . . . There are all kinds of dreams, Mr. Starbuck. Mine are small ones—like my name—Lizzie. But they're *real* like my name—real! So you can have yours—and I'll have mine!

[*Unable to control her tears, she starts to run away. This time he grabs her fully, holding her close.*]

STARBUCK Lizzie . . .

LIZZIE Please . . .

STARBUCK I'm sorry, Lizzie! I'm sorry!

LIZZIE It's all right—let me go!

STARBUCK I hope your dreams come true, Lizzie—I hope they do!

LIZZIE They won't—they never will!

STARBUCK Believe in yourself and they will!

LIZZIE I've got nothing to believe in.

STARBUCK You're a woman! Believe in that!

LIZZIE How can I when nobody else will?

STARBUCK *You* gotta believe it first! (*quickly*) Let me ask you, Lizzie— are you pretty?

LIZZIE (*with a wail*) No—I'm plain!

The Rainmaker 121

STARBUCK   There! You see? You don't know you're a woman!

LIZZIE   I am a woman! A plain one!

STARBUCK   There's no such thing as a plain woman! Every real woman is pretty! They're all pretty in a different way—but they're all pretty!

LIZZIE   Not me! When I look in the looking glass . . .

STARBUCK   Don't let Noah be your lookin' glass!

LIZZIE   He's not. My looking glass is right on the wall.

STARBUCK   It's in the wrong place. It's gotta be inside you.

LIZZIE   No . . .

STARBUCK   Don't be afraid—*look!* You'll see a pretty woman, Lizzie. Lizzie, you gotta be your own lookin' glass. And then one day the lookin' glass will be the man who loves you. It'll be his eyes, maybe. And you'll look in that mirror and you'll be more than pretty—you'll be beautiful!

LIZZIE   (*crying out*) It'll never happen!

STARBUCK   Make it happen! Lizzie, why don't you think "pretty" and take down your hair? (*He reaches for her hair.*)

LIZZIE   (*in panic*) No!

STARBUCK   Please, Lizzie! (*He is taking the pins out of her hair.*)

LIZZIE   No—no . . .

STARBUCK   Nobody sees you, Lizzie—nobody but me! (*taking her in his arms*) Now close your eyes, Lizzie—close them! (*as she obeys*) Now—say: "I'm pretty!"

LIZZIE   (*trying*) I'm—I'm—I can't!

STARBUCK   Say it! Say it, Lizzie!

LIZZIE   I'm . . . pretty.

STARBUCK   Say it again!

LIZZIE   (*with a little cry*) Pretty!

STARBUCK   Say it—mean it!

LIZZIE   (*exalted*) I'm pretty! I'm pretty! I'm pretty!

[*He kisses her. A long kiss and she clings to him, passionately, the bonds of her spinsterhood breaking away. The kiss over, she collapses on the cot, sobbing.*]

LIZZIE   (*through the sobs*) Why did you do that?

STARBUCK   (*going beside her on the cot*) Because when you said you were pretty, it was true!

[*Her sobs are louder, more heart-rending because, for the first time, she is happy.*]

STARBUCK   Lizzie—look at me!

LIZZIE   I can't!

STARBUCK   (*turning her to him*) Stop cryin' and look at me! Look at my eyes! What do you see?

LIZZIE (*gazing through her tears*) I can't *believe* what I see!

STARBUCK Tell me what you see!

LIZZIE (*with a sob of happiness*) Oh, is it me? Is it really me? (*Now she goes to him with all her giving.*)

Reference Key to Plays in Anthologies

A copy of the complete play may be found in *Theatre Arts*, March, 1956.

Further Reading on Nash and *The Rainmaker*

"Bright Galaxy of Playwrights." *Life*, Vol. 37, No. 17 (October 25, 1954), p. 78.

Nash, N. Richard. "Wanted: Some Wild-eyed Young Men." *Theatre Arts*, Vol. 39, No. 3 (March, 1955), pp. 30–31, 94–95.

Come Back, Little Sheba _____

WILLIAM INGE (1950)
From Act II, Scene 3

SCENE:	For one man, one woman
CHARACTERS:	Doc, a chiropractor Lola, his wife
SETTING:	An old house in a run-down neighborhood of a Midwestern city.
TIME:	The late 1940's. Five-thirty in the morning.
SITUATION:	Doc and Lola are an unhappy middle-aged couple unable to find comfort from each other. Doc is a former alcoholic; Lola has become fat and sloppy. She clings to a happier past symbolized by a dog she lost many years ago, Little Sheba; she pretends to believe that the dog will return any day. Marie, a college girl who rents a room from Doc and Lola, is having an affair with Turk, an athlete. Lola abets them, thus vicariously recapturing her youth. When Doc learns of Marie's behavior, his disgust at the situation drives him back to the bottle. This scene opens as Lola is trying desperately to reach one of Doc's fellow members of Alcoholics Anonymous for help. Doc has been out all night.

LOLA (*at telephone. She sounds frantic.*) Mr. Anderson? Mr. Anderson, this is Mrs. Delaney again. I'm sorry to call you so early, but I just *had* to. . . . Did you find Doc? . . . No, he's not home yet. I don't suppose he'll come home till he's drunk all he can hold and wants to sleep. . . . I don't know what else to think, Mr. Anderson. I'm scared, Mr. Anderson. I'm awful scared. Will you come right over? . . . Thanks, Mr. Anderson. (*She hangs up and goes to the kitchen to make coffee. She finds some left from the night before, so turns on the fire to warm it up. She wanders around vaguely, trying to get her thoughts in order, jumping at every sound. Pours herself a cup of coffee, then takes it to living room, sits and sips it. Very quietly* DOC *enters through the back way into the kitchen. He carries a big bottle of whiskey which he carefully places back in the pantry, not making a sound, hangs up overcoat, then puts suitcoat on back of chair. Starts to go upstairs. But* LOLA *speaks.*) Doc? That you, Doc? (*Then* DOC *quietly walks in from the kitchen. He is staggering drunk, but he is managing for a few minutes to appear as though he were perfectly sober and nothing had happened. His steps, however, are not too sure and his eyes are like blurred ink spots.* LOLA *is too frightened to talk. Her mouth is gaping and she is breathless with fear.*)

DOC Good morning, honey.

LOLA Doc! You all right?

DOC The morning paper here? I wanta see the morning paper.

LOLA Doc, we don't get a morning paper. *You* know that.

DOC Oh, then I suppose I'm drunk or something. That what you're trying to say?

LOLA No, Doc . . .

DOC Then give me the morning paper.

LOLA (*scampering to get last night's paper from console table*) Sure, Doc. Here it is. Now you just sit there and be quiet.

DOC (*resistance rising*) Why shouldn't I be quiet?

LOLA Nothin', Doc . . .

DOC (*has trouble unfolding paper. He places it before his face in order not to be seen. But he is too blind even to see.*) Nothing, Doc. (*mockingly*)

LOLA (*cautiously, after a few minutes' silence*) Doc, are you all right?

DOC Of course, I'm all right. Why shouldn't I be all right?

LOLA Where you been?

DOC What's it your business where I been? I been to London to see the Queen. What do you think of that? (*Apparently she doesn't know what to think of it.*) Just let me alone. That's all I ask. I'm all right.

LOLA (*whimpering*) Doc, what made you do it? You said you'd be home last night . . . 'cause we were having company. Bruce was here and I had a big dinner fixed . . . and you never came. What was the matter, Doc?

DOC (*mockingly*) We had a big dinner for *Bruce.*

LOLA Doc, it was for you, too.

DOC Well . . . I don't want it.

LOLA Don't get mad, Doc.

DOC (*threateningly*) Where's Marie?

LOLA I don't know, Doc. She didn't come in last night. She was out with Bruce.

DOC (*back to audience*) I suppose you tucked them in bed together and peeked through the keyhole and applauded.

LOLA (*sickened*) Doc, don't talk that way. Bruce is a nice boy. They're gonna get married.

DOC He probably *has* to marry her, the poor bastard. Just 'cause she's pretty and he got amorous one day . . . Just like I had to marry *you*.

LOLA Oh, Doc!

DOC You and Marie are both a couple of sluts.

LOLA Doc, please don't talk like that.

DOC What are you good for? You can't even get up in the morning and cook my breakfast.

LOLA (*mumbling*) I will, Doc. I will after this.

DOC You won't even sweep the floors, till some bozo comes along to make love to Marie, and then you fix things up like Buckingham Palace or a Chinese whorehouse with perfume on the lampbulbs, and flowers, and the gold-trimmed china *my mother* gave us. We're not going to use these any more. My mother didn't buy those dishes for whores to eat off of. (*He jerks the cloth off the table, sending the dishes rattling to the floor.*)

LOLA Doc! Look what you done.

DOC Look what I *did*, not *done*. I'm going to get me a drink. (*goes to kitchen*)

LOLA (*follows to platform*) Oh, no, Doc! You know what it does to you!

DOC You're damn right I know what it does to me. It makes me willing to come home here and look at you, you two-ton old heifer! (*takes a long swallow*) There! And pretty soon I'm going to have another, then another.

LOLA (*with dread*) Oh, Doc! (LOLA *takes phone.* DOC *sees this, rushes for the butcher-knife from kitchen-cabinet drawer. Not finding it, he gets a hatchet from the back porch.*) Mr. Anderson? Come quick, Mr. Anderson. He's back. He's *back!* He's got a hatchet!

DOC God damn you! Get away from that telephone. (*He chases her into living room where she gets the couch between them.*) That's right, phone! Tell the world I'm drunk. Tell the whole damn world. Scream your head off, you fat slut. Holler till all the neighbors think I'm beatin' hell outuv you. Where's Bruce now—under Marie's bed? You got all fresh and pretty for him, didn't you? Combed your hair for once—you even washed the back of your neck and put on a girdle. You were willing to harness all that fat into one bundle.

LOLA (*about to faint under the weight of the crushing accusations*) Doc, don't say any more . . . I'd rather you hit me with an axe, Doc . . . Honest I would. But I can't stand to hear you talk like that.

DOC I oughta hack off all that fat, and then wait for Marie and chop off those pretty ankles she's always dancing around on . . . then start lookin' for Turk and fix him too.

LOLA Daddy, you're talking crazy!

DOC I'm making sense for the first time in my life. You didn't know I knew about it, did you? But I saw him coming outa there, I saw him. You knew about it all the time and thought you were hidin' something . . .

LOLA Daddy, I didn't know anything about it at all. Honest, Daddy.

DOC Then *you're* the one that's crazy, if you think I didn't know. You were running a regular house, weren't you? It's probably been going on for years, ever since we were married.

[*He lunges for her. She breaks for kitchen. They struggle in front of sink.*]

LOLA Doc, it's not so; it's not so. You gotta believe me, Doc.

DOC You're lyin'. But none a that's gonna happen any more. I'm gonna fix you now, once and for all. . . .

LOLA Doc . . . don't do that to me. (LOLA, *in a frenzy of fear, clutches him around the neck holding arm with axe by his side.*) Remember, Doc. It's *me*, Lola! You said I was the prettiest girl you ever saw. Remember, Doc! It's me! Lola!

DOC (*The memory has overpowered him. He collapses, slowly mumbling.*) Lola . . . my pretty Lola.

[*He passes out on the floor.* LOLA *stands now, as though in a trance.*]

Reference Key to Plays in Anthologies

Copies of the complete play may be found in the following selected volumes: Numbers 30, 38, 62, 81.

Further Reading on Inge and *Come Back, Little Sheba*

Inge, William. "Forgotten Anger." *Theatre Arts*, Vol. 42, No. 2 (February, 1958), pp. 68–69, 94.

———. *Four Plays*. New York: Random House, 1958, pp. v–x.

————. "The Schizophrenic Wonder." *Theatre Arts*, Vol. 34, No. 5 (May, 1950), pp. 22–23. (An interesting analysis of *Come Back, Little Sheba* by the author.)

Shuman, Robert Baird. *William Inge*. New York: Twayne, 1965.

Weales, Gerald. *American Drama Since World War II*. New York: Harcourt, Brace & World, 1962, pp. 40–56.

Picnic

WILLIAM INGE (1953)
From Act III, Scene 1

SCENE: For one man, one woman

CHARACTERS: Howard, a small-town businessman
Rosemary Sydney, a schoolteacher

SETTING: A yard shared by two houses in a small Kansas town.

TIME: Very early in the morning, following a Labor Day picnic. It is still dark.

SITUATION: Rosemary Sydney, an old-maid schoolteacher, has long professed her freedom from men. However, her loneliness is all too real. She has returned home from the annual Labor Day picnic with Howard Bevans, a businessman of the town, who is rapidly approaching middle age. Normally Rosemary is light-hearted, but there is a change in her tonight.

[*We hear* HOWARD's *Chevrolet chugging to a stop by the house, then* HOWARD *and* ROSEMARY *come on,* ROSEMARY *first. Wearily, a groggy depression having set in, she makes her way to the doorstep and drops there, sitting limp. She seems preoccupied at first and her responses to* HOWARD *are mere grunts.*]

HOWARD Here we are, Honey. Right back where we started from.

ROSEMARY (*her mind elsewhere*) Uhh.

HOWARD You were awful nice to me tonight, Rosemary.

ROSEMARY Uhh.

HOWARD Do you think Mrs. Owens suspects anything?

ROSEMARY I don't care if she does.

HOWARD A businessman's gotta be careful of talk. And after all, you're a schoolteacher. (*fumbling to get away*) Well, I better be gettin' back to Cherryvale. I gotta open up the store in the morning. Good night, Rosemary.

ROSEMARY Uhh.

HOWARD   (*He pecks at her cheek with a kiss.*) Good night. Maybe I should say, good morning. (*He starts off.*)

ROSEMARY   (*just coming to*) Where you goin', Howard?

HOWARD   Honey, I gotta get home.

ROSEMARY   You can't go off without me.

HOWARD   Honey, talk sense.

ROSEMARY   You can't go off without me. Not after tonight. *That's* sense.

HOWARD   (*a little nervous*) Honey, be reasonable.

ROSEMARY   Take me with you.

HOWARD   What'd people say?

ROSEMARY   (*almost vicious*) To *hell* with what people'd say!

HOWARD   (*shocked*) Honey!

ROSEMARY   What'd people say if I thumbed my nose at them? What'd people say if I walked down the street and showed 'em my pink panties? What do I care what people say?

HOWARD   Honey, you're not yourself tonight.

ROSEMARY   Yes, I am. I'm more myself than I ever was. Take me with you, Howard. If you don't I don't know what I'll do with myself. I mean it.

HOWARD   Now look, Honey, you better go upstairs and get some sleep. You gotta start school in the morning. We'll talk all this over Saturday.

ROSEMARY   Maybe you won't be back Saturday. Maybe you won't be back ever again.

HOWARD   Rosemary, you know better than that.

ROSEMARY   Then what's the next thing in store for me? To be nice to the next man, then the next—till there's no one left to care whether I'm nice to him or not. Till I'm ready for the grave and don't have anyone to take me there.

HOWARD   (*in an attempt to be consoling*) Now, Rosemary!

ROSEMARY   You can't let that happen to me, Howard. I won't let you.

HOWARD   I don't understand. When we first started going together you were the best sport I ever saw, always good for a laugh.

ROSEMARY   (*in a hollow voice*) I can't laugh any more.

HOWARD   We'll talk it over Saturday.

ROSEMARY   We'll talk it over *now.*

HOWARD   (*squirming*) Well—Honey—I . . .

ROSEMARY   You said you were gonna marry me, Howard. You said when I got back from my vacation, you'd be waitin' with the preacher.

HOWARD   Honey, I've had an awful busy summer and . . .

ROSEMARY   Where's the preacher, Howard? Where is he?

HOWARD   (*walking away from her*) Honey, I'm forty-two years old. A person forms certain ways of livin', then one day it's too late to change.

ROSEMARY   (*grabbing his arm and holding him*) Come back here, Howard. I'm no spring chicken either. Maybe I'm a little older than you think *I* am. I've formed my ways too. But they can be changed. They *gotta* be changed. It's no good livin' like this, in rented rooms, meetin' a bunch of old maids for supper every night, then comin' back home alone.

HOWARD   *I* know how it is, Rosemary. My life's no bed of roses either.

ROSEMARY   Then why don't you do something about it?

HOWARD   I figure—there's some bad things about every life.

ROSEMARY   There's too much bad about mine. Each year, I keep tellin' myself, is the last. Something'll happen. Then nothing ever does—except I get a little crazier all the time.

HOWARD   (*hopelessly*) Well . . .

ROSEMARY   A *well's* a hole in the ground, Howard. Be careful you don't fall in.

HOWARD   I wasn't trying to be funny.

ROSEMARY   . . . and all this time you just been leadin' me on.

HOWARD   (*defensive*) Rosemary, that's not *so!* I've not been leading you on.

ROSEMARY   I'd like to know what else you call it.

HOWARD   Well—can't we talk about it Saturday? I'm dead tired and I got a busy week ahead, and . . .

ROSEMARY   (*She grips him by the arm and looks straight into his eyes.*) You gotta marry me, Howard.

HOWARD   (*tortured*) Well—Honey, I can't marry you *now.*

ROSEMARY   You can be over here in the morning.

HOWARD   Sometimes you're unreasonable.

ROSEMARY   You gotta marry me.

HOWARD   What'll you do about your job?

ROSEMARY   Alvah Jackson can take my place till they get someone new from the agency.

HOWARD   I'll have to pay Fred Jenkins to take care of the store for a few days.

ROSEMARY   Then get him.

HOWARD   Well . . .

ROSEMARY   I'll be waitin' for you in the morning, Howard.

HOWARD   (*after a few moments' troubled thought*) No.

ROSEMARY   (*a muffled cry*) Howard!

HOWARD   I'm not gonna marry anyone that says, "You gotta marry me, Howard." I'm not gonna. (*He is silent.* ROSEMARY *weeps pathetic tears. Slowly* HOWARD *reconsiders.*) If a woman wants me to marry her—she can at least say "please."

ROSEMARY   (*beaten and humble*) Please marry me, Howard.

HOWARD   Well—you got to give me time to think it over.

ROSEMARY (*desperate*) Oh, God! Please marry me, Howard. Please . . . (*She sinks to her knees.*) Please . . . please . . .

HOWARD (*embarrassed by her suffering humility*) Rosemary . . . I . . . I gotta have some time to think it over. You go to bed now and get some rest. I'll drive over in the morning and maybe we can talk it over before you go to school. I . . .

ROSEMARY You're not just tryin' to get out of it, Howard?

HOWARD I'll be over in the morning, Honey.

ROSEMARY Honest?

HOWARD Yah. I gotta go to the courthouse anyway. We'll talk it over then.

ROSEMARY Oh, God, please marry me, Howard. Please.

HOWARD (*trying to get away*) Go to bed, Honey. I'll see you in the morning.

ROSEMARY Please, Howard!

HOWARD I'll see you in the morning. Good night, Rosemary. (*starting off*)

ROSEMARY (*in a meek voice*) Please!

HOWARD Good night, Rosemary.

ROSEMARY (*after he is gone*) Please.

Reference Key to Plays in Anthologies

Copies of the complete play may be found in the following selected volumes:
Numbers 39, 47.
See also *Theatre Arts*, April, 1954.

Further Reading on Inge and *Picnic*

Bentley, Eric. "Pathetic Phalluses." *The Dramatic Event*. Boston: Beacon, 1956, pp. 102–06.

Brustein, R. "Men-Taming Women of William Inge." *Harper's*, Vol. 217, No. 1302 (November, 1958), pp. 52–57.

Inge, William. "Forgotten Anger." *Theatre Arts*, Vol. 42, No. 2 (February, 1958), pp. 68–69, 94.

———. *Four Plays*. New York: Random House, 1958, pp. v–x.

"Picnic's Provider." *New Yorker*, Vol. 29, No. 7 (April 4, 1953), pp. 24–25.

Weales, Gerald. *American Drama Since World War II*. New York: Harcourt, Brace & World, 1962, pp. 40–56.

A Streetcar Named Desire _____

TENNESSEE WILLIAMS (1947)
From Act II, Scene 2

SCENE: For one man, one woman

CHARACTERS: Blanche DuBois
              Harold Mitchell (Mitch)

SETTING: The living room of the Kowalski apartment in the French Quar-
              ter of New Orleans.

TIME: Two o'clock in the morning. The present.

SITUATION: Blanche DuBois is visiting her sister Stella, who is married to a
              virile brawler, Stanley Kowalski. Blanche is both attracted and
              repelled by Stanley. His coarseness disgusts her, but his un-
              abashed masculinity attracts her. Trying to forget her sordid
              past, the suicide of her perverted husband and the loss of her
              job as a schoolteacher for seducing one of her students,
              Blanche has retreated into a world of fantasy and has invented
              a story of a coming marriage to a millionaire.

              Unaware of Blanche's past, Mitch has taken a fancy to her.
              No longer a young man, Mitch has spent his life caring for his
              ailing mother. He thinks of Blanche as a potential wife. Blanche
              knows that Mitch may be her last means of escape from a sor-
              did and hopeless life.

              See also the following scene from *A Streetcar Named Desire*
              (p. 139), which occurs later in the play.

[BLANCHE *and* MITCH *come in. The utter exhaustion which only a
neurasthenic personality can know is evident in* BLANCHE'S *voice and
manner.* MITCH *is stolid but depressed. They have probably been out
to the amusement park on Lake Pontchartrain, for* MITCH *is bearing,
upside down, a plaster statuette of Mae West, the sort of prize won at
shooting-galleries and carnival games of chance.*]

BLANCHE   (*stopping lifelessly at the steps*) Well—(MITCH *laughs uneasily.*)
Well . . .

MITCH   I guess it must be pretty late—and you're tired.

BLANCHE   Even the hot tamale man has deserted the street, and he hangs
on till the end. (MITCH *laughs uneasily again.*) How will you get home?

MITCH   I'll walk over to Bourbon and catch an owl-car.

BLANCHE   (*laughing grimly*) Is that streetcar named Desire still grinding
along the tracks at this hour?

MITCH   (*heavily*) I'm afraid you haven't gotten much fun out of this
evening, Blanche.

BLANCHE   I spoiled it for *you*.

MITCH   No, you didn't, but I felt all the time that I wasn't giving you
much—entertainment.

BLANCHE   I simply couldn't rise to the occasion. That was all. I don't
think I've ever tried so hard to be gay and made such a dismal mess of
it. I get ten points for trying!—I *did* try.

MITCH   Why did you try if you didn't feel like it, Blanche?

BLANCHE   I was just obeying the law of nature.

MITCH   Which law is that?

BLANCHE   The one that says the lady must entertain the gentleman—or no
dice! See if you can locate my door-key in this purse. When I'm so
tired my fingers are all thumbs!

MITCH   (*rooting in her purse*) This it?

BLANCHE   No, Honey, that's the key to my trunk which I must soon be
packing.

MITCH   You mean you are leaving here soon?

BLANCHE   I've outstayed my welcome.

MITCH   This it?

· · ·

BLANCHE   Eureka! Honey, you open the door while I take a last look at
the sky. (*She leans on the porch rail. He opens the door and stands
awkwardly behind her.*) I'm looking for the Pleiades, the Seven Sisters,
but these girls are not out tonight. Oh, yes they are, there they are!
God bless them! All in a bunch going home from their little bridge
party. . . . Y' get the door open? Good boy! I guess you—want to go
now . . .

[*He shuffles and coughs a little.*]

MITCH   Can I—uh—kiss you—goodnight?

BLANCHE   Why do you always ask me if you may?

MITCH   I don't know whether you want me to or not.

BLANCHE   Why should you be so doubtful?

MITCH   That night when we parked by the lake and I kissed you, you—

BLANCHE Honey, it wasn't the kiss I objected to. I liked the kiss very much. It was the other little—familiarity—that I—felt obliged to—discourage. . . . I didn't resent it! Not a bit in the world! In fact, I was somewhat flattered that you—desired me! But, honey, you know as well as I do that a single girl, a girl alone in the world, has got to keep a firm hold on her emotions or she'll be lost!

MITCH (solemnly) Lost?

BLANCHE I guess you are used to girls that like to be lost. The kind that get lost immediately, on the first date!

MITCH I like you to be exactly the way that you are, because in all my—experience—I have never known anyone like you.

[BLANCHE looks at him gravely; then she bursts into laughter and then claps a hand to her mouth.]

MITCH Are you laughing at me?

BLANCHE No, honey. The lord and lady of the house have not yet returned, so come in. We'll have a night-cap. Let's leave the lights off. Shall we?

MITCH You just—do what you want to.

[BLANCHE precedes him into the kitchen. The outer wall of the building disappears and the interiors of the two rooms can be dimly seen.]

BLANCHE (remaining in the first room) The other room's more comfortable—go on in. This crashing around in the dark is my search for some liquor.

MITCH You want a drink?

BLANCHE I want you to have a drink! You have been so anxious and solemn all evening, and so have I; we have both been anxious and solemn and now for these few last remaining moments of our lives together—I want to create—joie de vivre! I'm lighting a candle.

MITCH That's good.

BLANCHE We are going to be very Bohemian. We are going to pretend that we are sitting in a little artists' cafe on the Left Bank in Paris! (She lights a candle stub and puts it in a bottle.) Je suis la Dame aux Camellias! Vous êtes—Armand! Understand French?

MITCH (heavily) Naw. Naw, I—

BLANCHE Voulez-vous coucher avec moi ce soir? Vous ne comprenez pas? Ah, quelle dommage!—I mean it's a damned good thing. . . . I've found some liquor! Just enough for two shots without any dividends, honey . . .

MITCH (heavily) That's—good.

[She enters the bedroom with the drinks and the candle.]

BLANCHE Sit down! Why don't you take off your coat and loosen your collar?

MITCH   I better leave it on.

BLANCHE   No. I want you to be comfortable.

MITCH   I am ashamed of the way I perspire. My shirt is sticking to me.

BLANCHE   Perspiration is healthy. If people didn't perspire they would die in five minutes. (*She takes his coat from him.*) This is a nice coat. What kind of material is it?

MITCH   They call that stuff alpaca.

BLANCHE   Oh. Alpaca.

MITCH   It's very lightweight alpaca.

BLANCHE   Oh. Lightweight alpaca.

MITCH   I don't like to wear a wash-coat even in summer because I sweat through it.

BLANCHE   Oh.

MITCH   And it don't look neat on me. A man with a heavy build has got to be careful of what he puts on him so he don't look too clumsy.

BLANCHE   You are not too heavy.

MITCH   You don't think I am?

BLANCHE   You are not the delicate type. You have a massive bone-structure and a very imposing physique.

MITCH   Thank you. Last Christmas I was given a membership to the New Orleans Athletic Club.

BLANCHE   Oh, good.

MITCH   It was the finest present I ever was given. I work out there with the weights and I swim and I keep myself fit. When I started there, I was getting soft in the belly but now my belly is hard. It is so hard now that a man can punch me in the belly and it don't hurt me. Punch me! Go on! See? (*She pokes lightly at him.*)

BLANCHE   Gracious. (*Her hand touches her chest.*)

MITCH   Guess how much I weigh, Blanche?

BLANCHE   Oh, I'd say in the vicinity of—one hundred and eighty?

MITCH   Guess again.

BLANCHE   Not that much?

MITCH   No. More.

BLANCHE   Well, you're a tall man and you can carry a good deal of weight without looking awkward.

MITCH   I weigh two hundred and seven pounds and I'm six feet one and one half inches tall in my bare feet—without shoes on. And that is what I weigh stripped.

BLANCHE   Oh, my goodness, me! It's awe-inspiring.

MITCH   (*embarrassed*) My weight is not a very interesting subject to talk about. (*He hesitates for a moment.*) What's yours?

BLANCHE   My weight?

MITCH   Yes.

BLANCHE Guess!

MITCH Let me lift you.

BLANCHE Samson! Go on, lift me. (*He comes behind her and puts his hands on her waist and raises her lightly off the ground.*) Well?

MITCH You are light as a feather.

BLANCHE Ha-ha! (*He lowers her but keeps his hands on her waist.* BLANCHE *speaks with an affectation of demureness.*) You may release me now.

MITCH Huh?

BLANCHE (*gaily*) I said unhand me, sir. (*He fumblingly embraces her. Her voice sounds gently reproving.*) Now, Mitch. Just because Stanley and Stella aren't at home is no reason why you shouldn't behave like a gentleman.

MITCH Just give me a slap whenever I step out of bounds.

BLANCHE That won't be necessary. You're a natural gentleman, one of the very few that are left in the world. I don't want you to think that I am severe and old maid schoolteacherish or anything like that. It's just—well—

MITCH Huh?

BLANCHE I guess it is just that I have—old-fashioned ideals!

Reference Key to Plays in Anthologies

Copies of the complete play may be found in the following selected volumes: Numbers 38, 46, 47, 62, 74.

Further Reading on Williams and *A Streetcar Named Desire*

Cole, Toby, and Helen Krich Chinoy, eds. *Directors on Directing*. Indianapolis: Bobbs-Merrill, 1963, pp. 364–79. (See "Elia Kazan, Notebook for *A Streetcar Named Desire*" in which the famous director offers his interpretation of the characters and his way of realizing them on the stage.)

Dusenbury, Winifred L. *The Theme of Loneliness in American Drama*. Gainesville: University of Florida Press, 1960, pp. 134–54.

Gibbs, Wolcott. "Lower Depths, Southern Style." *New Yorker*, Vol. 23, No. 43 (December 13, 1947), pp. 50–54.

Hurrell, John D. *Two Modern American Tragedies*. New York: Scribner's, 1961. (Includes a collection of reviews and criticisms of the play.)

McCarthy, Mary. "Streetcar Called Success." *Sights and Spectacles 1937–1956*. New York: Farrar, Straus and Cudahy, 1956, pp. 132 ff.

Nathan, George Jean. "*A Streetcar Named Desire*." *The Theatre Book of the Year 1947–1948*. New York: Knopf, 1948, pp. 163–66.

Popkin, Henry. "The Plays of Tennessee Williams." *Tulane Drama Review*, Vol. 4, No. 3 (March, 1960), pp. 45–61.

For additional sources that deal with Williams' work, see the data following the scene from *The Glass Menagerie* (p. 87).

A Streetcar Named Desire

TENNESSEE WILLIAMS (1947)

From Act III, Scene 2

SCENE:	For one man, two women
CHARACTERS:	Blanche DuBois Stella Kowalski, her sister Stanley Kowalski, Stella's husband
SETTING:	The living room of the Kowalski apartment in the French Quarter of New Orleans.
TIME:	Early evening. The present.
SITUATION:	See the preceding scene from *A Streetcar Named Desire* (p. 133), which occurs earlier in the play.

Several weeks have passed since the evening Mitch and Blanche had their date. Since that evening, Stanley has discovered the truth about Blanche's past and has told both Stella and Mitch what he has learned. Although Stanley has not revealed his knowledge to Blanche, she senses that something has happened. It is about three-quarters of an hour after Stanley has told Stella. Despite the strained atmosphere, they have gone through the motions of eating a dismal birthday dinner, "celebrating" Blanche's birthday. There is an empty chair at the table. Mitch has not come. Stella is embarrassed and sad; Blanche sits with a tight, artificial smile on her face. Stanley is watching Blanche sullenly as he gnaws a pork chop and licks his fingers.

BLANCHE   (*suddenly*) Stanley, tell us a joke, tell us a funny story to make us all laugh. I don't know what's the matter, we're all so solemn. Is it because I've been stood up by my beau? (STELLA *laughs feebly.*) It's the first time in my entire experience with men, and I've had a good deal of all sorts, that I've actually been stood up by anybody! Ha-ha! I don't know how to take it. . . . Tell us a funny little story, Stanley! Something to help us out.

STANLEY   I didn't think you liked my stories, Blanche.

BLANCHE   I like them when they're amusing but not indecent.

STANLEY   I don't know any refined enough for your taste.

BLANCHE   Then let me tell one.

STELLA   Yes, you tell one, Blanche. You used to know lots of good stories.

. . .

BLANCHE   Let me see, now. . . . I must run through my repertoire! Oh, yes—I love parrot stories! Do you all like parrot stories? Well, this one's about the old maid and the parrot. This old maid, she had a parrot that cursed a blue streak and knew more vulgar expressions than Mr. Kowalski!

STANLEY   Huh.

BLANCHE   And the only way to hush the parrot up was to put the cover back on its cage so it would think it was night and go back to sleep. Well, one morning the old maid had just uncovered the parrot for the day—when who should she see coming up the front walk but the preacher! Well, she rushed back to the parrot and slipped the cover back on the cage and then she let in the preacher. And the parrot was perfectly still, just as quiet as a mouse, but just as she was asking the preacher how much sugar he wanted in his coffee—the parrot broke the silence with a loud—(*She whistles.*)—and said—"God *damn*, but that was a short day!"

[*She throws back her head and laughs.* STELLA *also makes an ineffectual effort to seem amused.* STANLEY *pays no attention to the story but reaches way over the table to spear his fork into the remaining chop which he eats with his fingers.*]

BLANCHE   Apparently Mr. Kowalski was not amused.

STELLA   Mr. Kowalski is too busy making a pig of himself to think of anything else!

STANLEY   That's right, baby.

STELLA   Your face and your fingers are disgustingly greasy. Go and wash up and then help me clear the table.

[*He hurls a plate to the floor.*]

STANLEY   That's how I'll clear the table! (*He seizes her arm.*) Don't ever talk that way to me! "Pig—Polack—disgusting—vulgar—greasy!"—them kind of words have been on your tongue and your sister's too much around here! What do you two think you are? A pair of queens? Remember what Huey Long said—"Every Man Is a King!" And I am the king around here, so don't forget it! (*He hurls a cup and saucer to the floor.*) My place is cleared! You want me to clear your places?

[STELLA *begins to cry weakly.* STANLEY *stalks out on the porch and lights a cigarette. The Negro entertainers around the corner are heard.*]

BLANCHE   What happened while I was bathing? What did he tell you, Stella?

STELLA   Nothing, nothing, nothing!

BLANCHE   I think he told you something about Mitch and me! You know why Mitch didn't come but you won't tell me! (STELLA *shakes her head helplessly.*) I'm going to call him!

STELLA   I wouldn't call him, Blanche.

BLANCHE   I am, I'm going to call him on the phone.

STELLA   (*miserably*) I wish you wouldn't.

BLANCHE   I intend to be given some explanation from someone!

[*She rushes to the phone in the bedroom.* STELLA *goes out on the porch and stares reproachfully at her husband. He grunts and turns away from her.*]

STELLA   I hope you're pleased with your doings. I never had so much trouble swallowing food in my life, looking at that girl's face and the empty chair! (*She cries quietly.*)

BLANCHE   (*at the phone*) Hello. Mr. Mitchell, please. . . . Oh. . . . I would like to leave a number if I may. Magnolia 9047. And say it's important to call. . . . Yes, very important. . . . Thank you.

[*She remains by the phone with a lost, frightened look.* STANLEY *turns slowly back toward his wife and takes her clumsily in his arms.*]

STANLEY   Stell, it's gonna be all right after she goes and after you've had the baby. It's gonna be all right again between you and me the way that it was. You remember that way that it was? Them nights we had together? God, honey, it's gonna be sweet when we can make noise in the night the way that we used to and get the colored lights going with nobody's sister behind the curtains to hear us! (*Their upstairs neighbors are heard in bellowing laughter at something.* STANLEY *chuckles.*) Steve an' Eunice. . . .

STELLA   Come on back in. (*She returns to the kitchen and starts lighting the candles on the white cake.*) Blanche?

BLANCHE   Yes. (*She returns from the bedroom to the table in the kitchen.*) Oh, those pretty, pretty little candles! Oh, don't burn them, Stella.

STELLA   I certainly will.

[STANLEY *comes back in.*]

BLANCHE   You ought to save them for baby's birthdays. Oh, I hope candles are going to glow in his life and I hope that his eyes are going to be like candles, like two blue candles lighted in a white cake!

STANLEY   (*sitting down*) What poetry!

BLANCHE (*She pauses reflectively for a moment.*) I shouldn't have called him.

STELLA There's lots of things could have happened.

BLANCHE There's no excuse for it, Stella. I don't have to put up with insults. I won't be taken for granted.

STANLEY Goddamn, it's hot in here with the steam from the bathroom.

BLANCHE I've said I was sorry three times. . . . I take hot baths for my nerves. Hydro-therapy, they call it. You healthy Polack, without a nerve in your body, of course you don't know what anxiety feels like!

STANLEY I am not a Polack. People from Poland are Poles, not Polacks. But what I am is a one hundred percent American, born and raised in the greatest country on earth and proud as hell of it, so don't ever call me a Polack.

[*The phone rings.* BLANCHE *rises expectantly.*]

BLANCHE Oh, that's for me, I'm sure.

STANLEY *I'm* not sure. Keep your seat. (*He crosses leisurely to phone.*) H'lo. Aw, yeh, hello, Mac.

[*He leans against wall, staring insultingly in at* BLANCHE. *She sinks back in her chair with a frightened look.* STELLA *leans over and touches her shoulder.*]

BLANCHE Oh, keep your hands off me, Stella. What is the matter with you? Why do you look at me with that pitying look?

STANLEY (*bawling*) QUIET IN THERE!—We've got a noisy woman on the place.—Go on, Mac. At Riley's? No, I don't wanta bowl at Riley's. I had a little trouble with Riley last week. I'm the team-captain, ain't I? All right, then, we're not gonna bowl at Riley's, we're gonna bowl at the West Side or the Gala! All right, Mac. See you! (*He hangs up and returns to the table.* BLANCHE *fiercely controls herself, drinking quickly from her tumbler of water. He doesn't look at her but reaches in a pocket. Then he speaks slowly and with false amiability.*) Sister Blanche, I've got a little birthday remembrance for you.

BLANCHE Oh, have you, Stanley? I wasn't expecting any, I—I don't know why Stella wants to observe my birthday! I'd much rather forget it—when you—reach twenty-seven! Well—age is a subject that you'd prefer to—ignore!

STANLEY Twenty-seven?

BLANCHE (*quickly*) What is it? Is it for *me?*

[*He is holding a little envelope toward her.*]

STANLEY Yes, I hope you like it!

BLANCHE Why, why—Why, it's a—

STANLEY Ticket! Back to Laurel! On the Greyhound! Tuesday!

(. . . STELLA *rises abruptly and turns her back.* BLANCHE *tries to smile. Then she tries to laugh. Then she gives both up and springs from the table and runs into the next room. She clutches her throat and then runs into the bathroom. Coughing, gagging sounds are heard.*) Well!

STELLA   You didn't need to do that.

STANLEY   Don't forget all that I took off her.

STELLA   You needn't have been so cruel to someone alone as she is.

STANLEY   Delicate piece she is.

STELLA   She is. She was. You didn't know Blanche as a girl. Nobody, nobody, was tender and trusting as she was. But people like you abused her, and forced her to change. (*He crosses into the bedroom, ripping off his shirt, and changes into a brilliant silk bowling shirt. She follows him.*) Do you think you're going bowling now?

STANLEY   Sure.

STELLA   You're not going bowling. (*She catches hold of his shirt.*) Why did you do this to her?

STANLEY   I done nothing to no one. Let go of my shirt. You've torn it.

STELLA   I want to know why. Tell me why.

STANLEY   When we first met, me and you, you thought I was common. How right you was, baby. I was common as dirt. You showed me the snapshot of the place with the columns. I pulled you down off them columns and how you loved it, having them colored lights going! And wasn't we happy together, wasn't it all okay till she showed here? (STELLA *makes a slight movement. Her look goes suddenly inward as if some interior voice had called her name. She begins a slow, shuffling progress from the bedroom to the kitchen, leaning and resting on the back of the chair and then on the edge of a table with a blind look and listening expression.* STANLEY, *finishing with his shirt, is unaware of her reaction.*) And wasn't we happy together? Wasn't it all okay? Till she showed here. Hoity-toity, describing me as an ape. (*He suddenly notices the change in* STELLA.) Hey, what is it, Stel? (*He crosses to her.*)

STELLA   (*quietly*) Take me to the hospital.

[*He is with her now, supporting her with his arm, murmuring indistinguishably as they go outside.*]

For anthologies containing the complete text and for a list of suggested readings, see the preceding scene from *A Streetcar Named Desire* (p. 137).

The Barretts of Wimpole Street _____

RUDOLPH BESIER (1930)

From Act V, Scene 2

SCENE: For one man, one woman

CHARACTERS: Edward Moulton-Barrett
Elizabeth, his daughter

SETTING: Elizabeth Barrett's bed-sitting-room at Number 50, Wimpole Street, London.

TIME: An afternoon in 1845.

SITUATION: Edward Moulton-Barrett rules his family with an iron hand, controlling his children through fear rather than through love. Elizabeth, his favorite daughter, is a semi-invalid, but has become an accomplished poet. Robert Browning, already famous, has been a regular caller to her bed-sitting-room; their mutual admiration has ripened to love, and despite Barrett's opposition, Elizabeth and Browning have secretly married.

Barrett has always discouraged romantic attachments for his children; he has already forced his younger daughter, Henrietta, to give up her lover. At the time, Elizabeth took Henrietta's part, incurring her father's anger; Barrett refused to see Elizabeth again until she repented.

In this scene Barrett has just entered the room, dismissing Henrietta, who had been chatting with Elizabeth. He does not yet know that Elizabeth and Browning have been married for a week and that Elizabeth is now waiting for the coach that will take her from her father's house forever.

BARRETT   Do you know why I am back so early?

ELIZABETH   (*in a whisper*) No, Papa.

BARRETT   (*in a low, intense voice*) Because I could bear it no longer. . . . It's ten days since last I saw you. . . .

ELIZABETH   Am I to blame for that, Papa?

BARRETT *(with restrained fury)* You dare to ask me such a question? Weren't you a party in your sister's shameless conduct? Haven't you encouraged her? Haven't you helped her? Haven't you defended her? And did you expect to go scot-free of my displeasure? *(stopping himself with a violent gesture)* I've not come to speak about that—but to put it behind me—to forget it—to forget it. . . . I wonder, my child, have you been half so miserable these last ten days as your father?

ELIZABETH Miserable, Papa?

BARRETT Do you suppose I'm happy when I'm bitterly estranged from all I love in the world? Do you know that night after night I had to call up all my will power to hold me from coming here to forgive you?

ELIZABETH Papa—

BARRETT All my will power, I tell you—all my sense of duty and right and justice. . . . But today I could bear it no longer. The want of your face and your voice became a torment. I had to come. I am not so strong as they think me. I had to come. And I despise myself for coming—despise myself—hate myself. . . .

ELIZABETH No—no! *(suddenly rises and puts her hands on his shoulders)* Oh, Papa, can't you see, won't you ever see, that strength may be weakness, and your sense of justice and right and duty all mistaken and wrong?

BARRETT *(hoarsely, taking her hands from his shoulders)* Mistaken and wrong? What do you mean? . . . *(quickly stopping her from speaking)* No, be silent. Don't answer me. . . . Mistaken and wrong? You don't know what you're saying.

ELIZABETH If you'll only listen to me, Papa, I—

BARRETT No.

ELIZABETH But, Papa—

BARRETT No. *(He moves to the window and stands there, his face half averted from her. A pause. He turns.)* If there were even a vestige of truth in what you say, my whole life would be a hideous mockery. For always—through all misfortunes and miseries—I've been upheld by knowing, beyond a doubt, what was right, and doing it unflinchingly, however bitter the consequences. . . . And bitter they've been—how bitter, only God knows! It's been my heavy cross that those whom I was given to guide and rule have always fought against the right that I knew to be the right—and was in duty bound to impose upon them. . . . Even you. Even your mother.

ELIZABETH *(in a whisper)* My mother?

BARRETT Yes, your mother. . . . But not at first. . . . You—you, my eldest child, were born of love and only love. . . . But the others—long before they came the rift had begun to open between your mother and me. Not that she ever opposed me—never once. Or put into words what she felt. She was silent and dutiful and obedient. But love died out—and fear took its place—fear. . . .

ELIZABETH (*sharply*) No! No!

BARRETT And all because I saw the right—and did it.

ELIZABETH (*in a low voice, staring before her*) Oh . . . oh, dear God, what she must have suffered.

BARRETT She?—She? . . . And what of me? What of me?

ELIZABETH You? . . . Oh, Papa, then you—you still loved her—after her love for you had died?

BARRETT (*in a muffled voice, looking aside*) Love? . . . What's love? . . . She was my wife. . . . You—you don't understand. . . .

ELIZABETH (*in a horrified whisper*) And all those children . . . born in fear. . . . Oh, it's horrible—it's horrible—it's horrible. . . . (*With a shuddering sob, she covers her face with her hands.*)

BARRETT (*aghast and embarrassed*) Ba, my dear—don't—don't . . . I—I shouldn't have spoken—I shouldn't have told you all that. . . . Forget it, child. . . . (*He goes up to her.*) Take your hands from your face. . . . (*He gently touches her wrists. She starts away from him, looking at him with wide, frightened eyes.*) Don't look at me like that. (*in a low, thick voice, averting his eyes*) You don't understand. How should you? You know nothing of the brutal tyranny of—passion, and how even the strongest and best are driven by it to hell. Would you have abetted your sister in her—

ELIZABETH (*fiercely*) Henrietta's love—how dare you speak of it in the same breath as—

BARRETT (*brutally*) Her *love*? *You* ignorant little fool! What do *you* know of love? Love! The lust of the eye—the lowest urge of the body—

ELIZABETH (*springing to her feet*) I won't listen to you!

BARRETT (*seizing her wrist and forcing her back to her seat*) You must— you shall! It's time a little reality were brought into your dream of life. Do you suppose I should have guarded my house like a dragon from this so-called love if I hadn't known, from my own life, all it entails of cruelty and loathing and degradation and remorse? . . . (*He pulls himself together.*) With the help of God, and through years of torment- ing abstinence, I strangled it in myself. And so long as I have breath in my body, I'll keep it away from those I was given to protect and care for. You understand me?

ELIZABETH (*in a low voice, looking him full in the face*) Yes—I under- stand you . . . I understand you. . . .

BARRETT Very well. (*A pause.* ELIZABETH *sits quite still, looking before her. When he speaks again his voice has changed.*) This has been a hateful necessity. I had to speak—plainly—lest your very innocence should smirch the purity I am utterly resolved to maintain in my home. . . . And because I feel that you acted in innocence and ig-norance, I—I forgive you freely, my child. . . . We must turn over this ugly page—and forget what was on it. . . . (*He takes her hand.*) You're—cold as ice. . . . Why are you trembling?

ELIZABETH (*drawing her hand from his*) I shall never forget what you have said.

BARRETT Never forget—but—And yet, perhaps that's as well. . . . (*with sudden urgency*) But, for God's sake, my darling, don't let this raise any further barrier between us! I've told you how all these past months I've seemed to feel you slipping little by little away from me. . . . Your love is all I have left to me in the world.

ELIZABETH You had Mamma's love once. You might have had the love of all your children.

BARRETT Yes, if I'd played the coward's part, and taken the easier way, and shirked my duty. I'd rather be hated by the whole world than gain love like that.

ELIZABETH (*in a broken voice*) Oh, Papa, you—you don't know how I pity you. . . .

BARRETT (*roughly*) Pity? I don't want your pity. . . . But if I should ever lose you or your love—(*He seizes her unwilling hands.*) My darling, next week we shall have left this house, and I hope we shall never return here. I've grown to loathe it. In our new home we shall draw close to each other again. There will be little to distract you in the country—nothing and no one to come between us. (*He draws her stiffening form into his arms.*) My child, my darling, you want me to be happy. The only happiness I shall ever know is all yours to give or take. You must look up to me, and depend on me, and lean on me. You must share your thoughts with me, your hopes, your fears, your prayers. I want all your heart and all your soul. . . .

[*He holds her passionately close; she leans away from him, her face drawn with fear and pain.*]

ELIZABETH (*sobbingly*) I can't bear it—I can't bear any more. . . . Let me go, Papa—please let me go. . . .

[*He loosens his embrace, and she falls away from him, her arm covering her face. He rises and bends over her.*]

BARRETT Forgive me, dear. I've said too much. I was carried away. I'll leave you now.

ELIZABETH (*in a whisper*) Please . . .

BARRETT Shall I see you again tonight?

ELIZABETH (*as before*) Not tonight. . . .

BARRETT I shall pray for you.

ELIZABETH (*half to herself*) Pray for me? . . . Tonight. . . . (*She turns and looks up at him.*) Yes, pray for me tonight—if you will.

[*He kisses her forehead gently, and goes out.*]

Reference Key to Plays in Anthologies

Copies of the complete play may be found in the following selected volumes: Numbers 19, 45, 68, 72.

Further Reading on *The Barretts of Wimpole Street*

Bailey, R. S. "Those Barretts of Wimpole Street." *Theatre,* Vol. 53, No. 3 (March, 1931), pp. 19–20.
Hutchens, John. "The Actor's Month." *Theatre Arts Monthly,* Vol. 15, No. 4 (April, 1931), pp. 273–77.

Recorded Performances

Abridged performance: scenes from the play, Caedmon 1071, one record.

Angel Street

PATRICK HAMILTON (1938)
From Act III

SCENE:	For one man, one woman
CHARACTERS:	Mr. Manningham Nancy, the maid
SETTING:	The living room of a four-story house on Angel Street, located in the Pimlico district of London.
TIME:	1880.
SITUATION:	Fifteen years before the beginning of the play, Sydney Power murdered an old woman, Alice Barlow, in order to steal the Barlow rubies. The murderer was unable to find the rubies even after ransacking the house. Years later, the murderer returns, this time calling himself Manningham. He is married to a wealthy woman whose money he used to buy the old Barlow house. At last he is free to search the house carefully, but secretly, in order to find the rubies. As Manningham now has no further need of his wife, he has been carrying on an insidious campaign to drive her insane. Meanwhile, his taste in women has turned to unemployed actresses and domestic servants.

[*Footsteps can be heard, and* MANNINGHAM *appears outside. He stops to turn out the light in the passage. He enters the room and goes to the lamp on the c. table and turns it up. Then he lights the two brackets and crosses to table U.R. and puts his hat on it. He goes in a slow and deliberate way over to the bell-cord and pulls it. He is humming to himself as he goes over to the fireplace.*
NANCY *puts her head round the* L.C. *door. She has only just come in and is dressed for out-of-doors.*]

NANCY   Yes, sir. Did you ring, sir?

FROM *Angel Street* by Patrick Hamilton. Reprinted by permission of the estate of the late Patrick Hamilton.

MR. MANNINGHAM   Yes, Nancy, I did ring. It seems that the entire household has gone to bed without leaving me my milk and without leaving
me my biscuits.

NANCY   Oh, I'm sorry, sir. They're only just outside. I'll bring them in!
(*turns to door then stops and turns to* MR. MANNINGHAM) Mrs. Manningham usually gets them, doesn't she, sir? Cook's in bed and I've
only just come in.

MR. MANNINGHAM   Quite, Nancy. Then perhaps you will deputize for
Mrs. Manningham, and bring them into the room.

NANCY   Certainly, sir.

MR. MANNINGHAM   And after you do that, (*She stops in doorway.*) Nancy,
will you go upstairs and tell Mrs. Manningham that I wish to see her
down here.

NANCY   Yes, sir. Certainly, sir. (*exits* L.C. *and turns to* R.)

[MR. MANNINGHAM *walks into room* U.R. NANCY *returns. She has milk
in a jug, a glass and biscuits on a tray, and puts them on the table. She
goes upstairs. He enters from room* U.R. *crosses slowly to above table
then over to desk.* NANCY *comes downstairs and stops at the foot of the
stairs.*]

MR. MANNINGHAM   Well, Nancy?

NANCY   She says she has a headache, sir, and is trying to sleep.

MR. MANNINGHAM   Oh—she still has a headache, has she?

NANCY   Yes, sir. Is there anything else you want, sir?

MR. MANNINGHAM   Did you ever know a time when Mrs. Manningham
did not have a headache, Nancy?

NANCY   No, sir. Hardly ever, sir.

MR. MANNINGHAM   (*turns to* NANCY) Do you usually perform your domestic tasks in outdoor costume, Nancy?

NANCY   I told you, sir. I've only just come in, and I heard the bell by
chance.

MR. MANNINGHAM   Yes, that's just the point.

NANCY   How do you mean, sir?

MR. MANNINGHAM   Will you be so good as to come closer, Nancy, where
I can see you. (NANCY *comes down stage a step. They look at each
other in a rather strange way.*) Have you any idea of the time of the
day, or rather night, Nancy?

NANCY   Yes, sir. It's a little after eleven, sir.

MR. MANNINGHAM   Are you aware that you came in half a minute, or
even less, before myself?

NANCY   Yes, sir. I thought I saw you, sir.

MR. MANNINGHAM   Oh—you thought you saw me. Well, I certainly saw
you.

NANCY (*looking away*) Did you, sir?

MR. MANNINGHAM Have you ever reflected, Nancy, that you are given a great deal of latitude in this house?

NANCY I don't know, sir. I don't know what latitude means.

MR. MANNINGHAM Latitude, Nancy, means considerable liberty—liberty to the extent of two nights off a week.

NANCY (*pause*) Yes, sir.

MR. MANNINGHAM Well, that's all very well. It is not so well, however, when you return as late as the master of the house. We ought to keep up some pretences, you know.

NANCY Yes, sir. We must. (*She makes to go.*)

MR. MANNINGHAM Nancy.

NANCY (*stops*) Yes, sir?

MR. MANNINGHAM (*in a more human tone*) Where the devil have you been tonight, anyway?

NANCY (*pause—turns to him*) Only with some friends, sir.

MR. MANNINGHAM You know, Nancy, when you say friends, I have an extraordinary idea that you mean gentlemen friends.

NANCY (*looking at him*) Well, sir, possibly I might.

MR. MANNINGHAM You know, gentlemen friends have been known to take decided liberties with young ladies like yourself. Are you alive to such a possibility?

NANCY Oh, no, sir. Not with me. I can look after myself.

MR. MANNINGHAM Are you always so anxious to look after yourself?

NANCY No, sir, not always, perhaps.

MR. MANNINGHAM You know, Nancy, pretty as your bonnet is, it is not anything near so pretty as your hair beneath it. Won't you take it off and let me see it?

NANCY (*as she removes hat and crosses to R. of chair R. of table*) Very good, sir. It comes off easy enough. There—Is there anything more you want, sir?

MR. MANNINGHAM Yes. Possibly. Come here, will you, Nancy?

NANCY (*pause*) Yes, sir—(*drops hat on chair R. of table. Coming to him*) Is there anything you want, sir?—(*changing tone as he puts his arms on her shoulders*) What do you want?—eh—What do you want? (MANNINGHAM *kisses* NANCY *in a violent and prolonged manner. There is a pause in which she looks at him, and then she kisses him as violently.*) There! Can she do that for you? Can she do that?

MR. MANNINGHAM Who can you be talking about, Nancy?

NANCY You know who I mean all right.

MR. MANNINGHAM You know, Nancy, you are a very remarkable girl in many respects. I believe you are jealous of your mistress.

NANCY   She? She's a poor thing. There's no need to be jealous of her. You want to kiss me again, don't you? Don't you want to kiss me? (MR. MANNINGHAM *kisses* NANCY.) There! That's better than a sick headache —ain't it—a sick headache and a pale face all the day.

MR. MANNINGHAM   Why, yes, Nancy, I believe it is. I think, however, don't you, that it would be better if you and I met one evening in different surroundings.

NANCY   Yes. Where? I'll meet you when you like. You're mine now—ain't you—'cos you want me. You want me—don't you?

MR. MANNINGHAM   And what of you, Nancy. Do you want me?

NANCY   Oh, yes! I always wanted you, ever since I first clapped eyes on you. I wanted you more than all of them.

MR. MANNINGHAM   Oh—there are plenty of others?

NANCY   Oh, yes—there's plenty of others.

MR. MANNINGHAM   So I rather imagined. And only nineteen.

NANCY   Where can we meet? Where do you want us to meet?

MR. MANNINGHAM   (*slowly crossing to front of settee and facing fireplace*) Really, Nancy, you have taken me a little by surprise. I'll let you know tomorrow.

NANCY   (*crossing to front of table*) How'll you let me know, when she's about?

MR. MANNINGHAM   (*quietly, half turning to* NANCY) Oh, I'll find a way, Nancy, I don't believe Mrs. Manningham will be here tomorrow.

NANCY   Oh? Not that I care about her. (*crossing to him*) I'd like to kiss you under her very nose. That's what I'd like to do.

MR. MANNINGHAM   All right, Nancy. Now you had better go. I have some work to do.

NANCY   Go? I don't want to go.

MR. MANNINGHAM   (*turns away from her*) There, run along. I have some work to do.

NANCY   Work? What are you going to work at? What are you going to do?

MR. MANNINGHAM   (*turns to* NANCY) Oh—I'm going to write some letters. Then I—Go along, Nancy, that's a good girl.

NANCY   Oh, very well, sir. You shall be master for a little more. (*her arms around his neck. Kisses him*) Good night, your lordship. (*starts to door* L.C. *and picks up her hat on the way*)

MR. MANNINGHAM   Good night.

NANCY   (*at door stops and turns to him*) When shall you let me know tomorrow?

MR. MANNINGHAM   When I find time, Nancy, when I find time. Good night.

NANCY   Good night! (*goes out into the hall* L.C.—*closes doors*)

Reference Key to Plays in Anthologies

A copy of the complete play may be found in the following volume:
  Number 15.

An abridged version of the play may be found in

Mantle, Burns. *The Best Plays of 1941–1942.* New York: Dodd, Mead, 1942.

Further Reading on *Angel Street*

Gilder, Rosamond. "On the Boards—December, '41." *Theatre Arts,* Vol. 26, No. 2 (February, 1942), p. 87.

Traube, Shepard. "Production of *Angel Street.*" *Theatre Arts,* Vol. 26, No. 6 (June, 1942), pp. 374–78.

There Shall Be No Night ————————————

ROBERT E. SHERWOOD (1940)

From Act I, Scene 2

SCENE:	For one man, two women
CHARACTERS:	Miranda Valkonen Erik Valkonen, her son Kaatri Alquist, Erik's fiancée
SETTING:	The living room of the Valkonen house in the suburbs of Helsinki, Finland.
TIME:	An evening late in November, 1939.
SITUATION:	Europe is in the first throes of World War II. Poland has already been conquered and divided by Germany and Russia, and Finland is anxiously watching the troop movements of the Red Army near the Russo-Finnish border. Erik, son of the Nobel Prize winning Finnish scientist Dr. Kaarlo Valkonen and his American wife Miranda, echoes to a great extent his father's opinion that the Russians will not attack Finland. Kaatri, the girl he loves, disagrees, but both hope for peace for they plan to marry the next summer. Erik's mother, Miranda, has returned from visiting her husband in his laboratory as the scene begins.

MIRANDA   I stopped in at the American Legation on my way home and saw Mr. Walsh. I wanted to find out if he had any news. He told me that the State Department has ordered all Americans to leave Finland at once. He was very guarded in his choice of words—but he seems to think that things are rather serious.

ERIK   So does Uncle Waldemar. But that doesn't mean anything. The American government—all governments—are being pulverized with fear by this Soviet propaganda. (*He picks up the paper from the piano.*) They want to pulverize us, too, so that we'll give them what they want without a struggle. It's all bluff—it's all an imitation of the Nazis.

KAATRI   But when the bluff doesn't work, suppose they go on imitating the Nazis—suppose they do attack?

[MIRANDA *looks from* KAATRI *to* ERIK, *awaiting his reply.*]

ERIK   (*without emotion*) Then—we'll have to fight—that's all.

MIRANDA   But—how can we fight?

ERIK   To the best of our ability.

MIRANDA   And how long will that last?

ERIK   A few days—a few weeks—I don't know. (*He is looking out the window.*)

MIRANDA   Erik—*Erik!* (*He turns to her.*) Would *you* fight?

ERIK   Of course I would. Everybody would!

MIRANDA   Why? What good would that do?

ERIK   It would prove that this country has a right to live.

MIRANDA   And who will derive any benefit from that proof? Are you anxious to die just to get applause from the civilized world—applause and probably nothing else? The Czechs are fine, brave people—but they didn't offer any resistance to the Germans.

ERIK   They couldn't. Their resistance was stolen from them at Munich.

MIRANDA   Even so—they're better off now than the Poles, who did resist.

ERIK   That doesn't affect my feeling. I only know that if anyone is going to take my freedom from me, he's going to have to pay for it.

MIRANDA   Now you're talking like a boy scout.

ERIK   I'm your son, Mother. I have the same blood in me that you have—the blood of that gentleman up there. (*He points to the portrait of great-grandfather Eustis.*) He fought pirates in the Mediterranean. He fought with Jackson at New Orleans.

MIRANDA   Yes—and when he died, in honored old age, they had to pass the hat around among the neighbors to get enough to bury him . . . (*pointing to the portrait of her grandfather*) Whereas that unselfish hero who paid another man to take his place in the conscript army—when he died—the whole town turned out—the Chamber of Commerce, the Republican Club, the Knights of Pythias—all paying tribute to the memory of a good, substantial citizen. If you have to look to your ancestry for guidance, look to him. He was no hero. He was a despicable, slimy cheat. But he did very well . . . You say someone will have to pay for your freedom. But who will receive the payment? Not you, when you're dead.

KAATRI   (*fiercely*) Don't listen to her, Erik! Don't listen to her!

MIRANDA   (*amiably*) Why shouldn't he listen to me, Kaatri?

KAATRI   (*with too much vehemence*) Because you're an American! You don't understand.

MIRANDA (*patiently*) I understand one thing, Kaatri. Erik is my son. I want to save his life.

KAATRI What good is his life if it has to be spent in slavery? (*to* ERIK) And that's what it would be if he gave in to them. Slavery for you—for all of us. Oh, I know that you Americans don't like to think of such terrible things.

ERIK Kaatri! You mustn't say that—

MIRANDA (*gently*) You may say what you please about me, Kaatri. But you can't say it about Erik. He's as loyal as you are. He was born in this house, as his father was before him.

KAATRI Dr. Valkonen is like you. He doesn't really belong to this country. He is a great scientist. He has an international mind.

MIRANDA And is that a bad thing?

KAATRI Oh, no—it's a good thing—a noble thing. But for Erik—it would be weakness. I'm afraid for Erik—afraid that he belongs more to America than he does to us. Oh—I don't want to be rude, Mrs. Valkonen—to you or your country. But we're desperate people now. All the men in my family—my father, my brothers—they're all in the army now, on the frontier. It's the same with all families, rich and poor, men and women. All our lives we've had to be ready to fight, for everything we are, everything we believe in. Oh, I know—it's hard for you to understand that—or to see the *need* for it that is in our souls.

ERIK Kaatri! Of course Mother can understand! Americans fought for that same thing—for the same reason—the same need, that was in their souls. It was Americans who taught the whole world that it was *worth* fighting for!

KAATRI Yes. But—it's just as Dr. Valkonen says. When life becomes too easy for people, something changes in their character, something is lost. Americans now are too lucky. (*She looks straight at* MIRANDA.) In your blood is the water of those oceans that have made your country safe. But—don't try to persuade Erik that life here is as easy as it is in America. (*She is speaking passionately, desperately.*) He's a Finn, and the time has come when he must behave like one.

ERIK Kaatri—my dearest—(*crossing behind the sofa, he puts a hand on* KAATRI's *right shoulder. She buries her head against him.*) Don't—don't cry.

[*The word "dearest" makes an emphatic impression on* MIRANDA. *She stares at them.*]

MIRANDA Kaatri—Kaatri—are you and Erik really in love with each other?

ERIK Mother!

MIRANDA Darling, I started to talk to you as though you were still a child—and I wanted first to reason with you—and then if that failed, I would *forbid* you to throw your life away for a lost cause. And then Kaatri spoke up, and you called her "dearest," and that one word stopped me short. I asked Kaatri that question because I thought the answer might help me to understand this strange, new fact—that you're not my son any more. You're a man . . . Of course, you don't have to answer.

ERIK (*his hand on* KAATRI's *shoulder*) We do love each other. We are going to be married.

MIRANDA (*after a pause, kisses* KAATRI) Erik—Kaatri— I'm glad! I'm glad.

Reference Key to Plays in Anthologies

A copy of the complete play may be found in the following volume:
Number 32.

An abridged version of the play may be found in
Mantle, Burns. *The Best Plays of 1939–1940.* New York: Dodd, Mead, 1940.

Further Reading on Sherwood and *There Shall Be No Night*

Anderson, Maxwell. "Robert Sherwood." *Theatre Arts,* Vol. 40, No. 2 (February, 1956), pp. 26–27.

Brown, John Mason. "Mr. Sherwood's War Play." *Broadway in Review.* New York: Norton, 1940, pp. 154–59.

Gassner, John. "Robert Sherwood." *Atlantic,* Vol. 169, No. 1 (January, 1942), pp. 26–33.

Gilder, Rosamond. *"There Shall Be No Night."* *Theatre Arts,* Vol. 24, No. 6 (June, 1940), pp. 399–401.

The Crucible

ARTHUR MILLER (1953)

From Act II, Scene 2

SCENE: For one man, one woman

CHARACTERS: John Proctor
Abigail Williams

SETTING: A wood outside Salem, Massachusetts.

TIME: An evening in the spring of 1692.

SITUATION: The town of Salem has entered the period of the infamous witch trials. One of the accusers is Abigail Williams, a young woman who has served in John Proctor's house as a servant during the illness of his wife. She has accused a number of Salem citizens of practicing witchcraft. John knows that Abigail's charges are false and that she is far from being the innocent girl the court believes her to be. He hopes that she can be made to change her testimony.

Although Proctor was quiet during the initial development of the trials, an accusation brought against his wife forced him to face the problem. When Abigail was in the Proctor household, she and Proctor were intimate. Proctor believes that Abigail's accusation is an attempt to eliminate his wife Elizabeth as a rival. Abigail still desires Proctor, but he wishes only to be free of her so that he may be reconciled with his wife.

[PROCTOR *appears with lantern. He enters glancing behind him, then halts, holding the lantern raised.* ABIGAIL *appears with a wrap over her nightgown, her hair down. A moment of questioning silence*]

PROCTOR (*searching*) I must speak with you, Abigail. (*She does not move, staring at him.*) Will you sit?

ABIGAIL How do you come?

PROCTOR Friendly.

ABIGAIL (*glancing about*) I don't like the woods at night. Pray you, stand closer. (*He comes closer to her, but keeps separated in spirit.*) I knew it must be you. When I heard the pebbles on the window, before I opened up my eyes I knew. I thought you would come a good time sooner.

PROCTOR   I had thought to come many times.

ABIGAIL   Why didn't you? I am so alone in the world now.

PROCTOR   (*as a fact. Not bitterly*) Are you? I've heard that people come a hundred mile to see your face these days.

ABIGAIL   Aye, my face. Can you see my face?

PROCTOR   (*holds the lantern to her face*) Then you're troubled?

ABIGAIL   Have you come to mock me?

PROCTOR   (*sets lantern and sits down*) No, no, but I hear only that you go to the tavern every night, and play shovelboard with the Deputy Governor, and they give you cider.

ABIGAIL   (*as though that did not count*) I have once or twice played the shovelboard. But I have no joy in it.

PROCTOR   (*He is probing her.*) This is a surprise Abby. I'd thought to find you gayer than this. I'm told a troop of boys go step for step with you wherever you walk these days.

ABIGAIL   Aye, they do. But I have only lewd looks from the boys.

PROCTOR   And you like that not?

ABIGAIL   I cannot bear lewd looks no more, John. My spirit's changed entirely. I ought to be given Godly looks when I suffer for them as I do.

PROCTOR   Oh? How do you suffer, Abby?

ABIGAIL   (*pulls up dress*) Why, look at my leg. I'm holes all over from their damned needles and pins. (*touching her stomach*) The jab your wife gave me's not healed yet, y'know.

PROCTOR   (*seeing her madness now*) Oh, it isn't.

ABIGAIL   I think sometimes she pricks it open again while I sleep.

PROCTOR   Ah?

ABIGAIL   And George Jacobs . . . (*sliding up her sleeve*) He comes again and again and raps me with his stick—the same spot every night all this week. Look at the lump I have.

PROCTOR   Abby—George Jacobs is in the jail all this month.

ABIGAIL   Thank God he is, and bless the day he hangs and lets me sleep in peace again! Oh, John, the world's so full of hypocrites. (*astonished, outraged*) They pray in jail! I'm told they all pray in jail!

PROCTOR   They may not pray?

ABIGAIL   And torture me in my bed while sacred words are comin' from their mouths? Oh, it will need God himself to cleanse this town properly!

PROCTOR   Abby—you mean to cry out still others?

ABIGAIL   If I live, if I am not murdered, I surely will, until the last hypocrite is dead.

PROCTOR   Then there is no one good?

ABIGAIL   (*softly*) Aye, there is one. *You* are good.

PROCTOR   Am I? How am I good?

ABIGAIL   Why, you taught me goodness, therefore you are good. It were
a fire you walked me through, and all my ignorance was burned away.
It were a fire, John, we lay in fire. And from that night no woman
dare call me wicked anymore but I knew my answer. I used to weep
for my sins when the wind lifted up my skirts; and blushed for shame
because some old Rebecca called me loose. And then you burned my
ignorance away. As bare as some December tree I saw them all—walking like saints to church, running to feed the sick, and hypocrites in
their hearts! And God gave me strength to call them liars, and God
made men listen to me, and by God I will scrub the world clean for
the love of Him! Oh, John, I will make you such a wife when the world
is white again! (*She kisses his hand in high emotion.*) You will be
amazed to see me every day, a light of heaven in your house, a . . .
(*He rises and backs away, frightened, amazed.*) Why are you cold?

PROCTOR   (*in a business-like way, but with uneasiness, as though before
an unearthly thing*) My wife goes to trial in the morning, Abigail.

ABIGAIL   (*distantly*) Your wife?

PROCTOR   Surely you knew of it?

ABIGAIL   (*coming awake to that*) I do remember it now. (*as a duty*) How—
how—is she well?

PROCTOR   As well as she may be, thirty-six days in that place.

ABIGAIL   You said you came friendly.

PROCTOR   She will not be condemned, Abby.

ABIGAIL   (*her holy feelings outraged. But she is questioning.*) You brought
me from my bed to speak of her?

PROCTOR   I come to tell you, Abby, what I will do tomorrow in the court.
I would not take you by surprise, but give you all good time to think
on what to do to save yourself.

ABIGAIL   (*incredibly, and with beginning fear*) Save myself!

PROCTOR   If you do not free my wife tomorrow, I am set and bound to
ruin you, Abby.

ABIGAIL   (*her voice small—astonished*) How—ruin me?

PROCTOR   I have rocky proof in documents that you knew that poppet
were none of my wife's; and that you yourself bade Mary Warren stab
that needle into it.

ABIGAIL   (*A wildness stirs in her; a child is standing here who is unutter-
ably frustrated, denied her wish; but she is still grasping for her wits.*)
I bade Mary Warren . . . ?

PROCTOR   You know what you do, you are not so mad!

ABIGAIL   (*She calls upwards.*) Oh, hypocrites! Have you won him, too? (*directly to him*) John, why do you let them send you?

PROCTOR   I warn you, Abby.

ABIGAIL   They send you! They steal your honesty and . . .

PROCTOR   I have found my honesty.

ABIGAIL   No, this is your wife pleading, your sniveling, envious wife! This is Rebecca's voice, Martha Corey's voice. You were no hypocrite!

PROCTOR   (*He grasps her arm and holds her.*) I will prove you for the fraud you are!

ABIGAIL   And if they ask you why Abigail would ever do so murderous a deed, what will you tell them?

PROCTOR   (*It is hard even to say it.*) I will tell them why.

ABIGAIL   What will you tell? You will confess to fornication? In the court?

PROCTOR   If you will have it so, so I will tell it! (*She utters a disbelieving laugh.*) I say I will! (*She laughs louder, now with more assurance he will never do it. He shakes her roughly.*) If you can still hear, hear this! Can you hear! (*She is trembling, staring up at him as though he were out of his mind.*) You will tell the court you are blind to spirits; you cannot see them anymore, and you will never cry witchery again, or I will make you famous for the whore you are!

ABIGAIL   (*She grabs him.*) Never in this world! I know you, John—you are this moment singing secret Hallelujahs that your wife will hang!

PROCTOR   (*throws her down*) You mad, you murderous bitch!

ABIGAIL   (*rises*) Oh, how hard it is when pretense falls! But it falls, it falls! (*She wraps herself up as though to go.*) You have done your duty by her. I hope it is your last hypocrisy. I pray you will come again with sweeter news for me. I know you will—now that your duty's done. Good night, John. (*She is backing away, raising her hand in farewell.*) Fear naught. I will save you tomorrow. From yourself I will save you. (*She is gone.*)

[PROCTOR *is left alone, amazed in terror. He takes up his lantern and slowly exits as the curtain falls.*]

Reference Key to Plays in Anthologies

Copies of the complete play may be found in the following selected volumes:
    Numbers 26, 39, 58, 81.
    See also *Theatre Arts*, October, 1953.

Further Reading on Miller and *The Crucible*

Bentley, Eric. "The Innocence of Arthur Miller." *The Dramatic Event*. Boston: Beacon, 1954, pp. 90–94.

Hitchens, Gordon. *Attention Must Be Paid: A Study of Social Values in Four Plays by Arthur Miller*. Privately published, 1962.

Nathan, George Jean. "Henrik Miller." *Theatre Arts,* Vol. 37, No. 4 (April, 1953), pp. 24–26. (A particularly penetrating analysis of *The Crucible* and the technique of Miller's writing.)

Welland, Dennis. *Arthur Miller*. New York: Evergreen, 1961.

Liliom

Ferenc Molnar (1909)
translated by B. Glazer
From Scene 7

SCENE:	For one man, two women
CHARACTERS:	Liliom, a carousel barker Julie, his wife Louise, his daughter, aged sixteen
SETTING:	In front of a small, tumble-down house on a bare, unenclosed plot of ground. Before the house is a tiny garden enclosed by a hip-high hedge.
TIME:	A bright Sunday morning in spring near the beginning of this century.
SITUATION:	Several years before this scene begins, Liliom was killed while committing a robbery. His death left his wife Julie destitute. A heavenly judge sentenced Liliom to spend sixteen years in the crimson fires until his daughter is grown. At that time he will be permitted to return to earth for one day. During the period of his return, he is expected to take the opportunity to do a good deed for his daughter. Liliom's pathway to eternity will be determined by the nature of that one good deed.

The scene begins as Liliom arrives back on earth with two heavenly policemen. Liliom steps forward to a point just outside the tumble-down house of Julie and Louise.

LILIOM Good-day.

LOUISE Good-day.

JULIE Another beggar! What is it you want, my poor man?

LILIOM Nothing.

JULIE   We have no money to give, but if you care for a plate of soup—
(LOUISE *goes into the house.*) Have you come far to-day?

LILIOM   Yes—very far.

JULIE   Are you tired?

LILIOM   Very tired.

JULIE   Over there at the gate is a stone. Sit down and rest. My daughter
is bringing you the soup.

[LOUISE *comes out of the house.*]

LILIOM   Is that your daughter?

JULIE   Yes.

LILIOM   (*to* LOUISE) You are the daughter?

LOUISE   Yes, sir.

LILIOM   A fine, healthy girl.

[*takes the soup plate from her with one hand, while with the other he
touches her arm.* LOUISE *draws back quickly.*]

LOUISE   (*crosses to* JULIE) Mother!

JULIE   What, my child?

LOUISE   The man tried to take me by the arm.

JULIE   Nonsense! You only imagined it, dear. The poor, hungry man has
other things to think about than fooling with young girls. Sit down
and eat your soup.

[*They eat.*]

LILIOM   (*eats, too, but keeps looking at them*) You work at the factory,
eh?

JULIE   Yes.

LILIOM   Your daughter, too?

LOUISE   Yes.

LILIOM   And your husband?

JULIE   (*after a pause*) I have no husband. I'm a widow.

LILIOM   A widow?

JULIE   Yes.

LILIOM   Your husband—I suppose he's been dead a long time. (JULIE
does not answer.) I say—has your husband been dead a long time?

JULIE   A long time.

LILIOM   What did he die of?

[JULIE *is silent.*]

LOUISE   No one knows. He went to America to work and he died there—
in the hospital. Poor father, I never knew him.

LILIOM   He went to America?

LOUISE   Yes, before I was born.

LILIOM   To America?

JULIE Why do you ask so many questions? Did you know him, perhaps?

LILIOM (*puts the plate down*) Heaven knows! I've known so many people. Maybe I knew him, too.

JULIE Well, if you knew him, leave him and us in peace with your questions. He went to America and died there. That's all there is to tell.

LILIOM All right. All right. Don't be angry with me. I didn't mean any harm.

[*There is a pause.*]

LOUISE My father was a very handsome man.

JULIE Don't talk so much.

LOUISE Did I say anything—?

LILIOM Surely the little orphan can say that about her father.

LOUISE My father could juggle so beautifully with three ivory balls that people used to advise him to go on the stage.

JULIE Who told you that?

LOUISE Uncle Wolf.

LILIOM Who is that?

LOUISE Mr. Wolf Beifeld, who owns the Café Sorrento.

LILIOM The one who used to be a porter?

JULIE (*astonished*) Do you know him, too? It seems that you know all Budapest.

LILIOM Wolf Beifeld is a long way from being all Budapest. But I do know a lot of people. Why shouldn't I know Wolf Beifeld?

LOUISE He was a friend of my father.

JULIE He was not his friend. No one was.

LILIOM You speak of your husband so sternly.

JULIE What's that to you? Doesn't it suit you? I can speak of my husband any way I like. It's nobody's business but mine.

LILIOM Certainly, certainly—it's your own business.

[*takes up his soup plate again. All three eat.*]

LOUISE (*to* JULIE) Perhaps he knew father, too.

JULIE Ask him, if you like.

LOUISE (*crosses to* LILIOM. *He stands up.*) Did you know my father? (LILIOM *nods.* LOUISE *addresses her mother.*) Yes, he knew him.

JULIE (*rises*) You knew Andreas Zavocki?

LILIOM Liliom? Yes.

LOUISE Was he really a very handsome man?

LILIOM I wouldn't exactly say handsome.

LOUISE (*confidently*) But he was an awfully good man, wasn't he?

LILIOM He wasn't so good, either. As far as I know he was what they called a clown, a barker in a carousel.

LOUISE   (*pleased*) Did he tell funny jokes?

LILIOM   Lots of 'em. And he sang funny songs, too.

LOUISE   In the carousel?

LILIOM   Yes—but he was something of a bully, too. He'd fight any one. He even hit your dear little mother.

JULIE   That's a lie.

LILIOM   It's true.

JULIE   Aren't you ashamed to tell the child such awful things about her father? Get out of here, you shameless liar. Eats our soup and our bread and has the impudence to slander our dead!

LILIOM   I didn't mean—I—

JULIE   What right have you to tell lies to the child? Take that plate, Louise, and let him be on his way. If he wasn't such a hungry-looking beggar, I'd put him out myself.

[LOUISE *takes the plate out of his hand.*]

LILIOM   So he didn't hit you?

JULIE   No, never. He was always good to me.

LOUISE   (*whispers*) Did he tell funny stories, too?

LILIOM   Yes, and *such* funny ones.

JULIE   Don't speak to him any more. In God's name, go.

LOUISE   In God's name.

[JULIE *resumes her seat at the table and eats.*]

LILIOM   If you please, Miss—I have a pack of cards in my pocket. And if you like, I'll show you some tricks that'll make you split your sides laughing. (LOUISE *holds* LILIOM's *plate in her left hand. With her right she reaches out and holds the garden gate shut.*) Let me in, just a little way, Miss, and I'll do the tricks for you.

LOUISE   Go, in God's name, and let us be. Why are you making those ugly faces?

LILIOM   Don't chase me away, Miss; let me come in for just a minute— just for a minute—just long enough to let me show you something pretty, something wonderful. (*opens the gate*) Miss, I've something to give you.

[*takes from his pocket a big red handkerchief in which is wrapped a glittering star from Heaven. He looks furtively about him to make sure that the* POLICE *are not watching.*]

LOUISE   What's that?

LILIOM   Pst! A star!

[*With a gesture he indicates that he has stolen it out of the sky.*]

JULIE   (*sternly*) Don't take anything from him. He's probably stolen it somewhere. (*to* LILIOM) In God's name, be off with you.

LOUISE   Yes, be off with you. Be off.

[*She slams the gate.*]

LILIOM   Miss—please, Miss—I've got to do something good—or—do something   good—a good deed—

LOUISE   (*pointing with her right hand*) That's the way out.

LILIOM   Miss—

LOUISE   Get out!

LILIOM   Miss!

[*looks up at her suddenly and slaps her extended hand, so that the slap resounds loudly*]

LOUISE   Mother!

[*looks dazedly at* LILIOM, *who bows his head, dismayed, forlorn.* JULIE *rises and looks at* LILIOM *in astonishment. There is a long pause.*]

JULIE   (*comes over to them slowly*) What's the matter here?

LOUISE   (*bewildered, does not take her eyes off* LILIOM) Mother—the man—he hit me—on the hand—hard—I heard the sound of it—but it didn't hurt—it was like a caress—as if he had just touched my hand tenderly.

[*She hides behind* JULIE, LILIOM *sulkily raises his head and looks at* JULIE.]

JULIE   (*softly*) Go, my child. Go into the house. Go.

LOUISE   (*going*) But mother—I'm afraid—it sounded so loud—(*weepingly*) And it didn't hurt at all—just as if he'd—kissed my hand instead—mother!

[*She hides her face.*]

JULIE   Go in, my child, go in.

[LOUISE *goes slowly into the house.* JULIE *watches her until she has disappeared, then turns slowly to* LILIOM.]

JULIE   You struck my child.

LILIOM   Yes—I struck her.

JULIE   Is that what you came for, to strike my child?

LILIOM   No—I didn't come for that—but I did strike her—and now I'm going back.

JULIE   In the name of the Lord Jesus, who are you?

LILIOM   (*simply*) A poor, tired beggar who came a long way and who was hungry. And I took your soup and bread and I struck your child. Are you angry with me?

JULIE   (*her hand on her heart; fearfully, wonderingly*) Jesus protect me—I don't understand it—I'm *not* angry—not angry at all—

[LILIOM *goes to the doorway and leans against the doorpost, his back to the audience.* JULIE *goes to the table and sits.*]

JULIE   Louise! (LOUISE *comes out of the house.*) Sit down, dear, we'll finish eating.

LOUISE   Has he gone?

JULIE   Yes. (*They are both seated at the table.* LOUISE, *her head in her hands, is staring into space.*) Why don't you eat, dear?

LOUISE   What has happened, mother?

JULIE   Nothing, my child.

[*The* HEAVENLY POLICEMEN *appear outside.* LILIOM *walks slowly off at left. The* FIRST POLICEMAN *makes a deploring gesture. Both shake their heads deploringly and follow* LILIOM *slowly off at left.*]

LOUISE   Mother, dear, why won't you tell me?

JULIE   What is there to tell you, child? Nothing has happened. We were peacefully eating, and a beggar came who talked of bygone days, and then I thought of your father.

LOUISE   My father?

JULIE   Your father—Liliom.

[*There is a pause.*]

LOUISE   Mother—tell me—has it ever happened to you—has anyone ever hit you—without hurting you in the least?

JULIE   Yes, my child. It has happened to me, too.

[*There is a pause.*]

LOUISE   Is it possible for some one to hit you—hard like that—real loud and hard—and not hurt you at all?

JULIE   It is possible, dear—that some one may beat you and beat you and beat you—and not hurt you at all.—

[*There is a pause. Near by an organ-grinder has stopped. The music of his organ begins. The curtain falls.*]

Reference Key to Plays in Anthologies

Copies of the complete play may be found in the following selected volumes: Numbers 20, 42, 51, 71, 74.

Further Reading on Molnár and *Liliom*

Chandler, Frank W. *Modern Continental Playwrights.* New York: Harper, 1931, pp. 438–53.

Gassner, John. *Masters of the Drama.* New York: Dover, 1945, pp. 478–81.

————. *A Treasury of the Theatre.* Pt. 2, *From Ibsen to Ionesco.* 3rd ed. New York: Holt, Rinehart and Winston, 1960, pp. 354–55.

Of Mice and Men

JOHN STEINBECK (1937)
From Act III, Scene 1

SCENE: For one man, one woman

CHARACTERS: Lennie
Curley's wife

SETTING: One end of a great barn in an agricultural valley in Southern California.

TIME: Mid-afternoon on Sunday. The 1930's.

SITUATION: Lennie, an enormously powerful but simple-minded itinerant farm worker, and George, his friend, have taken jobs on a farm in the Salinas Valley in California. Lennie's great strength has gotten him into trouble in the past, and George has had to take care of his friend much as one takes care of a child. Both Lennie and George have been planning to save enough money to buy a small farm. It is Lennie's dream that he will be permitted to take care of the rabbits.

The owner's son Curley is a bully, who picks on the men and jealously guards his slatternly wife. Once Curley began to beat Lennie, but the powerful giant, instead of striking back, seized Curley's hand and crushed it. Curley's wife, lonely and bored on the farm, is attracted to Lennie. In this scene she comes upon him in the barn, where he has been petting a newborn puppy that had been given to him. Lennie is so strong that he has accidentally killed the puppy. Lennie is afraid of the woman's advances, knowing that George will be angry with him if he gets into trouble again.

[LENNIE, *alone, uncovers the pup. Lies down in the hay and sinks deep in it. Puts the pup on his arm and strokes it.* CURLEY'S WIFE *enters secretly. A little mound of hay conceals* LENNIE *from her. In her hand she carries a small suitcase, very cheap. She crosses the barn and buries the case in the hay. Stands up and looks to see whether it can be seen.* LENNIE *watching her quietly tries to cover the pup with hay. She sees the movement.*]

CURLEY'S WIFE   What—what you doin' here?

LENNIE   (*sullenly*) Jus' settin' here.

CURLEY'S WIFE   You seen what I done.

LENNIE   Yeah! you brang a valise.

CURLEY'S WIFE   (*comes near to him*) You won't tell—will you?

LENNIE   (*still sullen*) I ain't gonna have nothing to do with you. George tole me. I ain't to talk to you or nothing. (*covers the pup a little more*)

CURLEY'S WIFE   George give you all your orders?

LENNIE   Not talk nor nothing.

CURLEY'S WIFE   You won't tell about that suitcase? I ain't gonna stay here no more. Tonight I'm gonna get out. Come here an' get my stuff an' get out. I ain't gonna be run over no more. I'm gonna go in pitchers. (*sees* LENNIE'S *hand stroking the pup under the hay*) What you got there?

LENNIE   Nuthing. I ain't gonna talk to you. George says I ain't.

CURLEY'S WIFE   Listen. The guys got a horseshoe tenement out there. It's on'y four o'clock. Them guys ain't gonna leave that tenement. They got money bet. You don't need to be scared to talk to me.

LENNIE   (*weakening a little*) I ain't supposed to.

CURLEY'S WIFE   (*watching his buried hand*) What you got under there?

LENNIE   (*His woe comes back to him.*) Jus' my pup. Jus' my little ol' pup. (*sweeps the hay aside*)

CURLEY'S WIFE   Why! He's dead.

LENNIE   (*explaining sadly*) He was so little. I was jus' playin' with him— an' he made like he's gonna bite me—an' I made like I'm gonna smack him—an'—I done it. An' then he was dead.

CURLEY'S WIFE   (*consoling*) Don't you worry none. He was just a mutt. The whole country is full of mutts.

LENNIE   It ain't that so much. George gonna be mad. Maybe he won't let me—what he said I could tend.

CURLEY'S WIFE   (*sits down in the hay beside him, speaks soothingly*) Don't you worry. Them guys got money bet on that horseshoe tene- ment. They ain't gonna leave it. And tomorra I'll be gone. I ain't gonna let them run over me.

[*In the following scene it is apparent that neither is listening to the other and yet as it goes on, as a happy tone increases, it can be seen that they are growing closer together.*]

LENNIE   We gonna have a little place an' raspberry bushes.

CURLEY'S WIFE   I ain't meant to live like this. I come from Salinas. Well, a show come through an' I talked to a guy that was in it. He says I could go with the show. My ol' lady wouldn't let me, 'cause I was on'y fifteen. I wouldn't be no place like this if I had went with that show, you bet.

LENNIE   Gonna take a sack an' fill it up with alfalfa an'—

CURLEY'S WIFE   (*hurrying on*) 'Nother time I met a guy an' he was in pitchers. Went out to the Riverside Dance Palace with him. He said he was gonna put me in pitchers. Says I was a natural. Soon's he got back to Hollywood he was gonna write me about it. (*looks impressively at* LENNIE) I never got that letter. I think my ol' lady stole it. Well, I wasn't gonna stay no place where they stole your letters. So I married Curley. Met *him* out to the Riverside Dance Palace too.

LENNIE   I hope George ain't gonna be mad about this pup.

CURLEY'S WIFE   I ain't tol' this to nobody before. Maybe I oughtn' to. I don't like Curley. He ain't a nice fella. I might a stayed with him but last night him an' his ol' man both lit into me. I don't have to stay here. (*moves closer and speaks confidentially*) Don't tell nobody till I get clear away. I'll go in the night an' thumb a ride to Hollywood.

LENNIE   We gonna get out a here purty soon. This ain't no nice place.

CURLEY'S WIFE   (*ecstatically*) Gonna get in the movies an' have nice clothes—all them nice clothes like they wear. An' I'll set in them big hotels and they'll take pitchers of me. When they have them openings I'll go an' talk in the radio . . . an' it won't cost me nothing 'cause I'm in the pitcher. (*puts her hand on* LENNIE's *arm for a moment*) All them nice clothes like they wear . . . because this guy says I'm a natural.

LENNIE   We gonna go way . . . far away from here.

CURLEY'S WIFE   'Course, when I run away from Curley, my ol' lady won't never speak to me no more. She'll think I ain't decent. That's what she'll say. (*defiantly*) Well, we really ain't decent, no matter how much my ol' lady tries to hide it. My ol' man was a drunk. They put him away. There! Now I told.

LENNIE   George an' me was to the Sacramento Fair. One time I fell in the river an' George pulled me out an' saved me, an' then we went to the Fair. They got all kinds of stuff there. We seen long-hair rabbits.

CURLEY'S WIFE   My ol' man was a signpainter when he worked. He used to get drunk an' paint crazy pitchers an' waste paint. One night when I was a little kid, him an' my ol' lady had an awful fight. They was always fightin'. In the middle of the night he come into my room, and he says, "I can't stand this no more. Let's you an' me go away." I guess he was drunk. (*Her voice takes on a curious wondering tenderness.*) I remember in the night—walkin' down the road, and the trees was black. I was pretty sleepy. He picked me up, an' he carried me on his

back. He says, "We gonna live together. We gonna live together because you're my own little girl, an' not no stranger. No arguin' and
fightin'," he says, "because you're my little daughter." (*Her voice becomes soft.*) He says, "Why you'll bake little cakes for me, and I'll paint
pretty pitchers all over the wall." (*sadly*) In the morning they caught
us . . . an' they put him away. (*pause*) I wish we'd a' went.

LENNIE   Maybe if I took this here pup an' throwed him away George
wouldn't never know.

CURLEY'S WIFE   They locked him up for a drunk, and in a little while he
died.

LENNIE   Then maybe I could tend the rabbits without no trouble.

CURLEY'S WIFE   Don't you think of nothing but rabbits? (*sound of a horseshoe on metal*) Somebody made a ringer.

LENNIE   (*patiently*) We gonna have a house and a garden, an' a place for
alfalfa. And I take a sack and get it full of alfalfa, and then I take it
to the rabbits.

CURLEY'S WIFE   What makes you so nuts about rabbits?

LENNIE   (*moves closer to her*) I like to pet nice things. Once at a fair I
seen some of them long-hair rabbits. And they was nice, you bet.
(*despairingly*) I'd even pet mice, but not when I could get nothin'
better.

CURLEY'S WIFE   (*giggles*) I think you're nuts.

LENNIE   (*earnestly*) No, I ain't. George says I ain't. I like to pet nice things
with my fingers. Soft things.

CURLEY'S WIFE   Well, who don't? Everybody likes that. I like to feel silk
and velvet. You like to feel velvet?

LENNIE   (*chuckling with pleasure*) You bet, by God. And I had some too.
A lady give me some. And that lady was—my Aunt Clara. She give it
right to me. . . . (*measuring with his hands*) 'Bout this big a piece.
I wish I had that velvet right now. (*He frowns.*) I lost it. I ain't seen
it for a long time.

CURLEY'S WIFE   (*laughing*) You're nuts. But you're a kinda nice fella. Jus'
like a big baby. A person can see kinda what you mean. When I'm
doin' my hair sometimes I jus' set there and stroke it, because it's so
soft. (*runs her fingers over the top of her head*) Some people got kinda
coarse hair. You take Curley, his hair's just like wire. But mine is
soft and fine. Here, feel. Right here. (*takes* LENNIE's *hand and puts
it on her head*) Feel there and see how soft it is. (LENNIE's *fingers fall
to stroking her hair.*) Don't you muss it up.

LENNIE   Oh, that's nice. (*strokes harder*) Oh, that's nice.

CURLEY'S WIFE   Look out now, you'll muss it. (*angrily*) You stop it now,
you'll mess it all up. (*She jerks her head sideways and* LENNIE's *fingers
close on her hair and hang on. In a panic*) Let go. (*She screams.*) You

let go. (*She screams again. His other hand closes over her mouth and nose.*)

LENNIE   (*begging*) Oh, please don't do that. George'll be mad. (*She struggles violently to be free. A soft screaming comes from under* LENNIE'S *hand. Crying with fright*) Oh, please don't do none of that. George gonna say I done a bad thing. (*He raises his hand from her mouth and a hoarse cry escapes. Angrily*) Now don't. I don't want you to yell. You gonna get me in trouble just like George says you will. Now don't you do that. (*She struggles more.*) Don't you go yellin'. (*He shakes her violently. Her neck snaps sideways and she lies still. Looks down at her and cautiously removes his hand from her mouth*) I don't wanta hurt you. But George will be mad if you yell. (*When she doesn't answer he bends closely over her. He lifts her arm and lets it drop. For a moment he seems bewildered.*) I done a bad thing. I done another bad thing. (*He paws up the hay until it partly covers her. The sound of the horseshoe game comes from the outside. And for the first time* LENNIE *seems conscious of it. He crouches down and listens.*) Oh, I done a real bad thing. I shouldn't a did that. George will be mad. And . . . he said . . . and hide in the brush till he comes. That's what he said. (*He picks up the puppy from beside the girl.*) I'll throw him away. It's bad enough like it is.

[*He puts the pup under his coat, creeps to the barn wall and peers out between the cracks and then he creeps around to the end of the manger and disappears.*]

Reference Key to Plays in Anthologies

Copies of the complete play may be found in the following selected volumes: Numbers 25, 29, 44, 47.

Further Reading on Steinbeck and *Of Mice and Men*

Brown, John Mason. "Mr. Steinbeck's *Of Mice and Men.*" *Two on the Aisle.* New York: Norton, 1938, pp. 183–87.

Krutch, Joseph Wood. *American Drama Since 1918.* New York: Random House, 1939, pp. 73–133.

Shedd, Margaret. "*Of Mice and Men.*" *Theatre Arts Monthly,* Vol. 21, No. 10 (October, 1937), pp. 774–78.

two _____

COMEDY SCENES

THE world of comedy is vast: it ranges from the brilliant verbal wit of satire to the broad physical gestures of buffoonery. All the scenes in this section are comic; some of the comedy is broad, some is fairly subtle, but in every case it asks us to see ourselves as we really are and be willing to laugh at our follies.

To perform comedy successfully, the actor must understand the devices used by the playwright and must arrive at the proper combination of pointing and timing. The actor must grasp the playwright's vision and then make his audience accept this vision willingly.

No Time for Sergeants

IRA LEVIN AND MAC HYMAN (1955)

From Act I

SCENE: For two men

CHARACTERS: Will Stockdale, an Army private
An Army psychiatrist

SETTING: The office of a psychiatrist, a major in the United States Army.

TIME: Some of it is happening now and some of it happened a while back.

SITUATION: For anyone who has served in the armed forces, this scene should need no introduction. It is another comic view of a blundering recruit's upset of Army routine. Will's behavior at boot camp has hardly endeared him to the noncommissioned officers. Hoping to have him transferred, Will's sergeant sends him to the Army psychiatrist with an order to answer the psychiatrist's questions properly. When told that the psychiatrist might ask him what he dreams about, Will worries about how he should answer the question. But he solves this problem and the others that follow during his interview. The naiveté and common sense of Will's responses provide much of the humor of the play.

(The satirical handling of the Army psychiatrist is not unlike the treatment accorded another psychiatrist in *Teahouse of the August Moon*. See the scene from *Teahouse* on p. 181, immediately after this scene.)

[PSYCHIATRIST, *a major, signs and stamps a paper before him, then takes form from* WILL, *seated next to desk.* PSYCHIATRIST *looks at form, looks at* WILL. *A moment of silence.*]

WILL   I never have no dreams at all.

PSYCHIATRIST   (*a pause. He looks carefully at* WILL, *looks at form.*) Where you from, Stockdale?

WILL   Georgia.

PSYCHIATRIST   That's . . . not much of a state, is it?

WILL   Well . . . I don't live all over the state. I just live in this one little place in it.

PSYCHIATRIST   That's where "Tobacco Road" is, Georgia.

WILL   Not around my section. (*pause*) Maybe you're from a different part than me?

PSYCHIATRIST   I've never been there. What's more I don't think I would ever *want* to go there. What's your reaction to that?

WILL   Well, I don't know.

PSYCHIATRIST   I think I would sooner live in the rottenest pigsty in Alabama or Tennessee than in the fanciest mansion in all of Georgia. What about that?

WILL   Well, sir, I think where you want to live is your business.

PSYCHIATRIST   (*pause, staring*) You don't mind if someone says something bad about Georgia?

WILL   I ain't heared nobody say nothin' bad about Georgia.

PSYCHIATRIST   What do you think I've been saying?

WILL   Well, to tell you the truth, I ain't been able to get too much sense out of it. Don't you know?

PSYCHIATRIST   Watch your step, young man. (*pause*) We psychiatrists call this attitude of yours "resistance."

WILL   You do?

PSYCHIATRIST   You sense that this interview is a threat to your security. You feel yourself in danger.

WILL   Well, kind of I do. If'n I don't get classified Sergeant King won't give me the wrist watch. (PSYCHIATRIST *stares at* WILL *uncomprehendingly.*) He *won't!* He said I only gets it if I'm classified inside a week.

PSYCHIATRIST   (*turns forlornly to papers on desk. A bit subdued*) You get along all right with your mother?

WILL   No, sir, I can't hardly say that I do—

PSYCHIATRIST   (*cutting in*) She's very strict? Always hovering over you?

WILL   No, sir, just the opposite—

PSYCHIATRIST   She's never there.

WILL   That's right.

PSYCHIATRIST   You resent this neglect, don't you?

WILL   No, I don't resent nothin'.

PSYCHIATRIST   (*leaning forward paternally*) There's nothing to be ashamed of, son. It's a common situation. Does she ever beat you?

WILL   No!

PSYCHIATRIST   (*silkily*) So defensive. It's not easy to talk about your mother, is it.

WILL   No, sir. She died when I was borned.

PSYCHIATRIST (*a long, sick pause*) You . . . could have told me that sooner . . .

WILL (*looks hang-dog.* PSYCHIATRIST *returns to papers.* WILL *glances up at him.*) Do you hate *your* Mama? (PSYCHIATRIST's *head snaps up, glaring.*) I figgered as how you said it was so common . . .

PSYCHIATRIST I do not hate my mother.

WILL I should hope not! (*pause*) What, does she beat you or somethin'?

PSYCHIATRIST (*glares again, drums his fingers briefly on table. Steeling himself, more to self than* WILL) This is a transference. You're taking all your stored up antagonisms and loosing them in my direction. Transference. It happens every day. . . .

WILL (*excited*) It does? To the Infantry?

PSYCHIATRIST (*aghast*) The Infantry?

WILL You give Ben a transfer. I wish you'd give me one too. I'd sure love to go along with him.

PSYCHIATRIST Stop! (*The pause is a long one this time. Finally* PSYCHIATRIST *points at papers.*) There are a few more topics we have to cover. We will not talk about transfers, we will not talk about my mother. We will only talk about what *I* want to talk about, do you understand?

WILL Yes, sir.

PSYCHIATRIST Now then—your father. (*quickly*) Living?

WILL Yes, sir.

PSYCHIATRIST Do you get along with him okay?

WILL Yes, sir.

PSYCHIATRIST Does he ever beat you?

WILL You bet!

PSYCHIATRIST Hard?

WILL And how! Boy, there ain't nobody can beat like my Pa can!

PSYCHIATRIST (*beaming*) So *this* is where the antagonism comes from! (*pause*) You hate your father, don't you.

WILL No . . . I got an uncle I hate! Every time he comes out to the house he's always wantin' to rassle with the mule, and the mule gets all wore out, and *he* gets all wore out . . . Well, I don't really *hate* him; I just ain't exactly partial to him.

PSYCHIATRIST (*pause*) Did I ask you about your uncle?

WILL I thought you wanted to talk about hatin' people.

PSYCHIATRIST (*glares, drums his fingers, retreats to form. Barely audible*) Now—girls. How do you like girls?

WILL What girls is that, sir?

PSYCHIATRIST Just girls. Just any girls.

WILL Well, I don't like just any girls. There's one old girl back home that ain't got hair no longer than a hound-dog's and she's always—

PSYCHIATRIST No! Look, when I say girls I don't mean any one specific girl. I mean girls in general; women, sex! Didn't that father of yours ever sit down and have a talk with you?

WILL   Sure he did.

PSYCHIATRIST   Well?

WILL   Well what?

PSYCHIATRIST   What did he say?

WILL   (*with a snicker*) Well, there was this one about these two travelin' salesmen that their car breaks down in the middle of this terrible storm—

PSYCHIATRIST   Stop!

WILL   —so they stop at this farmhouse where the farmer has fourteen daughters who was—

PSYCHIATRIST   *Stop!*

WILL   You heared it already?

PSYCHIATRIST   (*writing furiously on form*) No, I did not hear it already . . .

WILL   Well, what did you stop me for? It's a real knee-slapper. You see, the fourteen daughters is all studyin' to be trombone players and—

PSYCHIATRIST   (*shoving form at* WILL) Here. Go. Good-by. You're through. You're normal. Good-by. Go. Go.

WILL   (*takes form and stands, a bit confused by it all*) Sir, if girls is what you want to talk about, you ought to come down to the barracks some night. The younger fellows there is always tellin' spicy stories and all like that.

Reference Key to Plays in Anthologies

A copy of the complete play may be found in the following volume:
Number 39.

An abridged version of the play may be found in:

Chapman, John. *Theatre '56.* New York: Random House, 1956.
Kronenberger, Louis. *The Best Plays of 1955–1956.* New York: Dodd, Mead, 1956.

Further Reading on *No Time for Sergeants*

"No Time for Sergeants." *Theatre Arts,* Vol. 39, No. 12 (December, 1955), pp. 28–29.

Teahouse of the August Moon _____

JOHN PATRICK (1953)
From Act II, Scene 3

SCENE:	For two men
CHARACTERS:	Captain Fisby, United States Army Captain McLean, an Army psychiatrist
SETTING:	Captain Fisby's makeshift office in the village of Tobiki, Okinawa.
TIME:	During the American occupation of Okinawa, following World War II.
SITUATION:	Captain Fisby, an ineffectual Army officer, but a humane and intelligent individual, has been given the assignment of bringing law, order, and democracy to the tiny village of Tobiki. Unfortunately, his progress reports do not please his commanding officer, Colonel Purdy. Instead of teaching the Okinawan children to sing "God Bless America" in English, he has attempted to introduce some industry into the village, such as manufacturing cricket cages and getas (a type of thonged wooden sandal) and raising goats. The disconcerted colonel decides to send Captain McLean, a psychiatrist, to look into the situation. The psychiatrist soon discovers that Captain Fisby has gone quite native.

[CAPTAIN MC LEAN *enters. He is an intense, rather wild-eyed man in his middle forties. He glances about furtively, then begins to examine the papers on* FISBY'S *desk. He makes several notes in a notebook. He picks up* FISBY'S *cricket cage and is examining it intently when* FISBY *enters behind him. He halts upon seeing* MC LEAN. FISBY *is wearing his blue bathrobe, his getas, and a native straw hat.*]

FISBY   Well, who are you?

MC LEAN   (*gasps in surprise*) Oh, you startled me.

FISBY   Can I do anything for you? I'm Captain Fisby.

MC LEAN   I'm Captain McLean. There was no one here . . . so I came in.

FISBY (*He looks at his insignia.*) Oh, medical corps. What brings you to Tobiki?

MC LEAN Well, I'm—I'm on leave. Thought I'd spend it making some—ethnological studies. (*He adds quickly*) Of the natives.

FISBY Well, you couldn't have come to a more interesting spot. Sit down, Captain.

MC LEAN (*sits*) Thank you. Would you have any objection to my spending a week or so making my studies, Captain?

FISBY Not at all. Make yourself at home. I'll take that if it's in your way. (*He reaches out to relieve* MC LEAN *of the cricket cage he still holds.*)

MC LEAN (*glances at the cage in his hand and laughs awkwardly*) Oh, yes. I was just examining it.

FISBY (*pleased at his authority on the subject*) It's a cricket cage.

MC LEAN (*pauses*) You . . . like crickets?

FISBY I haven't found one yet. But at least I've got the cage. I've got two . . . if you want one.

MC LEAN Thank you, no. Thank you very much. (*He looks at* FISBY's *attire.*) What happened to your uniform, Captain?

FISBY It's around. I find getas and a kimono much more comfortable in this climate.

MC LEAN But isn't that a bathrobe?

FISBY (*shrugs*) It passes for a kimono. Would you like to take off your shoes, Captain?

MC LEAN Thank you . . . no. I'll keep them on if you don't mind.

FISBY Can I offer you some tsukemono? You eat these during the day between meals. (*He extends a platter.*) Tsukemono means fragrant things.

MC LEAN I just had a chocolate bar, thank you. (*He rises and looks out the door.*) May I ask what you're building down the road?

FISBY (*proudly*) That's my cha ya. (*He pops a few tsukemonos into his mouth.*) It's really going to be something to write home about.

MC LEAN Cha ya?

FISBY Well, it just so happens, Captain, that I own a geisha girl. That might sound strange to you, but you get used to these things after a while. And if you have a geisha, you've got to have a cha ya. Sure you don't want some tsukemono?

MC LEAN I really couldn't eat a thing. (*He glances out the door again.*) May I ask what the men are doing down there wading in that irrigation ditch?

FISBY They're not wading, they're building a lotus pond. You can't have a cha ya without a lotus pond.

MC LEAN (*sits opposite* FISBY) How have you felt lately, Fisby?

FISBY McLean, I'll tell you something. I've never been happier. I feel reckless and free. And it all happened the moment I decided not to build that damned pentagon-shaped school.

MC LEAN That what?

FISBY The good colonel ordered me to build a pentagon-shaped schoolhouse down here. But the people wanted a teahouse. Believe it or not, someone gave me a geisha girl. So I'm giving this village what it wants. That must all sound pretty crazy to you, Mac.

MC LEAN Well, yes and no.

FISBY These are wonderful people with a strange sense of beauty. And hardworking . . . when there's a purpose. You should have seen them start out day before yesterday, great bundles of things they'd made piled high on their heads. Getas, cricket cages, lacquer ware—things to sell as souvenirs up north. Don't let anyone tell you these people are lazy.

MC LEAN Oh. I see. I see.

FISBY No, you don't. But you'll have a chance to study them.

MC LEAN So you're building them a teahouse.

FISBY Next thing I'm going to do for them is find out if this land here will grow anything besides sweet potatoes. I'm going to send for fertilizers and DDT and—

MC LEAN (*leaps to his feet*) Chemicals!

FISBY Sure, why not?

MC LEAN Do you want to poison these people?

FISBY No, but—

MC LEAN Now you've touched on a subject that is very close to me. For years I've planned to retire and buy a farm—raise specialties for big restaurants. So let me tell you this. Chemicals will kill all your earthworms, and earthworms aerate your soil.

FISBY They do?

MC LEAN Do you know an earthworm leaves castings eight times its own weight every day?

FISBY That much!

MC LEAN Organic gardening is the only thing. Nature's way—compost, manure, but no chemicals.

FISBY Hey! You know a lot about this.

MC LEAN (*modestly*) I should. I've subscribed to all the farm journals for years.

FISBY Say, you could help these people out while you're here—if you would. Do you think you could take over supervision—establish a sort of experimental station for them?

MC LEAN Well, I—no—no—I haven't time.

FISBY Take time. This is a chance for you to put some of your theories into practice.

MC LEAN (*haughtily*) They are not theories. They are proven facts.

FISBY I'll give you a couple of men to help, and all you'd have to do is tell us how.

MC LEAN (*hesitates*) Is your soil acid or alkaline?

FISBY Gosh, I don't know.

MC LEAN Well, that's the very *first* thing you have to find out. Do you have bees?

FISBY I haven't seen any.

MC LEAN (*shakes his head sadly*) People always underestimate the importance of bees for pollinating.

FISBY (*slaps him on the back*) Mac, you're just the man we've needed down here. You're a genius!

MC LEAN I'll want plenty of manure.

FISBY You'll get it.

MC LEAN And I'll want to plan this program scientifically. I wish I had some of my books . . . and my seed catalogues. (*He measures from the floor.*) I've got a stack of catalogues that high.

FISBY Why don't you make a list, and I'll get the boys over at the airstrip to fly us in seeds from the States.

MC LEAN (*The gardener fever possesses the doctor as he begins to make his list.*) Every spring I've made lists of seeds and never had any soil to put them in. And now . . . I could actually germinate. (*He writes*) Corn—Golden Bantam. (*then adds enthusiastically*) And Country Gentleman! Hybrid.

FISBY Why don't I just leave you with your list while I check on the lotus pond? (MC LEAN *doesn't hear him.*) Well, I'll be back for tea. We have tea in the pine grove and watch the sun go down.

[*He goes out.*]

MC LEAN (*continues with his list reading aloud*) Cucumbers—Extra Early Green Prolific. (*His enthusiasm mounts.*) Radishes—Crimson Giant! (*The telephone begins to ring; he ignores it as he writes.*) Tomatoes—Ponderosa Earliana. (*The telephone rings insistently.*) Watermelon! (*He closes his eyes ecstatically.*)

Reference Key to Plays in Anthologies

Copies of the complete play may be found in the following selected volumes: Numbers 41, 47.

See also *Theatre Arts*, June, 1955.

An abridged version of the play may be found in:

Chapman, John. *Theatre '54.* New York: Random House, 1954.

Kronenberger, Louis. *The Best Plays of 1953–1954.* New York: Dodd, Mead, 1954.

Further Reading on *Teahouse of the August Moon*

Bentley, Eric. "Tea, Sympathy, and the Noble Savage." *The Dramatic Event.* Boston: Beacon, 1956, pp. 222–25.

Gilroy, Harry. "Playwright of the August Moon." *New York Times Magazine Section,* November 15, 1953, pp. 17 ff.

"Teahouse of the August Moon." *Theatre Arts,* Vol. 37, No. 12 (December, 1953), pp. 22–23.

Gigi

ANITA LOOS (1951)

(*from the novel by* COLETTE)

From Act I, Scene 2

SCENE:	For two women
CHARACTERS:	Gigi Aunt Alicia, a retired courtesan
SETTING:	The boudoir of Madame Alicia de St. Ephlam. Luxuriously but discretely furnished, it almost resembles a jewel case.
TIME:	About 1900.
SITUATION:	Gigi is the youngest in a long line of famous courtesans who have had highly successful careers. A teenager rapidly approaching womanhood, Gigi is about to enter the profession, and the family has decided that it is necessary to teach her the fine points of her trade. Alicia de St. Ephlam is acknowledged the most successfully living member of the family, and Gigi has come to her Aunt Alicia's for the proper instructions.

ALICIA   Gilberte, just how old are you, exactly?

GIGI   Same as the other day, Aunty—sixteen.

ALICIA   Whom do you have as friends?

GIGI   Nobody. Grandma only allows me to play with the very little children. She doesn't want me going around with anyone my own age.

ALICIA   She's right, for once.

GIGI   Oh, but I do adore the little ones. It's such fun to play house, and pretend that I'm their mother.

ALICIA   And that amuses you?

GIGI   Oh, yes, they're so divine, those youngsters! I wish they belonged to me, every one of them.

ALICIA   Perhaps it's just as well they don't. Now, tell me, Gilberte, whether or not you've got any bees in your bonnet?

GIGI   Bees in my bonnet?

ALICIA   Any young men hanging about? Any college student with his books still under his arm? Any middle-aged gentleman? If you lie, I'll know it.

GIGI   But there's nobody, Aunty. Has someone been telling stories about me?

ALICIA   (*patting her cheek*) No, child. I just wanted to be sure.

GIGI   But why does Grandma forbid me to accept any invitations?

ALICIA   Because you'd only be asked out by very ordinary people, who wouldn't be of any use to you.

GIGI   And we're not ordinary people?

ALICIA   No, indeed, we are not!

GIGI   But what makes us different from those ordinary people, Aunty?

ALICIA   In the main, Gilberte, it's because they marry.

GIGI   Is that the reason why I'm forbidden ever to talk to any young men?

ALICIA   Yes. (*unlocks jewel-case*)

GIGI   But, Aunty, why is it we're not supposed to get married?

ALICIA   Well, marriage with us is not forbidden. But in place of marrying "at first," it's always possible that we may marry "at last."

GIGI   But why not "at first"?

ALICIA   Because if we marry "at first," he's certain to be the sort who will—vulgarize us.

GIGI   You mean somebody like a shopkeeper?

ALICIA   Exactly.

GIGI   But won't he be just the same sort, if we marry him "at last"?

ALICIA   Yes, he's likely to be. But by that time, one has one's memories. (*She opens case, displaying array of jewels.*) Now, we'll begin the lesson for today.

GIGI   Oh, oh, Aunty!

ALICIA   You never dreamed I had so many jewels, did you?

GIGI   I didn't know there were that many in all of France!

ALICIA   (*takes ring from box, and holds it up for inspection*) Now, what is this, Gilberte?

GIGI   (*speaking as an attentive pupil*) A diamond.

ALICIA   What kind?

GIGI   A—an oblong one.

ALICIA   Yes. (*putting ring on* GIGI's *finger*) And the weight of it is five carats.

GIGI   It is?

ALICIA   (*taking another jewel*) Now, take these diamonds, which are set around this ruby. Their weight is half a carat each. (*pins jewel on* GIGI's *dress*) Anything less than that, I call a chip. Will you remember that?

GIGI   Yes, Aunty.

ALICIA (*selecting another jewel*) Ah, this ring! What memories it brings up!

GIGI It's a very large stone, Aunty.

ALICIA It was given to me by my mother, when I was only fifteen. She put it on my finger and said, "Always wear this, my child, and nobody will ever dare give you one that's smaller"—and it worked. (*puts ring on* GIGI *and picks up another jewel*) Now, what is this?

GIGI (*studies it*) Mmmmmm—a—topaz!

ALICIA A topaz! A topaz, among my jewels!

GIGI I'm sorry, Aunty.

ALICIA Why not an agate? Or a cat's eye?

GIGI Then—then what *is* it, Aunt Alicia?

ALICIA It's a jonquil diamond, you little barbarian. (*holding ring closer to* GIGI) And study it closely for color, or you'll wind up your career with topazes. (*places it on* GIGI's *finger and reaches for another ring*) And—this?

GIGI (*entranced*) Why, that's an emerald! Oh—it's beautiful!

ALICIA There are very few emeralds in this world that have ever possessed such a miracle of evanescent blue.

GIGI Who gave you that emerald, Aunty?

ALICIA A king.

GIGI (*holding the rings at arm's length, surveys them*) A great king?

ALICIA No, a little one. Great kings don't give away very valuable stones.

GIGI Why not?

ALICIA If you want my opinion, it's because they're rather stingy. But you must learn never to accept a second-rate jewel, even from a king.

GIGI (*obediently*) Yes, Aunt Alicia.

ALICIA It's much better to wait until first-rate ones come along.

GIGI What if they don't come along?

ALICIA (*removing the jewels from* GIGI's *hands, and returning them to the box*) Then hold firmly to your ideals, just the same. Better to wear a ring that costs 100 sous, than a bad diamond costing 3000 francs. At least you can say it's a memento from some female relative.

GIGI Aunty, who does give away the most valuable jewels?

ALICIA Men who are timid—men who are conceited. Climbers, because they think giving away monstrous jewels is proof of culture. And, speaking of culture, never, under any circumstances, wear artistic jewels. And *always* protect yourself against family heirlooms.

GIGI But Grandma wears a very beautiful cameo around her neck, on a ribbon.

ALICIA There is no such thing as a beautiful cameo! You must only recognize precious stones and pearls.

GIGI (*stretching her legs, leans back against the chaise-longue*) Aunty, I just adore opals!

ALICIA That's all right, dear, so long as you don't wear them.

GIGI You think they bring people bad luck?

ALICIA I think nothing of the kind. But a good, healthy set of superstitions is a necessity when dealing with men.

GIGI Why, Aunty?

ALICIA Because the poor things are not as intelligent as we are. So it's only good manners to play the fool for them. That's where superstitions come in handy.

GIGI Aunty, what is a bracelet set in—malachite?

ALICIA Always a calamity! Where did you ever hear of such a thing! Get up, child! Stand over there! (GIGI *rises.* ALICIA *follows, lifting* GIGI's *head to the light.*) Beautiful jaws, my child! (*opening* GIGI's *mouth*) What teeth! With teeth like that I'd have been able to eat up all France. As it was, I was able to get away with rather a large slice of it. (*resuming her inspection of* GIGI) An impossible little nose—undistinguished mouth—cheekbones like a Russian moujik's . . .

GIGI (*distressed*) Oh, Aunty!

ALICIA Never mind, you have all the equipment necessary in your eyes, your eyelashes, your teeth and your hair. . . . And, as for your figure, possibilities . . . (*She slowly outlines the contour of* GIGI's *bosom.*) Very nice—possibilities. (GIGI's *glance observes first the right and then the left breast.*) I wonder if you're going to have any taste in dress. When you think of being well-turned-out, Gilberte, how do you see yourself?

GIGI (*with great excitement*) Oh, but I understand very well what's becoming to me, Aunty! I saw the picture of a dress in a fashion book that was designed for Mme. Lucie Gerard. (*gestures elaborately, to describe the effect*) Hundreds of little pin-tucks in pearl-gray chiffon, from top to bottom . . .

ALICIA Don't gesticulate, dear. It makes you look common.

GIGI And I saw another picture—in color—a dress of brocade, a sort of lavender blue, on a background of black velvet—cut-out, so that the train looks like the tail of a peacock! (*another gesture describing the tail of a peacock*)

ALICIA Just like an actress!

GIGI (*pleased with herself*) Yes.

ALICIA It wasn't meant as a compliment. I tell you what I'm going to do, child . . . (*takes note-pad and pencil from table*) I'm going to give you a note to the head saleswoman at Paquin.

GIGI (*excited*) Pa—Pa—

ALICIA (*starts to scratch off note*) Paquin. She's an old colleague of mine—
she failed and had to go to work.

GIGI Oh, Aunt Alicia, a dress from Paquin's!

ALICIA But I thought you weren't interested in clothes?

GIGI I'm just not interested in the clothes they make me at the house.

ALICIA (*folding the note*) I don't wonder! Here, child. One who risks
nothing gains nothing.

GIGI (*throwing her arms around* ALICIA) Oh, Aunty, thanks, thanks,
thanks!

ALICIA Not too rough, dear. Don't disarrange my hair!

Reference Key to Plays in Anthologies

A copy of the complete play may be found in
   Theatre Arts, July, 1952.

An abridged version of the play may be found in
Chapman, John. *The Best Plays of 1951–1952.* New York: Dodd, Mead, 1952.

Further Reading on Colette and *Gigi*

Miller, Gilbert. "The Search for Gigi." *Theatre Arts,* Vol. 36, No. 7 (July, 1952),
   pp. 48–51.
"Mr. Nathan Goes to the Play." *Theatre Arts,* Vol. 36, No. 2 (February, 1952),
   pp. 30 ff. (See especially p. 31.)
Scott, J. "Colette." In John Hadfield, ed., *Saturday Book, Twelfth Year.* New
   York: Macmillan, 1952, pp. 209–15.

Send Me No Flowers

NORMAN BARASCH AND
CARROLL MOORE (1960)
From Act I

SCENE:	For two men
CHARACTERS:	George Kimball Dr. Ralph Morrissey
SETTING:	The living room of George Kimball's surburban ranch house.
TIME:	A Saturday morning. The present.
SITUATION:	George Kimball is a hypochondriac. When Whitey Ford had bone chips removed from his elbow, George suffered pains in the same region. In this scene, he has severe pains in his chest. Afraid of heart trouble, he decided not to butter his toast, in order to avoid cholesterol. He also had grave doubts about eating the toast because it is roughage. He has called his doctor for an examination. It has been about two weeks since his last checkup and George knows that "your body can turn on you, just like that!"

As the scene begins, George is waiting for Dr. Morrissey to arrive. He goes to his medical dictionary to diagnose his chest pains.

See also the following scene from *Send Me No Flowers* (p. 196), which occurs later in the play.

Send Me No Flowers **191**

GEORGE   Hmph! (*He rubs his chest, and his eye falls on the bookcase. He goes to bookcase and takes down a large medical dictionary. He riffles through it, until he finds the page he is looking for. He reads aloud.*) "Angina pectoris. A muscular spasm of the chest, often accompanied by an affection of the heart. Frequently fatal." (*He looks up. Pause*) They shouldn't be allowed to print stuff like this. (*The front door bell rings.* GEORGE *goes to the front door and opens it.*) Good morning, Ralph.

DOCTOR   Hello, George.

[DOCTOR *enters.* GEORGE *follows to below dinette table—places dictionary on it.*]

Oh, boy. Eleven in the morning, and this is my eighth call already. I'm pooped. (*puts hat and bag on end of sofa*)

GEORGE   Can I get you something, Ralph?

DOCTOR   No, I just want to rest a minute. Why in hell didn't I specialize, so I could sleep in the morning! You never hear of an ear, nose and throat man being yanked out of bed at five A.M. Or those damn allergists! Jeez, they've got hours like a banker. And the same kind of money, too. I know one has a hundred-thousand-dollar house just built on ragweed. What a business! When the pollen count goes up it's just like the stock market.

GEORGE   (*touching his chest*) Well, Ralph, I have this pain. . . .

DOCTOR   Boy, I'm pooped! Thank God I'm going fishing this week end. Friend of mine has a cabin cruiser. Gastro-enterologist. Won't look at anything but gall bladders. He's cleaning up. *Cleaning up!*

GEORGE   (*anxiously*) You'll be on a boat? For a whole week end?

DOCTOR   Yes, sir!

GEORGE   Well, isn't it wonderful that you can just take off? Although . . . what happens . . . if somebody has to reach you? Like an emergency? I mean, when you're out on a boat like that?

DOCTOR   Emergency? What emergencies? Hell, ninety per cent of my patients have nothing wrong with them. The five per cent who've got something serious, I send to a specialist. The other five per cent you can't do anything for, anyway. What's your trouble, George?

GEORGE   What? Oh. I have this pain.

DOCTOR   M-hm. Show me where.

GEORGE   (*indicating the spot*) Right here. (*He presses his chest.*) It hurts like the devil when I press it.

DOCTOR   Well, don't press it! Now, is it a sharp pain, or a dull pain, or does it grip like a vise . . . ?

GEORGE   (*eagerly*) Yes! Yes!

DOCTOR   No, no. Pick one.

GEORGE   Oh. Well, then I'd say it was more of a sharp pain.

DOCTOR   M-hm. Was the pain severe enough to wake you up during the night?

GEORGE   Actually, I never got to sleep. So I don't know.

DOCTOR   Couldn't sleep, eh? Worried about something?

GEORGE   Yes. This pain.

DOCTOR   M-hm. I'd better take a listen. (*reaches into his bag for his stethoscope.* GEORGE *takes chair and sits on it and opens shirt.*)

GEORGE   (*anxiously*) Do you have any idea what it might be, Ralph?

DOCTOR   Not yet.

GEORGE   (*trying to be casual*) It's probably nothing. But you know how much Judy worries.

DOCTOR   Yeah! (*applies the stethoscope to* GEORGE'S *chest*)
Deep breath.
Good. Another one.
Okay. One more.
Good. You can button up.

[GEORGE *buttons his shirt, as the* DOCTOR *puts his stethoscope in the bag.*]

GEORGE   Well . . . what's the bad news, Ralph?

DOCTOR   (*vaguely*) What?

GEORGE   This pain in my chest . . . is there some medical term for it?

DOCTOR   Yes. It's called indigestion. (*reaching into his bag*) Here. (*pulls out bottle of pills*) I want you to take these pills. One before each meal, and one before retiring.

GEORGE   Oh. What kind of pills are they?

DOCTOR   You wouldn't know if I told you. Just take them. (*crosses to bar and opens bottle of 7-Up*)

GEORGE   All right. (*pause*) Oh, Ralph . . .

DOCTOR   Yes?

GEORGE   About that cardiogram I had taken—when I had my checkup . . . ?

DOCTOR   (*pouring 7-Up into glass*) What about it?

GEORGE   That's what I was going to ask you . . . what about it?

DOCTOR   What do you mean? (*puts bottle down*)

GEORGE   Well . . . how did it turn out?

DOCTOR   I don't know. I won't get the results from Dr. Petersen for another week.

GEORGE   He had it for two weeks. He's certainly studying it for quite a while, isn't he?

DOCTOR   Well, Petersen's a busy man. Biggest cardiologist in the city. Got a gold mine there!

Send Me No Flowers   193

GEORGE   Then in your considered opinion, everything is okay?

DOCTOR   Sound as a bell. I wish all my patients were as healthy as you . . . speaking nonprofessionally, of course.

GEORGE   And this pain in my chest . . . I can just go right ahead and live a normal life?

DOCTOR   I would. Take one of those pills right now, with a glass of water.

GEORGE   Right now? You make it sound sort of urgent.

DOCTOR   Then take it whenever you want. It doesn't make much difference.

GEORGE   No, no. I'll take it right away, if it's that important.

[GEORGE *exits to the kitchen with the pills.* DR. MORRISSEY *goes to phone and dials.*]

DOCTOR   (*on phone*) Hello, Dr. Petersen, please. Dr. Morrissey . . . Hello, Petersen? Morrissey . . . Thank you. Same to you. Say, I'm on my way now to see that patient of mine, William Malone. . . . That's right, William Malone, that old feller down in Yonkers. . . . I don't want to rush you, but I'm leaving town for a few days, (GEORGE *enters from kitchen unseen by* DOCTOR)—and I was wondering if you got the results of his cardiogram. . . . Uh-huh . . . uh-huh. . . . What! That's a damn shame. Well, what can you do? Give him a few pills to ease the pain in his chest. . . . There's not much you can do when the old ticker goes. (*On hearing this,* GEORGE *retreats into foyer, out of sight.*) . . . How much time you figure the poor devil's got? . . . M-hm . . . a few weeks. . . . Oh, I know, I've seen 'em go like that! (*snaps his fingers*) Well, whataya gonna do? I'll tell you what I'm gonna do. I'm going fishing! (*big, hearty laugh*) Damn right! Gotta beat 'em out of a week end once in a while. Well, thanks Dr. Petersen. . . . What? . . . No, I'm not going to tell him. He's better off not knowing . . . Right. You have a nice week end, too. 'Bye, Doctor.

[*He hangs up the phone. Crosses to sofa and closes bag.* GEORGE *enters with pills. He appears pale and shaken. He comes into the room, to below dinette table.*]

GEORGE   (*weakly*) I'm back, Ralph.

DOCTOR   Good.

GEORGE   (*pause, then holds up the bottle*) Do you . . . still want me to take these pills?

DOCTOR   Sure. Ease that pain in your chest. Well, I guess I'll be off, George. Got a couple of more calls.

GEORGE   Ralph, wait a minute. . . .

DOCTOR   Yes?

GEORGE   Do you mind if I ask you a sort of hypothetical question?

DOCTOR   Shoot.

GEORGE   Well . . . suppose you had a patient, and you knew he didn't have much longer to live . . . I mean, if you knew he could go . . . (*snaps his fingers*) just like that. In a few weeks?

DOCTOR   Yeah?

GEORGE   Would you tell him?

DOCTOR   Hmmm . . . well, now that decision often confronts a doctor. Offhand, I'd say it would all depend on the circumstances.

GEORGE   Circumstances?

DOCTOR   Yes. If I knew that the man's affairs were in order, will made out properly, insurance paid up, no loose ends—why—I'd see no reason to tell him.

GEORGE   Well, suppose this patient were an old friend, like me?

DOCTOR   Your affairs in order, will made out, insurance paid up?

GEORGE   Yes.

DOCTOR   (*flatly*) Then I wouldn't tell you. . . . Anything else, George?

GEORGE   No, no. I . . . I guess that's it.

DOCTOR   Right. (*slaps* GEORGE *on the shoulder*) Well, so long, boy. See you in church!

[*He exits.* GEORGE *waves weakly. He looks stricken.*]

GEORGE   Oh, my God! My God!

[*He paces around, then goes to dinette table and sits. After a moment, he reaches for a piece of toast, butters it heavily and takes a large bite.*]

Reference Key to Plays in Anthologies

A copy of the complete play may be found in
Theatre Arts, June, 1961.

Further Reading on *Send Me No Flowers*

"Alan Pryce-Jones at the Theatre." *Theatre Arts,* Vol. 45, No. 2 (February, 1961), pp. 9–11, 70.

Send Me No Flowers

NORMAN BARASCH AND
CARROLL MOORE (1960)
From Act I

SCENE: For two men

CHARACTERS: George Kimball
Arnold Nash, his helpful neighbor

SETTING: The living room of George Kimball's surburban ranch house.

TIME: A Saturday morning. The present.

SITUATION: See the preceding scene from *Send Me No Flowers* (p. 191), which occurs earlier in the play.

After Dr. Morrissey's departure, George sits down at the dinette table, "reaches for a piece of toast, butters it heavily and takes a large bite." He is eating as the scene begins.

[ARNOLD NASH *enters through the patio.*]

ARNOLD Morning, George.

GEORGE Arnold.

ARNOLD Thanks for the loan of the hedge clipper. It's back in your garage. Well, I just put Ruth on the train to her Mother's. (*reflective pause*) Gee, y'know, tomorrow will be the only club dance in ten years that the four of us haven't been together? Oh, well, we'll make it up when she gets back. Oh, listen, George, we changed the golf date. We're teeing off at ten tomorrow. Okay, kid? I think we'll take 'em this week. I was out at the driving range last night, and boy! I was really belting those woods. I think I got this game licked. You know what does it? (*does a nice slow backswing, and as he follows through he sees* GEORGE *with the toast*) Hey, what are you doing?

GEORGE I'm eating.

ARNOLD You ought to go easy on the butter—haven't you ever heard of cholesterol? I won't let Ruth even bring butter in the house any more. I'm telling you, these days you've got to watch every bite you put in your mouth. I don't want to worry you, George, but do you know what we're doing every time we sit down at the table to eat? We're poisoning ourselves! They spray all the fruits and vegetables with arsenic, and DDT, and God-knows-what. Frankly, we don't eat a thing any more that grows above ground! (*pause*) What's the matter, George? You seem kind of down today.

GEORGE Yes, I suppose I am.

ARNOLD Anything wrong?

GEORGE Well. . . . Arnold, can I take you into my confidence?

ARNOLD Sure, George. What?

GEORGE Well, I just heard some rather bad news. But you've got to promise to keep it quiet. I wouldn't want it to get around the neighborhood.

ARNOLD It's nothing that's going to affect property values, is it?

GEORGE I wouldn't think so.

ARNOLD That's a relief. Then what?

GEORGE Well, do you know this little pain in my chest I've complained about?

ARNOLD You mean your indigestion.

GEORGE Well, it's not indigestion. . . .

ARNOLD Anything serious?

GEORGE (*nods. Pause*) It's curtains, Arnold.

ARNOLD Curtains? What do you mean . . . curtains?

GEORGE The doctor was just here. He only gives me a few weeks more to live.

ARNOLD My God! I can't believe it.

GEORGE Well, it's true.

ARNOLD What is it, George?

GEORGE It's the old ticker, Arnold.

ARNOLD   Holy cow! Are they sure?

GEORGE   I had Petersen, the biggest cardiologist in the city.

ARNOLD   . . . Holy cow! (*pause*) Gee, George, I don't know what to say.
. . . Dammit, George, if you're going to die shouldn't you do something about it?

GEORGE   What?

ARNOLD   . . . Shouldn't you at least be in bed? . . . I mean, saving your
strength for it? . . . I'm sorry, George. I'm just so shocked, I don't
know what I'm saying.

GEORGE   That's all right, Arnold.

ARNOLD   I mean, it's so sudden! How old are you, George?

GEORGE   Forty-one.

ARNOLD   Forty-one! My God! *I'm* forty-one! Oh, excuse me, George. Here
I am thinking about me . . . when it's you who's going to—May I
have a drink, George?

GEORGE   Of course, Arnold. By God I'll have one with you. (*goes to the
bar*)

ARNOLD   George . . . how are you going to . . . tell Judy?

GEORGE   Judy? Oh, I'm not going to tell her.

ARNOLD   No?

GEORGE   (*putting ice in glasses*) I couldn't bear it. She'd probably go to
pieces . . . weeping and wailing . . . You know Judy! (*picks up bottle of scotch—pours a drink*)

ARNOLD   Yeah. I remember how she was when the dog died . . . (GEORGE
slams bottle down.) I don't mean there's any comparison! (GEORGE
pours another drink.) This would be much worse!

[GEORGE *slams bottle down again.*]

(*thinks about this, then*) Well, you know what I mean, George.

GEORGE   (*coming back with the drinks*) Of course, Arnold. (*hands* ARNOLD
a drink)

ARNOLD   Thanks. (*Both take long sips of their drinks.*) George . . . is
there anything I can do? Anything at all? Not only as a lawyer, but as
your best friend.

GEORGE   I—I don't know, Arnold. I really haven't had time to think. Yes.
There is something you can do . . .

ARNOLD   Just name it!

GEORGE   I'd like you to take care of the funeral details.

ARNOLD   Oh, my God!

GEORGE   Well, you understand the reason. It's Judy. Anybody can sell her
anything, especially at a time like this. If she had her way she'd probably have me buried like King Tut! And this is no time for extrav-
agance. Will you do it, Arnold?

ARNOLD   (*with great emotion*) Yes, George. Of course I will. (*He gets up and goes quickly to the bar and pours himself a stiff drink.*) George, are you fixed all right—I mean, financially?

GEORGE   Well, it's largely insurance. Like most of us, I'm in lousy shape now, but I'll be all right after I'm gone.

ARNOLD   Well, your house is free and clear now, isn't it?

GEORGE   No more. It was free and clear last year . . . but I took out another mortgage to build that den on. Then we stopped watching television, and I haven't been in the damn thing since!

ARNOLD   George, if you'd asked me, I'd have advised you against it. No matter what you put into a house, you never get it out when you sell.

GEORGE   I know, Arnold.

ARNOLD   It's the damndest thing about a house. Everybody can stick you, but you can never stick anybody else!

GEORGE   Judy'll probably have to sell, anyway, so keep an eye on it, will you? See that she gets something out of it.

ARNOLD   I will, George.

GEORGE   Poor Judy. How will she possibly get along? She depends on me for everything. Alone, she'll be absolutely helpless. What's wrong with us, anyway, Arnold?

ARNOLD   Who, George?

GEORGE   Us husbands! Why don't we teach our wives to be self-sufficient so they can be sensible, practical widows! I mean it! We know we're going to go first, so . . . instead of taking them to the theatre, and restaurants, and parties, we should send them to night school!

For sources containing the complete text and for a list of suggested readings, see the preceding scene from *Send Me No Flowers* (p. 195).

Mister Roberts _____

THOMAS HEGGEN AND
JOSHUA LOGAN (1948)
From Act I

SCENE:	For three men
CHARACTERS:	Lieutenant (J.G.) Roberts Ensign Pulver Doc
SETTING:	The stateroom of Pulver and Roberts aboard a Navy cargo ship, somewhere in the South Pacific.
TIME:	1945.
SITUATION:	*Mister Roberts* is a war play, but a war play somewhat different from those that deal with the bravery of men in combat. It deals with the tedium and monotony found in the backwaters of war—as real a part of the conflict as the more frequently dramatized aspects.
	Lieutenant Roberts is the central figure in the crew's battle against the tyrannical captain of U.S. Navy supply ship *Reluctant*. Roberts' closest companions are Doc, the ship's medical officer, and Pulver, an immature ensign who spends most of his time dreaming about women or trying to devise ways of making life miserable for the captain.
	In this scene Roberts and Doc do their best to help Pulver solve a tactical problem he faces in luring a Navy nurse on board the *Reluctant*.

ROBERTS (*sitting in chair and searching through desk drawer*) Hey, Frank, has Dolan been in here yet with my letter?

PULVER (*innocently*) I don't know, Doug boy. I just came in here myself.

DOC You don't know anybody on the island, do you, Doug?

ROBERTS Yes. The Port Director—the guy who decides where to send this ship next. He confided to me that he used to drink a quart of whiskey every day of his life. So this morning when I broke up that fight it came to me that he might just possibly sell his soul for a quart of Scotch.

PULVER (*rises*) Doug, you didn't give that shoe box to the Post Director!

ROBERTS I did. "Compliments of the Captain."

DOC You've had a quart of Scotch in a shoe box?

ROBERTS Johnny Walker! I was going to break it out the day I got off this ship—Resurrection Day!

PULVER Oh, my God! It's really gone! (*He sinks to the bunk.*)

DOC Well, did the Port Director say he'd send us to a Liberty Port?

ROBERTS Hell, no. He took the Scotch and said, "Don't bother me, Roberts. I'm busy." The rummy!

PULVER How could you do it!

DOC Well, where there's a rummy, there's hope. Maybe when he gets working on that Scotch he'll mellow a little.

PULVER You gave that bottle to a goddamn *man!*

ROBERTS Man! Will you name me another sex within a thousand miles . . . (PULVER, *dejected, goes up to porthole.*) What the hell's eating you anyhow, Frank?

[DOC *crosses to bunk. He sees two fancy pillows on bottom bunk, picks up one and tosses it to* ROBERTS. *He picks up the other.*]

DOC Well, look here. Somebody seems to be expecting company!

ROBERTS Good Lord!

DOC (*reads lettering on pillowcase*) "Toujours l'amour . . . Souvenir of San Diego . . . Oh, you kid!"

ROBERTS (*reading from his pillowcase*) "Tonight or never . . . Compliments of Allis-Chalmers, Farm Equipment . . . We plow deep while others sleep." (*He looks at* DOC, *then rises.*) Doc—that new hospital over there hasn't got nurses, has it?

DOC Nurses! It didn't have yesterday!

PULVER (*turning from porthole*) It has today!

DOC But how did you find out they were there?

PULVER (*trying to recall*) Now let me think . . . it just came to me all of a sudden. This morning it was so hot I was just lying on my bunk—thinking . . . There wasn't a breath of air. And then, all of a sudden, a funny thing happened. A little breeze came up and I took a big deep breath and said to myself, "Pulver boy, there's women on that island."

ROBERTS Doc, a thing like this could make a bird dog self-conscious as hell.

PULVER (*warming up*) They just flew in last night. There's eighteen of them—all brunettes except for two beautiful blondes—twin sisters! I'm working on one of those. I asked her out to the ship for lunch and she said she was kind of tired. So then I got kind of desperate and turned on the old personality—and I said, "Ain't there anything in the world that'll make you come out to the ship with me?" And she said, "Yes, there is, one thing and one thing only—" (*crosses to* ROBERTS, *looks at him accusingly*) "A good stiff drink of Scotch!" (*He sinks into the chair.*)

ROBERTS   (*after a pause*) I'm sorry, Frank. I'm really sorry. Your first assignment in a year. (*He pats* PULVER *on the shoulder.*)

PULVER   I figured I'd bring her in here . . . I fixed it up real cozy . . . (*fondling pillow on desk*) . . . and then I was going to throw a couple of fast slugs of Scotch into her and . . . but, hell, without the Scotch, she wouldn't . . . she just wouldn't, that's all.

ROBERTS   (*after a pause*) Doc, let's make some Scotch!

DOC   Huh?

ROBERTS   As naval officers we're supposed to be resourceful. Frank here's got a great opportunity and I've let him down. Let's fix him up!

DOC   Right! (*He goes to desk.* ROBERTS *begins removing bottles from medicine chest.*) Frank, where's the rest of that alcohol we were drinking last night?

PULVER   (*pulling a large vinegar bottle half filled with colorless liquid from the waste basket and handing it to* DOC) Hell, that ain't even the right color.

DOC   (*taking the bottle*) Quiet! (*thinks deeply*) Color . . . (*with sudden decision*) Coca-Cola! Have you got any?

ROBERTS   I haven't seen a Coke in four months—no, by God, it's five months!

PULVER   Oh, what the hell! (*He rises, crosses to bunk, reaches under mattress of top bunk and produces a bottle of Coca-Cola. The others watch him.* DOC *snatches the bottle.* PULVER *says apologetically*) I forgot I had it.

[DOC *opens the bottle and is about to pour the Coca-Cola into the vinegar bottle when he suddenly stops.*]

DOC   Oh—what shade would you like? Cutty Sark . . . Haig and Haig . . . Vat 69 . . .

PULVER   (*interested*) I told her Johnny Walker.

DOC   Johnny Walker it is! (*He pours some of the Coca-Cola into the bottle.*)

ROBERTS   (*looking at color of the mixture*) Johnny Walker Red Label!

DOC   Red Label!

PULVER   It may look like it—but it won't taste like it!

ROBERTS   Doc, what does Scotch taste like?

DOC   Well, it's a little like . . . uh . . . it tastes like . . .

ROBERTS   Do you know what it's always tasted like to me? Iodine.

DOC   (*shrugs as if to say "Of course" and rises. He takes dropper from small bottle of iodine and flicks a drop in the bottle.*) One drop of iodine—for taste. (*shakes the bottle and pours some in glass*)

PULVER Lemme taste her, Doc!

DOC (*stops him with a gesture*) No. This calls for a medical opinion. (*takes a ceremonial taste while the others wait for his verdict*)

PULVER How about it?

DOC We're on the right track! (*sets glass down. Rubs hands professionally*) Now we need a little something extra—for age! What've you got there, Doug?

ROBERTS (*reading labels of bottles on desk*) Bromo-Seltzer . . . Wildroot Wave Set . . . Eno Fruit Salts . . . Kreml Hair Tonic . . .

DOC Kreml! It has a coal tar base! And it'll age the hell out of it! (*pours a bit of Kreml into mixture. Shakes bottle solemnly*) One drop Kreml for age. (*sets bottle on desk, looks at wrist watch for a fraction of a second*) That's it! (*pours drink into glass. PULVER reaches for it. ROBERTS pushes his arm aside and tastes it.*)

ROBERTS By God, it does taste a little like Scotch!

[PULVER *again reaches for glass.* DOC *pushes his arm aside and takes a drink.*]

DOC By God, it does!

[PULVER *finally gets glass and takes a quick sip.*]

PULVER It's delicious. That dumb little blonde won't know the difference.

DOC (*hands the bottle to PULVER*) Here you are, Frank. Doug and I have made the Scotch. The *nurse* is your department.

[PULVER *takes the bottle and hides it under the mattress, then replaces the pillows.*]

PULVER (*singing softly*) Won't know the difference . . . won't know the difference. (*DOC starts to drink from Coca-Cola bottle as PULVER comes over and snatches it from his hand.*) Thanks, Doc. (*puts cap on the bottle and hides it under the mattress. Turns and faces the others*) Thanks, Doug. Jeez, you guys are wonderful to me.

ROBERTS (*putting bottles back in medicine chest*) Don't mention it, Frank. I think you almost deserve it.

PULVER You do—really? Or are you just giving me the old needle again? What do you really think of me, Doug—honestly?

ROBERTS (*turning slowly to face PULVER*) Frank, I like you. No one can get around the fact that you're a hell of a likable guy.

PULVER (*beaming*) Yeah—yeah . . .

ROBERTS *But . . .*

PULVER But what?

ROBERTS But I also think you are the most hapless . . . lazy . . . disorganized . . . and, in general, the most lecherous person I've ever known in my life.

Reference Key to Plays in Anthologies

Copies of the complete play may be found in the following selected volumes:
Numbers 38, 50, 67.

Further Reading on *Mister Roberts*

Brown, John Mason. "Order of the Palm." *Seeing More Things*. New York:
McGraw-Hill, 1948, pp. 282–88.
Nathan, George Jean. *"Mister Roberts." Theatre Book of the Year, 1947–1948*.
New York: Knopf, 1948, pp. 283–86.

Born Yesterday

GARSON KANIN (1946)

From Act I

SCENE: For one man, one woman

CHARACTERS: Billie Dawn
Paul Verral, a reporter

SETTING: The sitting room of the best suite in the best hotel in Washington, D.C.

TIME: September, 1945.

SITUATION: Billie Dawn is the mistress of the successful but unscrupulous junk dealer Harry Brock, who made a fortune dealing in surplus materials after the Second World War. In Washington in order to obtain some legislation favorable to his schemes, Brock has decided that Billie might be an asset if she were better educated and more refined. She is beautiful but dumb. Brock hires an idealistic young journalist, Paul Verral, to "improve her mind."

See also the following scene from *Born Yesterday* (p. 210), which occurs later in the play.

PAUL   Your—friend, Mr. Brock, has an idea he'd like us to spend a little time together. You and me, that is.

BILLIE   You don't say.

PAUL   Yes.

BILLIE   What are you? Some kind of gigolo?

PAUL   Not exactly.

BILLIE   What's the idea?

PAUL   Nothing special. (*He sits on the sofa, some distance from* BILLIE.) He just wants me to put you wise to a few things. Show you the ropes. Answer any questions.

BILLIE   I got no questions.

PAUL   I'll give you some.

BILLIE   Thanks.

PAUL   Might be fun for you, in a way. There's a lot to see down here. I'd be glad to show you around.

BILLIE   You know this Supreme Court?

PAUL   Yes.

BILLIE   I'd like to take that in.

PAUL   Sure. We're on, then?

BILLIE   How do you mean?

PAUL   The arrangement.

BILLIE   I don't mind. I got nothin' much to do.

PAUL   Good.

BILLIE   What's he payin' you?

PAUL   Two hundred.

BILLIE   You're a sucker. You could of got more. He's got plenty.

PAUL   I'd have done it for nothing. (BILLIE *looks at him with rare disbelief and gives a mirthless little laugh.*) I would.

BILLIE   Why?

PAUL   This isn't work. I like it.

[BILLIE *smiles.*]

BILLIE   He thinks I'm too stupid, huh?

PAUL   Why, no—

BILLIE   He's right. I'm stupid and I like it.

PAUL   You do?

BILLIE   Sure. I'm happy. I got everything I want. Two mink coats. Everything. If there's somethin' I want, I ask. And if he don't come across—I don't come across. (*This candor has* PAUL *off balance.*) If you know what I mean.

PAUL   (*with a gulp*) Yes, I do.

BILLIE   So long as I know how to get what I want, that's all I want to know.

PAUL   As long as you know what you want.

BILLIE   Sure. What?

PAUL   As long as you know what you want.

BILLIE   You tryin' to mix me up?

PAUL   No.

[*a pause*]

BILLIE   I'll tell you what I *would* like.

PAUL   Yes?

BILLIE   I'd like to learn how to talk good.

PAUL   All right.

BILLIE   Is it hard to learn?

PAUL   I don't think so.

BILLIE   What do I have to do?

PAUL   Well, I might give you a few books to start with. Then, if you don't mind, I'll correct you now and then.

BILLIE   Go ahead.

PAUL   When *I* know, that is. I don't—talk so good myself.

BILLIE   You'll do.

PAUL   Fine.

BILLIE   I never say "ain't." Did you notice that? Never.

PAUL   I do.

BILLIE   Well, I'll correct *you* then.

PAUL   Do that.

BILLIE   Since I was very small, I never say it. We had this teacher. She used to slug you if you did it.

PAUL   Did what?

BILLIE   Said ain't.

PAUL   Oh.

BILLIE   So I got out of the habit.

PAUL   I wonder if it was worth the slugging.

BILLIE   Well, not hard.

PAUL   It's the principle of the thing. There's too much slugging. I don't believe in it.

BILLIE   All right, I don't believe in it either.

PAUL   Good.

BILLIE   I learn pretty fast, don't I?

PAUL   (*smiling*) You're great, Miss Dawn.

BILLIE   Billie.

PAUL   Billie. (*a tiny pause*) Sort of an odd name, isn't it?

BILLIE   What are you talkin'? Half the kids I know are named it. Anyway, it's not my real name.

PAUL   What is?

[*She has to think a moment before she can answer.*]

BILLIE   My God! Emma.

PAUL   What's the matter?

BILLIE   Do I look to you like an Emma?

PAUL   No. You don't look like a Billie, either.

BILLIE   So what do I look like?

PAUL   To me?

BILLIE   Yuh, to you.

PAUL   You look like a little angel.

[*a pause*]

BILLIE   Lemme ask you. Are you one of these talkers, or would you be interested in a little action?

PAUL   (*stunned*) Huh?

BILLIE   I got a yen for you right off.

PAUL   Do you get many?

BILLIE   Now and then.

PAUL   What do you do about them?

BILLIE   Stick around. You'll find out.

PAUL   All right, I will.

BILLIE   And if you want a tip, I'll tell you. Sweet-talk me. I like it. Like that angel line. (PAUL *looks upstairs with a frown.*) Don't worry about him. He don't see a thing. He's too dizzy from being a big man.

PAUL   (*rising and moving away*) This is going to be a little different than I thought.

BILLIE   You mind?

PAUL   No.

BILLIE   It's only fair. We'll educate each other.

PAUL   (*in a weak attempt to get on safer ground*) Now, about those books.

BILLIE   Yes?

PAUL   I'll get them for you tomorrow. I'll look around my place, too. If there's anything interesting, I'll drop it by later.

BILLIE   All right.

PAUL   We can figure out time every day the day before.

[BILLIE *beckons.* PAUL *comes to her. She reaches up, takes his lapel, and brings his ear close.*]

BILLIE   Or the night.

PAUL   (*straightening*) Sure.

Reference Key to Plays in Anthologies

A copy of the complete play may be found in the following volume:
   Number 37.

An abridged version of the play may be found in
   Mantle, Burns. *The Best Plays of 1945–1946.* New York: Dodd, Mead, 1946.

Further Reading on Kanin and *Born Yesterday*

Gilder, Rosamond. "From Far to Near." *Theatre Arts,* Vol. 30, No. 4 (April, 1946), pp. 200–201.

Houghton, Norris. "Kanins on Broadway." *Theatre Arts,* Vol. 30, No. 12 (December, 1946), pp. 731–33.

Nathan, George Jean. "*Born Yesterday.*" *Theatre Book of the Year, 1945–1946.* New York: Knopf, 1946, pp. 296–98.

Born Yesterday —————————————————————

GARSON KANIN (1946)

From Act II

SCENE:	For two men, one woman
CHARACTERS:	Paul Verral, a reporter Harry Brock, a millionaire Billie Dawn, Brock's mistress
SETTING:	The sitting room of the best suite in the best hotel in Washington, D.C.
TIME:	November, 1945.
SITUATION:	See the preceding scene from *Born Yesterday* (p. 205), which occurs earlier in the play.
	Paul has been taking his tutoring assignment very seriously. He has given Billie a number of books to read, and in this scene he is checking her progress in reading. Billie's mind, however, is on different matters, and Paul, too, finds it difficult to concentrate.

BILLIE (*softly*) You're crazy about me, aren't you.

PAUL Yes.

BILLIE That's why you get so mad at Harry.

PAUL Billie, listen, I hate his life, what he does, what he stands for. Not him. He just doesn't know any better.

BILLIE I go for you, too.

PAUL I'm glad, Billie.

BILLIE That's why I started doing all this. I guess you know.

PAUL No, I didn't.

BILLIE A lot of good it did me. I never had this kind of trouble before, I can tell you.

PAUL Trouble?

BILLIE   After that first night when I met you—I figured it was all going to work dandy. Then, when you wouldn't step across the line—I figured maybe the way to *you* was through your head.

PAUL   (*very slowly*) Well—no.

BILLIE   Anyway, it doesn't matter now—but I like you anyway. Too late for the rest.

PAUL   Why?

BILLIE   Why? Look, Paul, there's a certain time between a fellow and a girl when it either comes off or not and if it doesn't then, then it never does.

PAUL   Maybe we haven't got to our time yet.

BILLIE   I think we did. And you dropped the ball.

PAUL   Don't be so sure.

BILLIE   I know. I've had lots of fellas and I *haven't* had lots of fellas. If you know what I mean.

PAUL   Yes.

BILLIE   (*moving away*) But I sure never thought I'd go through a thing like this for anybody.

PAUL   Like what?

BILLIE   Like getting all mixed up in my head. Wondering and worrying and *thinking*—and stuff like that. And, I don't know if it's good to find out so much so quick. (*She sits on the sofa.*)

PAUL   What the hell, Billie. Nobody's *born* smart. You know what's the stupidest thing on earth? An infant.

BILLIE   What've you got against babies all of a sudden?

PAUL   Nothing. I've got nothing against a brain three weeks old and empty. But when it hangs around for thirty years without absorbing anything, I begin to think something's the matter with it.

BILLIE   (*rising in fury*) What makes you think I'm thirty?

PAUL   I didn't mean you, especially.

BILLIE   Yes, you did.

PAUL   I swear.

BILLIE   You certainly know how to get me sore.

PAUL   I'm sorry.

BILLIE   Thirty! Do I look thirty to you?

PAUL   No.

BILLIE   Then what'd you say it for?

PAUL   I don't know. (*a short pause*) How old *are* you?

BILLIE   Twenty-nine.

[*They look at each other.* PAUL *smiles. She responds. He comes over and kisses her, softly.*]

PAUL   Don't stop. (*She kisses him.*) I meant don't stop studying.

BILLIE   Oh.

PAUL   Will you?

BILLIE   I don't know why it's so important to you.

PAUL   It's sort of a cause. I want everybody to be smart. As smart as they can be. A world full of ignorant people is too dangerous to live in.

BILLIE   *(sitting again)* I know. That's why I wish I was doing better.

PAUL   You're doing wonderfully.

BILLIE   Yeah, but it's just no use. I bet most people would laugh at me if they knew what I was trying to do.

PAUL   I'm not laughing.

BILLIE   I am. I'm sort of laughing at myself. Who do I think I am anyway?

PAUL   What's the matter?

BILLIE   All them books!

PAUL   *(coming to her)* It isn't only books, Billie. I've told you a hundred times.

BILLIE   It's mostly.

PAUL   *(sitting beside her)* Not at all. Listen, who said this? "The proper study of Mankind is Man."

BILLIE   I don't know.

PAUL   You should.

BILLIE   Why?

PAUL   I've told you.

BILLIE   I forgot.

PAUL   Pope.

BILLIE   The Pope?

PAUL   No, not the Pope. Alexander Pope.

BILLIE   "The proper study of—

PAUL   —Mankind is Man."

BILLIE   —Mankind is Man." Of course, that means women, too.

PAUL   Yes.

BILLIE   Yes, I know.

PAUL   Don't worry about books so much.

BILLIE   I *been* studying different mankind lately. The ones you told me. Jane Addams last week, and this week Tom Paine. And then all by myself I got to thinking about Harry. He works so hard to get what he wants, for instance, but he doesn't know what he wants.

PAUL   More of what he's got, probably.

BILLIE   Money.

PAUL   Money, more people to push around, money.

BILLIE   He's not so bad as you think he is.

PAUL   I know. He's got a brain of gold.

[*There is the sound of a key in the door.* BROCK *comes in.*]

BROCK   Hello.

PAUL   Hello, Harry. We were just talking about you.

BROCK   (*removing his hat and coat and putting them on a chair*) Yeah? Well, that ain't what I pay you for. She knows enough about me. Too much, in fact. Ed here?

BILLIE   No.

BROCK   God damn it! He's supposed to meet me. (*He sits down and removes his shoes.*)

PAUL   (*to* BILLIE) What did you find out about Tom Paine?

BILLIE   Well, he was quite a fella.

PAUL   Where was he born? Do you remember?

BILLIE   London. Or England. Some place like that.

BROCK   What do you mean London or England? It's the same thing.

BILLIE   It is?

BROCK   London is *in* England. It's a city. London. England is a whole country.

BILLIE   I forgot.

BROCK   (*to* PAUL) Honest to God, boy. You got some patience.

PAUL   Take it easy.

BROCK   How can anybody get so dumb?

PAUL   We can't all know everything, Harry.

BILLIE   (*to* BROCK) Who's Tom Paine, for instance?

BROCK   What?

BILLIE   You heard me. Tom Paine.

BROCK   What the hell do I care who he is?

BILLIE   *I* know.

BROCK   So what? If I wanted to know who he is I'd know who he is. I just don't care. (*to* PAUL) Go ahead. Don't let me butt in.

PAUL   (*to* BILLIE) Which of his books did you like best?

BILLIE   Well, I didn't read *by* him yet—only about him.

PAUL   Oh.

BILLIE   But I made a list of—

BROCK   (*suddenly*) Who's Rabbit Maranville?

BILLIE   Who?

BROCK   Rabbit Maranville.

BILLIE   I don't know any rabbits.

BROCK   Think you're so smart.

PAUL   Used to play shortstop for the Braves, didn't he?

BROCK   (*to* PAUL) What are you? Some kind of genius?

PAUL   No.

BROCK   I hire and fire geniuses every day.

PAUL   I'm sure you do. (*He turns to* BILLIE.) Where's that list?

BILLIE   (*handing it over*) Here.

PAUL   (*studying it*) Well, suppose you start with *The Age of Reason.*

BILLIE   (*writing it down*) *The—Age—of—Reason.*

PAUL   Then, next, you might—

BROCK   Who's Willie Hop?

PAUL   (*turning slightly*) National billiard champion. And I think it's pronounced—Hoppe.

BROCK   That's what I said. Anyway, I didn't ask you, I asked her.

PAUL   Sorry. (*He turns back to* BILLIE.) Where were we?

BILLIE   *Age of Reason.*

PAUL   All right, then try *The Rights of Man.*

BILLIE   (*writing*) *The—Rights—of—Man.*

PAUL   I think that'll give you a rough idea of what—

BROCK   (*coming over to them*) What's a peninsula?

BILLIE   Sshhh!!

BROCK   Don't give me that shush—! You think you know so much—what's a peninsula?

PAUL   It's a—

BROCK   Not you.

BILLIE   (*with condescending superiority*) It's that new medicine!

BROCK   It is not.

BILLIE   What then?

BROCK   It's a body of land surrounded on three sides by water.

BILLIE   So what's that to know?

BROCK   So what's this Sam Paine to know?

BILLIE   Some difference! Tom Paine—not Sam Paine—*Tom* Paine practically started this whole country.

BROCK   You mean he's dead?

BILLIE   Of course.

BROCK   (*to* PAUL) What the hell are you learnin' her about dead people? I just want her to know how to act with live people.

PAUL   Education is a difficult thing to control or to channel, Harry. One thing leads to another. It's a matter of awakening curiosity—stimulating imagination—developing a sense of independence.

BROCK   (*cutting in*) Work on her, not me.

PAUL   No extra charge.

BROCK   I don't need nothin' you can tell me.

PAUL   Oh, I'm sure we could tell each other lots of interesting things, Harry.

BROCK   (*a warning tone*) What the hell does that mean?

PAUL   Just trying to be friendly.

BROCK   Who asked you? You know, every time I see you I don't like you as much. For a chump who's got no place, you're pretty fresh. You better watch out—I got an eye on you.

PAUL   All right. Let's both watch out.

BROCK   You know, I could knock your block off, if I wanted.

PAUL   Yes, I know.

BROCK   All right, then—just go ahead and do what you're supposed to—and that's all.

PAUL   It's all right—we'll stop for now.

BROCK   No, go ahead. I want to see how you do it.

PAUL   Not just now, if you don't mind—I've got to lie down. You don't realize how hard I work.

BILLIE   Ha ha. Some joke.

BROCK   (petulant) Two hundred bucks a week and I can't even watch!

PAUL   (to BILLIE) See you later.

BILLIE   Goodbye, Paul. Thanks.

PAUL   Not a bit.

[He leaves.]

BROCK   London or England. Honest to God.

[He opens an envelope on the desk and studies its contents throughout the following, without once looking at BILLIE.]

BILLIE   Harry.

BROCK   Yeah?

BILLIE   What's this business we're in down here? Could you tell me?

BROCK   What do you mean—we?

BILLIE   Well, I figure I'm sort of a partner, in a way.

BROCK   A silent partner.

BILLIE   So?

BROCK   So shut up.

BILLIE   I got a right to know.

BROCK   You got a right to get the hell out of my hair. Just put your nose in your book and keep it.

BILLIE   I don't want to do anything if it's against the law. That's one sure thing.

BROCK   You'll do what I tell you.

BILLIE   I think I know what it is—only I'm not sure.

BROCK   You should worry. You're doin' all right. Somethin' you want you ain't got maybe?

BILLIE   Yuh.

BROCK   What?

BILLIE   I want to be like the happy peasant.

BROCK   I'll buy it for you.

For anthologies containing the complete text and for a list of suggested readings, see the preceding scene from *Born Yesterday* (p. 208).

Blithe Spirit

NOEL COWARD (1941)

From Act II, Scene 1

SCENE: For one man, two women

CHARACTERS: Charles Condomine
Ruth Condomine, his second wife
The ghost of Elvira Condomine, his first wife

SETTING: The living room of Charles Condomine's house in Kent, England.

TIME: A summer morning. The present.

SITUATION: Gathering material for a book, author Charles Condomine invited a spiritualist, Madame Arcati, to hold a seance. Unfortunately, she brought back the spirit of Charles' first wife, Elvira. However, Elvira is visible only to Charles. As a result, his present wife, Ruth, believes that Charles is either losing his mind or else deliberately insulting her. All his explanations have been of no avail. Just as Elvira makes one of her appearances, Ruth is trying to determine whether or not Charles is still seeing things. "You're not hearing or seeing anything in the least unusual?" she asks. "Not a thing," replies Charles.

[ELVIRA *comes in from the garden, carrying an armful of roses. The roses are as grey as the rest of her.*]

ELVIRA You've absolutely ruined that border by the sundial—it looks like a mixed salad.

CHARLES O my God!

RUTH What's the matter now?

CHARLES She's here again!

RUTH What do you mean? Who's here again?

CHARLES Elvira.

RUTH Pull yourself together and don't be absurd.

FROM *Blithe Spirit* by Noel Coward. Copyright 1941 by Noel Coward. Reprinted by permission of Doubleday & Company, Inc.

ELVIRA It's all those nasturtiums—they're so vulgar.

CHARLES I like nasturtiums.

RUTH You like what?

ELVIRA (*putting her grey roses into a vase*) They're all right in moderation but in a mass like that they look beastly.

CHARLES Help me, Ruth—you've got to help me—

RUTH (*rises*) What did you mean about nasturtiums?

CHARLES Never mind about that now—I tell you she's here again.

ELVIRA You have been having a nice scene, haven't you? I could hear you right down the garden.

CHARLES Please mind your own business.

RUTH If your behaving like a lunatic isn't my business nothing is.

ELVIRA I expect it was about me, wasn't it? I know I ought to feel sorry but I'm not—I'm delighted.

CHARLES How can you be so inconsiderate?

RUTH (*shrilly*) Inconsiderate—I like that, I must say—

CHARLES Ruth—darling—please . . .

RUTH I've done everything I can to help—I've controlled myself admirably—I should like to say here and now that I don't believe a word about your damned hallucinations—you're up to something, Charles—there's been a certain furtiveness in your manner for weeks— Why don't you be honest and tell me what it is?

CHARLES You're wrong—you're dead wrong—I haven't been in the least furtive—I—

RUTH You're trying to upset me—for some obscure reason you're trying to goad me into doing something that I might regret—I won't stand for it any more— You're making me utterly miserable—(*She bursts into tears and collapses on sofa.*)

CHARLES Ruth—please— (*sits on sofa beside* RUTH)

RUTH Don't come near me—

ELVIRA Let her have a nice cry—it'll do her good.

CHARLES You're utterly heartless!

RUTH Heartless!

CHARLES (*wildly*) I was not talking to you—I was talking to Elvira.

RUTH Go on talking to her then, talk to her until you're blue in the face but don't talk to me—

CHARLES Help me, Elvira—

ELVIRA How?

CHARLES Make her see you or something.

ELVIRA I'm afraid I couldn't manage that—it's technically the most difficult business—frightfully complicated, you know—it takes years of study—

CHARLES You are here, aren't you? You're not an illusion?

ELVIRA   I may be an illusion but I'm most definitely here.

CHARLES   How did you get here?

ELVIRA   I told you last night—I don't exactly know—

CHARLES   Well, you must make me a promise that in future you only come and talk to me when I'm alone—

ELVIRA   (*pouting*) How unkind you are—making me feel so unwanted—I've never been treated so rudely—

CHARLES   I don't mean to be rude, but you must see—

ELVIRA   It's all your own fault for having married a woman who is incapable of seeing beyond the nose on her face—if she had a grain of real sympathy or affection for you she'd believe what you tell her.

CHARLES   How could you expect anybody to believe this?

ELVIRA   You'd be surprised how gullible people are—we often laugh about it on the other side.

[RUTH, *who has stopped crying and been staring at* CHARLES *in horror, suddenly gets up.*]

RUTH   (*gently*) Charles—

CHARLES   (*surprised at her tone*) Yes, dear—

RUTH   I'm awfully sorry I was cross—

CHARLES   But, my dear—

RUTH   I understand everything now, I do really—

CHARLES   You do?

RUTH   (*patting his arm reassuringly*) Of course I do.

ELVIRA   Look out—she's up to something—

CHARLES   Will you please be quiet?

RUTH   Of course, darling—we'll all be quiet, won't we? We'll be as quiet as little mice.

CHARLES   Ruth dear, listen—

RUTH   I want you to come upstairs with me and go to bed—

ELVIRA   The way that woman harps on bed is nothing short of erotic.

CHARLES   I'll deal with you later—

RUTH   Whenever you like, darling. Come along.

CHARLES   Ruth dear—I'd really rather not go to bed in the middle of the morning—

ELVIRA   How you've changed, darling!

CHARLES   Don't be disgusting.

RUTH   (*sweetly*) I'm sorry, dear—I didn't mean to be.

CHARLES   What are you up to?

RUTH   I'm not up to anything—I just want you to go quietly to bed and wait there until Doctor Bradman comes—

CHARLES   No, Ruth—you're wrong—

RUTH   (*firmly*) Come, dear—

ELVIRA   She'll have you in a strait jacket before you know where you are.

CHARLES   (*frantically*) Help me—you must help me—

ELVIRA   (*enjoying herself*) My dear, I would with pleasure, but I can't think how—

CHARLES   I can—listen, Ruth—

RUTH   Yes, dear?

CHARLES   If I promise to go to bed will you let me stay here for five minutes longer?

RUTH   I really think it would be better—

CHARLES   Bear with me—however mad it may seem—bear with me for just five minutes longer—

RUTH   (*letting go of him*) Very well—what is it?

CHARLES   Sit down then.

RUTH   (*sitting down*) All right—there.

CHARLES   Now listen—listen carefully—

ELVIRA   Have a cigarette, it will soothe your nerves.

CHARLES   I don't want a cigarette.

RUTH   (*indulgently*) Then you shan't have one, darling.

CHARLES   Ruth, I want to explain to you clearly and without emotion that beyond any shadow of doubt the ghost or shade or whatever you like to call it of my first wife Elvira is in this room now.

RUTH   Yes, dear.

CHARLES   I know you don't believe it and are trying valiantly to humour me but I intend to prove it to you.

RUTH   Why not lie down and have a nice rest and you can prove anything you want to later on?

CHARLES   She may not be here later on.

ELVIRA   Don't worry—she will!

CHARLES   O God!

RUTH   Hush, dear.

CHARLES   (*to* ELVIRA) Promise you'll do what I ask?

ELVIRA   That all depends what it is.

CHARLES   Ruth—you see that bowl of flowers on the piano?

RUTH   Yes, dear—I did it myself this morning.

ELVIRA   Very untidily if I may say so.

CHARLES   You may not.

RUTH   Very well—I never will again—I promise.

CHARLES   Elvira will now carry that bowl of flowers to the mantelpiece and back again. You will, Elvira, won't you—just to please me?

ELVIRA   I don't really see why I should—you've been quite insufferable to me ever since I materialized.

CHARLES   Please.

ELVIRA All right, I will just this once—not that I approve of all these Herman The Great carryings on. (*She goes over to the piano.*)

CHARLES Now, Ruth—watch carefully.

RUTH (*patiently*) Very well, dear.

CHARLES Go on, Elvira—bring it to the mantelpiece and back again.

[ELVIRA *does so, taking obvious pleasure in doing it in a very round-about way. At one moment she brings it up to within an inch of* RUTH's *face.* RUTH *shrinks back with a scream and then jumps to her feet.*]

RUTH (*furiously*) How dare you, Charles! You ought to be ashamed of yourself!

CHARLES What on earth for?

RUTH (*hysterically*) It's a trick—I know perfectly well it's a trick—you've been working up to this—it's all part of some horrible plan—

CHARLES It isn't—I swear it isn't—Elvira—do something else for God's sake—

ELVIRA Certainly—anything to oblige.

RUTH (*becoming really frightened*) You want to get rid of me—you're trying to drive me out of my mind—

CHARLES Don't be so silly.

RUTH You're cruel and sadistic and I'll never forgive you— (ELVIRA *lifts up a light chair and waltzes solemnly round the room with it, then she puts it down with a bang. Making a dive for the door*) I'm not going to put up with this any more.

CHARLES (*holding her*) You must believe it—you must—

RUTH Let me go immediately—

CHARLES That was Elvira—I swear it was—

RUTH (*struggling*) Let me go—

CHARLES Ruth—please—

[RUTH *breaks away from him and runs towards the windows.* ELVIRA *gets there just before her and shuts them in her face.* RUTH *starts back, appalled.*]

RUTH (*looking at* CHARLES *with eyes of horror*) Charles—this is madness—sheer madness! It's some sort of auto-suggestion, isn't it—some form of hypnotism, swear to me it's only that? Swear to me it's only that.

ELVIRA (*taking an expensive vase from the mantelpiece and crashing it into the grate*) Hypnotism my foot!

[RUTH *gives a scream and goes into violent hysterics as the curtain falls.*]

Reference Key to Plays in Anthologies

Copies of the complete play may be found in the following selected volumes:
Numbers 36, 42, 54, 78.

Further Reading on Coward and *Blithe Spirit*

Gassner, John. *A Treasury of the Theatre*. Pt. 2, *From Ibsen to Ionesco*. 3rd ed. New York: Holt, Rinehart and Winston, 1960, pp. 730–31.

Greacen, Robert. *The Art of Noel Coward*. Aldington, England: The Hand and Flower Press, 1953.

Mander, Raymond and J. Mitchenson. *Theatrical Companion to Coward*. London: Rockliff, 1957.

Present Laughter

NOEL COWARD (1943)

From Act 1

SCENE: For two men

CHARACTERS: Garry Essendine, a famous actor
Roland Maule, an aspiring playwright

SETTING: The studio flat of Garry Essendine in London.

TIME: The present.

SITUATION: Garry Essendine is a famous matinee idol who is trying to convince himself that he is not gradually slipping into middle age. Vain, theatrical, articulate, and smug, he finds pleasure in making love to young women and in insulting his colleagues. When a strange young playwright, Roland Maule, comes to him for advice, Garry finds that his usual insults have no effect.

GARRY   *(motions* ROLAND *into a chair)* Do sit down, won't you?
ROLAND   *(sitting)* Thank you.
GARRY   Cigarette?
ROLAND   No, thank you.
GARRY   Don't you smoke?
ROLAND   No.
GARRY   Drink?
ROLAND   No, thank you.
GARRY   How old are you?
ROLAND   Twenty-five. Why?
GARRY   It doesn't really matter—I just wondered.
ROLAND   How old are you?
GARRY   Forty in December. Jupiter, you know—very energetic.
ROLAND   Yes, of course. *(He gives a nervous braying laugh.)*
GARRY   You've come all the way from Uckfield?
ROLAND   It isn't very far.

GARRY   Well, it sort of sounds far, doesn't it?

ROLAND   (*defensively*) It's quite near Lewes.

GARRY   Then there's nothing to worry about, is there?

．　．　．

I want to talk to you about your play.

ROLAND   (*gloomily*) I expect you hated it.

GARRY   Well, to be candid, I thought it was a little uneven.

ROLAND   I thought you'd say that.

GARRY   I'm glad I'm running so true to form.

ROLAND   I mean it really isn't the sort of thing you would like, is it?

GARRY   In that case why on earth did you send it to me?

ROLAND   I just took a chance. I mean I know you only play rather trashy stuff as a rule, and I thought you just might like to have a shot at something deeper.

GARRY   What is there in your play that you consider so deep, Mr. Maule? Apart from the plot, which is completely submerged after the first four pages.

ROLAND   Plots aren't important; it's ideas that matter. Look at Chekhov.

GARRY   In addition to ideas I think we might concede Chekhov a certain flimsy sense of psychology, don't you?

ROLAND   You mean my play isn't psychologically accurate?

GARRY   (*gently*) It isn't very good, you know, really it isn't.

ROLAND   I think it's very good indeed.

GARRY   I understand that perfectly, but you must admit that my opinion, based on a lifelong experience of the theatre, might be the right one.

ROLAND   (*contemptuously*) The commercial theatre.

GARRY   Oh dear, oh dear, oh dear.

ROLAND   I suppose you'll say that Shakespeare wrote for the commercial theatre and that the only point of doing anything with the drama at all is to make money! All those old arguments. What you don't realize is that the theatre of the future is the theatre of ideas.

GARRY   That may be, but at the moment I am occupied with the theatre of the present.

ROLAND   (*heatedly*) And what do you do with it? Every play you appear in is exactly the same, superficial, frivolous, and without the slightest intellectual significance. You have a great following and a strong personality, and all you do is prostitute yourself every night of your life. All you do with your talent is to wear dressing-gowns and make witty remarks when you might be really helping people, making them think! Making them feel!

GARRY   There can be no two opinions about it. I am having a most discouraging morning.

ROLAND (*rising and standing over* GARRY) If you want to live in people's memories, to go down to posterity as an important man, you'd better do something about it quickly. There isn't a moment to be lost.

GARRY I don't give a hoot about posterity. Why should I worry about what people think of me when I'm dead as a doornail anyway? My worst defect is that I am apt to worry too much about what people think of me when I'm alive. But I'm not going to do that any more. I'm changing my methods and you're my first experiment. As a rule, when insufferable young beginners have the impertinence to criticize me, I dismiss the whole thing lightly because I'm embarrassed for them and consider it not quite fair game to puncture their inflated egos too sharply. But this time, my highbrow young friend, you're going to get it in the neck. To begin with, your play is not a play at all. It's a meaningless jumble of adolescent, pseudo-intellectual poppycock. It bears no relation to the theatre or to life or to anything. And you yourself wouldn't be here at all if I hadn't been bloody fool enough to pick up the telephone when my secretary wasn't looking. Now that you are here, however, I would like to tell you this. If you wish to be a playwright you just leave the theatre of tomorrow to take care of itself. Go and get yourself a job as a butler in a repertory company if they'll have you. Learn from the ground up how plays are constructed and what is actable and what isn't. Then sit down and write at least twenty plays one after the other, and if you can manage to get the twenty-first produced for a Sunday-night performance you'll be damned lucky!

ROLAND (*hypnotized*) I had no idea you were like this. You're wonderful!

GARRY (*flinging up his hands*) My God!

ROLAND I'm awfully sorry if you think I was impertinent, but I'm awfully glad too because if I hadn't been you wouldn't have got angry, and if you hadn't got angry I shouldn't have known what you were really like.

GARRY You don't in the least know what I'm really like.

ROLAND Oh yes, I do—now.

GARRY I can't see that it matters anyway.

ROLAND It matters to me.

GARRY Why?

ROLAND Do you really want to know?

GARRY What on earth are you talking about?

ROLAND It's rather difficult to explain really.

GARRY What is difficult to explain?

ROLAND What I feel about you.

GARRY But—

ROLAND No, please let me speak. You see in a way I've been rather unhappy about you—for quite a long time. You've been a sort of obsession with me. I saw you in your last play forty-seven times; one week I came every night, in the pit, because I was up in town trying to pass an exam.

GARRY   Did you pass it?

ROLAND   No, I didn't.

GARRY   I'm not entirely surprised.

ROLAND   My father wants me to be a lawyer, that's what the exam was for, but actually I've been studying psychology a great deal because I felt somehow that I wasn't at peace with myself and gradually, bit by bit, I began to realize that you signified something to me.

GARRY   What sort of something?

ROLAND   I don't quite know—not yet.

GARRY   That "not yet" is one of the most sinister remarks I've ever heard.

ROLAND   Don't laugh at me, please. I'm always sick if anyone laughs at me.

GARRY   You really are the most peculiar young man.

ROLAND   I'm all right now, though, I feel fine!

GARRY   I'm delighted.

ROLAND   Can I come and see you again?

GARRY   I'm afraid I'm going to Africa.

ROLAND   Would you see me if I came to Africa too?

GARRY   I really think you'd be happier in Uckfield.

ROLAND   I expect you think I'm mad, but I'm not really. I just mind deeply about certain things. But I feel much better now because I think I shall be able to sublimate you all right.

GARRY   Good! Now I'm afraid I shall have to turn you out because I'm expecting my manager and we have some business to discuss.

ROLAND   It's all right. I'm going immediately.

GARRY   Shall I get you your script?

ROLAND   No, no—tear it up. You were quite right about it—it was only written with part of myself. I see that now. Good-bye.

GARRY   Good-bye.

[ROLAND *goes out.*]

Reference Key to Plays in Anthologies

A copy of the complete play may be found in
Theatre Arts, August, 1949.

Further Reading on Coward and *Present Laughter*

Brown, John Mason. "English Laughter—Past and Present." *Seeing More Things.* New York: McGraw-Hill, 1948, pp. 200–08.

Greacen, Robert. *The Art of Noel Coward.* Aldington, England: The Hand and Flower Press, 1953.

Mander, Raymond and J. Mitchenson. *Theatrical Companion to Coward.* London: Rockliff, 1957.

Nathan, George Jean. *"Present Laughter." Theatre Book of the Year, 1946–1947.* New York: Knopf, 1947, pp. 142–45.

The Importance of Being Earnest _____

OSCAR WILDE (1895)

From Act I

SCENE: For one man, one woman

CHARACTERS: Jack Worthing (also known as Ernest)
Gwendolen Fairfax

SETTING: The morning room of Algernon Moncrieff's flat in Half-moon Street, London.

TIME: An afternoon in the 1890's.

SITUATION: In an interview given to a journalist just before *Earnest* opened, Wilde reportedly said that his new play was "exquisitely trivial, a delicate bubble of fancy," and that it had its "philosophy." Wilde offered this definition of the play's philosophy: "We should treat all the trivial things of life seriously, and all the serious things of life with sincere and studied triviality."

Jack is in love with Gwendolen in as passionately trivial a manner as possible. He takes the opportunity to propose marriage to her while her mother is out of the room. Gwendolen does not know that her suitor's real name is Jack; she believes it to be Ernest, the name Jack assumes while carrying on his bachelor escapades. His name is "Ernest in town and Jack in the country." He is proposing to Gwendolen in town.

See also the following scene from *The Importance of Being Earnest* (p. 232), which occurs later in the play.

JACK Charming day it has been, Miss Fairfax.
GWENDOLEN Pray don't talk to me about the weather, Mr. Worthing. Whenever people talk to me about the weather, I always feel quite certain that they mean something else. And that makes me so nervous.
JACK I do mean something else.
GWENDOLEN I thought so. In fact, I am never wrong.
JACK And I would like to be allowed to take advantage of Lady Bracknell's temporary absence . . .
GWENDOLEN I would certainly advise you to do so. Mamma has a way of

coming back suddenly into a room that I have often had to speak to her about.

JACK (*nervously*) Miss Fairfax, ever since I met you I have admired you more than any girl . . . I have ever met since . . . I met you.

GWENDOLEN Yes, I am quite aware of the fact. And I often wish that in public, at any rate, you had been more demonstrative. For me you have always had an irresistible fascination. Even before I met you I was far from indifferent to you. (JACK *looks at her in amazement.*) We live, as I hope you know, Mr. Worthing, in an age of ideals. The fact is constantly mentioned in the more expensive monthly magazines, and has reached the provincial pulpits I am told: and my ideal has always been to love some one of the name of Ernest. There is something in that name that inspires absolute confidence. The moment Algernon first mentioned to me that he had a friend called Ernest, I knew I was destined to love you.

JACK You really love me, Gwendolen?

GWENDOLEN Passionately!

JACK Darling! You don't know how happy you've made me.

GWENDOLEN My own Ernest!

JACK But you don't really mean to say that you couldn't love me if my name wasn't Ernest?

GWENDOLEN But your name is Ernest.

JACK Yes, I know it is. But supposing it was something else? Do you mean to say you couldn't love me then?

GWENDOLEN (*glibly*) Ah! that is clearly a metaphysical speculation, and like most metaphysical speculations has very little reference at all to the actual facts of real life, as we know them.

JACK Personally, darling, to speak quite candidly, I don't much care about the name of Ernest . . . I don't think that name suits me at all.

GWENDOLEN It suits you perfectly. It is a divine name. It has a music of its own. It produces vibrations.

JACK Well, really, Gwendolen, I must say that I think there are lots of other much nicer names. I think, Jack, for instance, a charming name.

GWENDOLEN Jack? . . . No, there is very little music in the name Jack, if any at all, indeed. It does not thrill. It produces absolutely no vibrations. . . . I have known several Jacks, and they all, without exception, were more than usually plain. Besides, Jack is a notorious domesticity for John! And I pity any woman who is married to a man called John. She would probably never be allowed to know the entrancing pleasure of a single moment's solitude. The only really safe name is Ernest.

JACK Gwendolen, I must get christened at once—I mean we must get married at once. There is no time to be lost.

GWENDOLEN   Married, Mr. Worthing?

JACK   (*astounded*) Well . . . surely. You know that I love you, and you led me to believe, Miss Fairfax, that you were not absolutely indifferent to me.

GWENDOLEN   I adore you. But you haven't proposed to me yet. Nothing has been said at all about marriage. The subject has not even been touched on.

JACK   Well . . . may I propose to you now?

GWENDOLEN   I think it would be an admirable opportunity. And to spare you any possible disappointment, Mr. Worthing, I think it only fair to tell you quite frankly beforehand that I am fully determined to accept you.

JACK   Gwendolen!

GWENDOLEN   Yes, Mr. Worthing, what have you got to say to me?

JACK   You know what I have got to say to you.

GWENDOLEN   Yes, but you don't say it.

JACK   Gwendolen, will you marry me? (*goes on his knees*)

GWENDOLEN   Of course I will, darling. How long you have been about it! I am afraid you have had very little experience in how to propose.

JACK   My own one, I have never loved anyone in the world but you.

GWENDOLEN   Yes, but men often propose for practice. I know my brother Gerald does. All my girl-friends tell me so. What wonderfully blue eyes you have, Ernest! They are quite, quite blue. I hope you will always look at me just like that, especially when there are other people present.

Reference Key to Plays in Anthologies

Copies of the complete play may be found in the following selected volumes: Numbers 2, 3, 4, 5, 12, 14, 19, 42, 54, 74, 81.

Further Reading on Wilde and *The Importance of Being Earnest*

Gassner, John. "Bernard Shaw and the British Compromise." *Masters of the Drama*. 3rd ed. New York: Dover, 1954, pp. 587–91.

Pearson, Hesketh. *Oscar Wilde: His Life and Wit*. New York: Grosset and Dunlap, 1946.

Reinert, Otto. "The Courtship Dance in *The Importance of Being Earnest*." *Modern Drama*, Vol. 1, No. 4 (February, 1959), pp. 256–57.

Shaw, G. Bernard. "Old New Play and a New Old One." *Plays and Players: Essays on the Theatre*. Oxford: Oxford University Press, 1952, pp. 17–25.

Winwar, Frances. *Oscar Wilde and the Yellow Nineties*. New York: Harper, 1940.

Woodcock, George. *The Paradox of Oscar Wilde*. London: T. V. Boardman, 1949.

Recorded Performances

Slightly abridged performance: Sir John Gielgud as Jack, Dame Edith Evans as Lady Bracknell, and Pamela Brown as Gwendolen, Angel 3504, two records.

The Importance of Being Earnest

OSCAR WILDE (1895)

From Act I

SCENE:	For one man, one woman
CHARACTERS:	Lady Bracknell, Gwendolen's mother Jack Worthing
SETTING:	The morning room of Algernon Moncrieff's flat in Half-moon Street, London.
TIME:	An afternoon in the 1890's.
SITUATION:	See the preceding scene from *The Importance of Being Earnest* (p. 228), which occurs earlier in the play.
	This scene follows almost immediately the preceding scene. Lady Bracknell has entered the room as Jack is kneeling before Gwendolen. She assumes that Jack wishes to propose to her daughter, and she dismisses Gwendolen in order to talk to him to determine if he will be a suitable husband. Gwendolen has just left the room as Lady Bracknell begins the interview.

LADY BRACKNELL   (*sitting down*) You can take a seat, Mr. Worthing. (*looks in her pocket for note-book and pencil*)

JACK   Thank you, Lady Bracknell, I prefer standing.

LADY BRACKNELL   (*pencil and note-book in hand*) I feel bound to tell you that you are not down on my list of eligible young men, although I have the same list as the dear Duchess of Bolton has. We work together, in fact. However, I am quite ready to enter your name, should your answers be what a really affectionate mother requires. Do you smoke?

JACK   Well, yes, I must admit I smoke.

LADY BRACKNELL   I am glad to hear it. A man should always have an occupation of some kind. There are far too many idle men in London as it is. How old are you?

JACK   Twenty-nine.

LADY BRACKNELL A very good age to be married at. I have always been of opinion that a man who desires to get married should know either everything or nothing. Which do you know?

JACK (*after some hesitation*) I know nothing, Lady Bracknell.

LADY BRACKNELL I am pleased to hear it. I do not approve of anything that tampers with natural ignorance. Ignorance is like a delicate exotic fruit; touch it and the bloom is gone. The whole theory of modern education is radically unsound. Fortunately in England, at any rate, education produces no effect whatsoever. If it did, it would prove a serious danger to the upper classes, and probably lead to acts of violence in Grosvenor Square. What is your income?

JACK Between seven and eight thousand a year.

LADY BRACKNELL (*makes a note in her book*) In land, or in investments?

JACK In investments, chiefly.

LADY BRACKNELL That is satisfactory. What between the duties expected of one during one's lifetime, and the duties exacted from one after one's death, land has ceased to be either a profit or a pleasure. It gives one position, and prevents one from keeping it up. That's all that can be said about land.

JACK I have a country house with some land, of course, attached to it, about fifteen hundred acres, I believe; but I don't depend on that for my real income. In fact, as far as I can make out, the poachers are the only people who make anything out of it.

LADY BRACKNELL A country house! How many bedrooms? Well, that point can be cleared up afterwards. You have a town house, I hope? A girl with a simple, unspoiled nature, like Gwendolen, could hardly be expected to reside in the country.

JACK Well, I own a house in Belgrave Square, but it is let by the year to Lady Bloxham. Of course, I can get it back whenever I like, at six months' notice.

LADY BRACKNELL Lady Bloxham? I don't know her.

JACK Oh, she goes about very little. She is a lady considerably advanced in years.

LADY BRACKNELL Ah, now-a-days that is no guarantee of respectability of character. What number in Belgrave Square?

JACK 149.

LADY BRACKNELL (*shaking her head*) The unfashionable side. I thought there was something. However, that could easily be altered.

JACK Do you mean the fashion, or the side?

LADY BRACKNELL (*sternly*) Both, if necessary, I presume. What are your politics?

JACK Well, I am afraid I really have none. I am a Liberal Unionist.

LADY BRACKNELL Oh, they count as Tories. They dine with us. Or come in the evening, at any rate. Now to minor matters. Are your parents living?

JACK I have lost both my parents.

LADY BRACKNELL To lose one parent, Mr. Worthing, may be regarded as a misfortune; to lose both looks like carelessness. Who was your father? He was evidently a man of some wealth. Was he born in what the Radical papers call the purple of commerce, or did he rise from the ranks of the aristocracy?

JACK I am afraid I really don't know. The fact is, Lady Bracknell, I said I had lost my parents. It would be nearer the truth to say that my parents seem to have lost me . . . I don't actually know who I am by birth. I was . . . well, I was found.

LADY BRACKNELL Found!

JACK The late Mr. Thomas Cardew, an old gentleman of a very charitable and kindly disposition, found me, and gave me the name of Worthing, because he happened to have a first-class ticket for Worthing in his pocket at the time. Worthing is a place in Sussex. It is a seaside resort.

LADY BRACKNELL Where did the charitable gentleman who had a first-class ticket for this seaside resort find you?

JACK (*gravely*) In a hand-bag.

LADY BRACKNELL A hand-bag?

JACK (*very seriously*) Yes, Lady Bracknell. I was in a hand-bag—a somewhat large, black leather hand-bag, with handles to it—an ordinary hand-bag in fact.

LADY BRACKNELL In what locality did this Mr. James, or Thomas, Cardew come across this ordinary hand-bag?

JACK In the cloak-room at Victoria Station. It was given to him in mistake for his own.

LADY BRACKNELL The cloak-room at Victoria Station?

JACK Yes. The Brighton line.

LADY BRACKNELL The line is immaterial. Mr. Worthing, I confess I feel somewhat bewildered by what you have just told me. To be born, or at any rate bred, in a hand-bag, whether it had handles or not, seems to me to display a contempt for the ordinary decencies of family life that remind one of the worst excesses of the French Revolution. And I presume you know what that unfortunate movement led to? As for the particular locality in which the hand-bag was found, a cloak-room at a railway station might serve to conceal a social indiscretion—has probably, indeed, been used for that purpose before now—but it could hardly be regarded as an assured basis for a recognized position in good society.

JACK May I ask you then what you would advise me to do? I need hardly say I would do anything in the world to ensure Gwendolen's happiness.

LADY BRACKNELL I would strongly advise you, Mr. Worthing, to try and acquire some relations as soon as possible, and to make a definite effort to produce at any rate one parent, of either sex, before the season is quite over.

JACK Well, I don't see how I could possibly manage to do that. I can produce the hand-bag at any moment. It is in my dressing-room at home. I really think that should satisfy you, Lady Bracknell.

LADY BRACKNELL Me, sir! What has it to do with me? You can hardly imagine that I and Lord Bracknell would dream of allowing our only daughter—a girl brought up with the utmost care—to marry into a cloakroom, and form an alliance with a parcel? Good morning, Mr. Worthing!

[LADY BRACKNELL *sweeps out in majestic indignation.*]

JACK Good morning!

For anthologies containing the complete text and for a list of suggested readings, see the preceding scene from *The Importance of Being Earnest* (p. 230).

Private Lives ———————————————

From Act III

SCENE:	For two men
CHARACTERS:	Elyot Chase Victor Prynne
SETTING:	An attractive flat in Paris.
TIME:	Morning. (Although the play may be performed in a modern setting, the period intended is the era between the two World Wars.)
SITUATION:	After an exciting but stormy marriage, Elyot and Amanda were divorced. Each remarried a mate who was totally different from his former spouse. Coincidentally, both Amanda and Elyot were honeymooning on the Riveria at the same time, in the same hotel, and in adjoining rooms. When they met, they discovered that they were still very much attracted to each other; they fled to Paris together to resume their loving and fighting. Amanda's stuffy second husband, Victor, is disturbed by this strange behavior. He traces the pair to Paris, and the scene begins as Victor confronts Elyot. Victor soon discovers, however, that Elyot is decidedly his intellectual superior.

VICTOR (*belligerently*) Now then!

ELYOT Now then what?

VICTOR Are you going to take back those things you said to Amanda?

ELYOT Certainly, I'll take back anything, if only you'll stop bellowing at me.

VICTOR (*contemptuously*) You're a coward, too.

ELYOT They want us to fight, don't you see?

VICTOR No, I don't; why should they?

FROM *Private Lives* by Noel Coward. Copyright 1930 by Doubleday & Company, Inc. Reprinted by permission of the publisher.

ELYOT   Primitive feminine instincts—warring males—very enjoyable.

VICTOR   You think you're very clever, don't you?

ELYOT   I think I'm a bit cleverer than you, but apparently that's not saying much.

VICTOR   (violently) What?

ELYOT   Oh, do sit down.

VICTOR   I will not.

ELYOT   Well, if you'll excuse me, I will, I'm extremely tired. (He sits down.)

VICTOR   Oh, for God's sake, behave like a man.

ELYOT   (patiently) Listen a minute, all this belligerency is very right and proper and highly traditional, but if only you'll think for a moment, you'll see that it won't get us very far.

VICTOR   To hell with all that.

ELYOT   I should like to explain that if you hit me, I shall certainly hit you, probably equally hard, if not harder. I'm just as strong as you I should imagine. Then you'd hit me again, and I'd hit you again, and we'd go on until one or the other was knocked out. Now if you'll explain to me satisfactorily how all that can possibly improve the situation, I'll tear off my coat, and we'll go at one another hammer and tongs, immediately.

VICTOR   It would ease my mind.

ELYOT   Only if you won.

VICTOR   I should win all right.

ELYOT   Want to try?

VICTOR   Yes.

ELYOT   (jumping up) Here goes then—(He tears off his coat.)

VICTOR   Just a moment.

ELYOT   Well?

VICTOR   What did you mean about them wanting us to fight?

ELYOT   It would be balm to their vanity.

VICTOR   Do you love Amanda?

ELYOT   Is this a battle or a discussion? If it's the latter I shall put on my coat again, I don't want to catch a chill.

VICTOR   Answer my question, please.

ELYOT   Have a cigarette?

VICTOR   (stormily) Answer my question.

ELYOT   If you analyze it, it's rather a silly question.

VICTOR   Do you love Amanda?

ELYOT   (confidentially) Not very much this morning; to be perfectly frank, I'd like to wring her neck. Do you love her?

VICTOR   That's beside the point.

ELYOT   On the contrary, it's the crux of the whole affair. If you do love her still, you can forgive her, and live with her in peace and harmony until you're ninety-eight.

VICTOR You're apparently even more of a cad than I thought you were.

ELYOT You are completely in the right over the whole business—don't imagine I'm not perfectly conscious of that.

VICTOR I'm glad.

ELYOT It's all very unfortunate.

VICTOR Unfortunate! My God!

ELYOT It might have been worse.

VICTOR I'm glad you think so.

ELYOT I do wish you'd stop being so glad about everything.

VICTOR What do you intend to do? That's what I want to know. What do you intend to do?

ELYOT (suddenly serious) I don't know, I don't care.

VICTOR I suppose you realize that you've broken that poor little woman's heart?

ELYOT Which poor little woman?

VICTOR Sibyl, of course.

ELYOT Oh, come now, not as bad as that. She'll get over it, and forget all about me.

VICTOR I sincerely hope so . . . for her sake.

ELYOT Amanda will forget all about me too. Everybody will forget all about me. I might just as well lie down and die in fearful pain and suffering, nobody would care.

VICTOR Don't talk such rot.

ELYOT You must forgive me for taking rather a gloomy view of everything but the fact is, I suddenly feel slightly depressed.

VICTOR I intend to divorce Amanda naming you as co-respondent.

ELYOT Very well.

VICTOR And Sibyl will divorce you for Amanda. It would be foolish of either of you to attempt any defense.

ELYOT Quite.

VICTOR And the sooner you marry Amanda again, the better.

ELYOT I'm not going to marry Amanda.

VICTOR What?

ELYOT She's a vile-tempered wicked woman.

VICTOR You should have thought of that before.

ELYOT I did think of it before.

VICTOR (firmly) You've got to marry her.

ELYOT I'd rather marry a ravening leopard.

VICTOR (angrily) Now look here. I'm sick of all this shilly-shallying. You're getting off a good deal more lightly than you deserve; you can consider yourself damned lucky I didn't shoot you.

ELYOT   (*with sudden vehemence*) Well, if you'd had a spark of manliness in you, you would have shot me. You're all fuss and fume, one of these cottonwool Englishmen. I despise you.

VICTOR   (*through clenched teeth*) You despise me?

ELYOT   Yes, utterly. You're nothing but a rampaging gas bag!

[*He goes off into his room and slams the door, leaving* VICTOR *speechless with fury.*]

Reference Key to Plays in Anthologies

Copies of the complete play may be found in the following selected volumes:
Numbers 22, 23.

Further Reading on Coward and *Private Lives*

Brown, John Mason. *Two on the Aisle.* New York: Norton, 1938, pp. 108–13.

Coward, Noel. *Present Indicative.* New York: Doubleday, Doran, 1937.

Mander, Raymond and J. Mitchenson. *Theatrical Companion to Coward.* London: Rockliff, 1957.

Nathan, George Jean. "*Private Lives.*" *Theatre Book of the Year, 1948–1949.* New York: Knopf, 1949, pp. 110–13.

"*Private Lives.*" *Theatre,* Vol. 53, No. 4 (April, 1931), p. 25.

Short, Ernest. *Theatrical Cavalcade.* London: Eyre, 1942, pp. 188–93.

Arms and the Man _____

GEORGE BERNARD SHAW (1894)

From Act II

SCENE: For one man, one woman

CHARACTERS: Sergius, an accidental military hero
Louka, a servant

SETTING: The garden of Major Petkoff's house in a small town in Bulgaria.

TIME: A fine spring morning, 1886.

SITUATION: Major Sergius Saranoff, a pompous cavalry officer, became a Bulgarian national hero when he led a successful cavalry charge against the Serbs. He would not have been so heroic had his horse not charged too quickly in the direction of the Serbian lines. The unfortunate Serbs had the wrong ammunition and were easily overrun. Otherwise, Sergius and his soldiers would have been destroyed.

The war over, Sergius has returned home with Major Petkoff, whose daughter, Raina, Sergius presumably loves. However, Sergius finds their platonic relationship rather uninteresting and begins to look about for other more accommodating women. He has just caught sight of Louka as the scene begins.

SERGIUS *(His eye gleams at once. He takes a stealthy look at her, and begins to twirl his moustache nervously, with his left hand akimbo on his hip. Finally, striking the ground with his heels in something of a cavalry swagger, he strolls over to the left of the table, opposite her, and says)* Louka: do you know what the higher love is?

LOUKA *(astonished)* No, sir.

SERGIUS Very fatiguing thing to keep up for any length of time, Louka. One feels the need of some relief after it.

LOUKA *(innocently)* Perhaps you would like some coffee, sir? *(She stretches her hand across the table for the coffee pot.)*

SERGIUS *(taking her hand)* Thank you, Louka.

FROM *Arms and the Man* by George Bernard Shaw. Reprinted by permission of The Public Trustee and The Society of Authors.

LOUKA (*pretending to pull*) Oh, sir, you know I didn't mean that. I'm surprised at you!

SERGIUS (*coming clear of the table and drawing her with him*) I am surprised at myself, Louka. What would Sergius, the hero of Slivnitza, say if he saw me now? What would Sergius, the apostle of the higher love, say if he saw me now? What would the half dozen Sergiuses who keep popping in and out of this handsome figure of mine say if they caught us here? (*letting go her hand and slipping his arm dexterously round her waist*) Do you consider my figure handsome, Louka?

LOUKA Let me go, sir. I shall be disgraced. (*She struggles: he holds her inexorably.*) Oh, *will* you let go?

SERGIUS (*looking straight into her eyes*) No.

LOUKA Then stand back where we can't be seen. Have you no common sense?

SERGIUS Ah, that's reasonable. (*He takes her into the stableyard gateway, where they are hidden from the house.*)

LOUKA (*complaining*) I may have been seen from the windows: Miss Raina is sure to be spying about after you.

SERGIUS (*stung—letting her go*) Take care, Louka. I may be worthless enough to betray the higher love; but do not you insult it.

LOUKA (*demurely*) Not for the world, sir, I'm sure. May I go on with my work please, now?

SERGIUS (*again putting his arm round her*) You are a provoking little witch, Louka. If you were in love with me, would you spy out of windows on me?

LOUKA Well, you see, sir, since you say you are half a dozen different gentlemen all at once, I should have a great deal to look after.

SERGIUS (*charmed*) Witty as well as pretty. (*He tries to kiss her.*)

LOUKA (*avoiding him*) No, I don't want your kisses. Gentlefolk are all alike—you making love to me behind Miss Raina's back, and she doing the same behind yours.

SERGIUS (*recoiling a step*) Louka!

LOUKA It shews how little you really care!

SERGIUS (*dropping his familiarity and speaking with freezing politeness*) If our conversation is to continue, Louka, you will please remember that a gentleman does not discuss the conduct of the lady he is engaged to with her maid.

LOUKA It's so hard to know what a gentleman considers right. I thought from your trying to kiss me that you had given up being so particular.

SERGIUS (*turning from her and striking his forehead as he comes back into the garden from the gateway*) Devil! Devil!

LOUKA Ha! ha! I expect one of the six of you is very like me, sir, though I am only Miss Raina's maid.

[*She goes back to her work at the table, taking no further notice of him.*]

SERGIUS (*speaking to himself*) Which of the six is the real man?—that's the question that torments me. One of them is a hero, another a buffoon, another a humbug, another perhaps a bit of a blackguard. (*He pauses and looks furtively at* LOUKA, *as he adds with deep bitterness*) And one, at least, is a coward—jealous, like all cowards. (*He goes to the table.*) Louka.

LOUKA Yes?

SERGIUS Who is my rival?

LOUKA You shall never get that out of me, for love or money.

SERGIUS Why?

LOUKA Never mind why. Besides, you would tell that I told you; and I should lose my place.

SERGIUS (*holding out his right hand in affirmation*) No; on the honor of a— (*He checks himself, and his hand drops nerveless as he concludes, sardonically*)—of a man capable of behaving as I have been behaving for the last five minutes. Who is he?

LOUKA I don't know. I never saw him. I only heard his voice through the door of her room.

SERGIUS Damnation! How dare you?

LOUKA (*retreating*) Oh, I mean no harm: you've no right to take up my words like that. The mistress knows all about it. And I tell you that if that gentleman ever comes here again, Miss Raina will marry him, whether he likes it or not. I know the difference between the sort of manner you and she put on before one another and the real manner.

[SERGIUS *shivers as if she had stabbed him. Then, setting his face like iron, he strides grimly to her, and grips her above the elbows with both hands.*]

SERGIUS Now listen to me!

LOUKA (*wincing*) Not so tight: you're hurting me!

SERGIUS That doesn't matter. You have stained my honor by making me a party to your eavesdropping. And you have betrayed your mistress—

LOUKA (*writhing*) Please—

SERGIUS That shews that you are an abominable little clod of common clay, with the soul of a servant.

[*He lets her go as if she were an unclean thing, and turns away, dusting his hands of her, to the bench by the wall, where he sits down with averted head, meditating gloomily.*]

LOUKA (*whimpering angrily with her hands up her sleeves, feeling her bruised arms*) You know how to hurt with your tongue as well as with your hands. But I don't care, now I've found out that whatever clay I'm made of, you're made of the same. As for her, she's a liar; and her fine airs are a cheat; and I'm worth six of her.

[*She shakes the pain off hardily; tosses her head; and sets to work to put the things on the tray. He looks doubtfully at her once or twice. She finishes packing the tray, and laps the cloth over the edges, so as to carry all out together. As she stoops to lift it, he rises.*]

SERGIUS Louka! (*She stops and looks defiantly at him with the tray in her hands.*) A gentleman has no right to hurt a woman under any circumstances. (*with profound humility, uncovering his head*) I beg your pardon.

LOUKA That sort of apology may satisfy a lady. Of what use is it to a servant?

SERGIUS (*thus rudely crossed in his chivalry, throws it off with a bitter laugh and says slightingly*) Oh, you wish to be paid for the hurt? (*He puts on his shako, and takes some money from his pocket.*)

LOUKA (*her eyes filling with tears in spite of herself*) No, I want my hurt made well.

SERGIUS (*sobered by her tone*) How? (*She rolls up her left sleeve; clasps her arm with the thumb and fingers of her right hand; and looks down at the bruise. Then she raises her head and looks straight at him. Finally, with a superb gesture she presents her arm to be kissed. Amazed, he looks at her; at the arm; at her again; hesitates; and then, with shuddering intensity, exclaims*) Never! (*and gets away as far as possible from her.*)

Reference Key to Plays in Anthologies

Copies of the complete play may be found in the following selected volumes: Numbers 3, 30, 45, 63.

Further Reading on Shaw and *Arms and the Man*

Ervine, St. John. *Bernard Shaw.* New York: Morrow, 1956.
Gassner, John. "Bernard Shaw and the British Compromise." *Masters of the Drama.* 3rd ed. New York: Dover, 1954, pp. 575–628.

Henderson, Archibald. *Bernard Shaw: Man of the Century.* New York: Apple-ton-Century-Crofts, 1956. (A detailed and comprehensive study of G.B.S. by his official biographer.)

Pearson, Hesketh. *George Bernard Shaw: His Life and Personality.* New York: Atheneum, 1963.

Purdom, C. B. *A Guide to the Plays of Bernard Shaw.* London: Methuen, 1963.

three ———————————————

MODERN
VERSE DRAMA

WE generally associate verse drama with the theatre of the past, with the Greeks, the Elizabethans, the Renaissance Italians, and the French neo-classic dramatists, Racine and Corneille. We tend to assume that the realistic movement in literature, which developed in the latter half of the nineteenth century, put an end to stage speech that did not try to imitate everyday speech. In recent years, however, various playwrights, Maxwell Anderson, T. S. Eliot, Christopher Fry, and Archibald MacLeish among the best known, have broken away from this realistic stage speech. These playwrights felt that prose drama did not offer a full range of connotative speech.

The actor will find in this section a representative selection of scenes from verse plays whose settings are both modern and historical. *Winterset* takes place in the present-day streets of New York; *Elizabeth the Queen* and *Mary of Scotland,* on the other hand, are set in sixteenth-century England, and *The Lady's Not for Burning* is set even earlier. *Cyrano de Bergerac* takes place in seventeenth-century France.

In each of these scenes the actor will need to communicate the *meaning* of the dialogue. This is the primary function of the actor with all dialogue, prose or poetry. But here, in addition, he must not neglect the beauty of the phrasing and rhythm. In modern verse plays, as in Greek and Elizabethan drama, poetic speech may produce an exhilaration difficult to achieve through prose.

The Lady's Not for Burning _____

CHRISTOPHER FRY (1948)

From Act III

SCENE: For one man, one woman

CHARACTERS: Humphrey Devize

Jennet Jourdemayne, an alleged witch

SETTING: A large room in the house of Hebble Tyson, Mayor of the little market town of Cool Clary, in England.

TIME: A lovely April evening sometime during the fifteenth century, "either more or less exactly."

SITUATION: The superstitious townspeople of the little English town of Cool Clary have become convinced that Jennet Jourdemayne is a witch. Jennet has been given the evening off to enjoy herself at a party before she faces the rather unpleasant business arranged for the next day. In the spirit of the evening she has joined in the merrymaking, although her heart is not quite in it. It seems she has no wish to burn. She has developed an attachment for a disillusioned soldier named Thomas Mendip, who is so fed up with the world that he wishes to be hanged and tells anyone who will listen that *he* is the devil. But no one believes him.

Humphrey Devize, a lecherous young man and the Mayor's nephew, has taken a fancy to Jennet and offers her a proposition which will help her escape her fate. Despite his seemingly serious theme, the author handles the material in a light-handed manner. We may classify the play simply as a comedy in verse.

HUMPHREY (*moves* D. *to* R. *of* JENNET)

. . . You have bewitched me. But not by scents

Of new-mown hell. For all I know you may

Have had some by-play with the Devil, and your eyes
May well be violets in a stealthy wood
Where souls are lost. If so, you will agree
The fire is fair, as fair goes: you have
To burn.

JENNET   It is hard to live last hours
As the earth deserves. Must you bring closer the time
When, as night yawns under my feet,
I shall be cast away in the chasm of dawn?
I am tired with keeping my thoughts clear of that verge.

HUMPHREY   But need you? These few hours of the night
Might be lived in a way which wouldn't end
In fire. It would be insufferable
If you were burned while you were strange to me.
I should never sit at ease in my body again.

JENNET   Must we talk of this? All there is
To be said has been said, and all in a heavy sentence;
There's nothing to add except a grave silence.

HUMPHREY   (*rises, moving* D.C.)
Listen, will you listen? There is more to say,
      (*breaks* L., *then leans on back of chair* L., *facing*
      her)
I am able to save you,
      (JENNET *sits chair* C.)
                              since all official action
Can be given official hesitation. I happen
To be on the Council, and a dozen reasons
Can be found to postpone the moment of execution:
Legal reasons, monetary reasons . . .
They've confiscated your property, and I can question
Whether your affairs may not be too disordered.
And once postponed, a great congestion of quibbles
Can be let loose over the Council table . . .

JENNET   Hope can break the heart, Humphrey. Hope
Can be too strong.

HUMPHREY   But this is true: actual
As my body is. And as for that . . . now, impartially
Look what I risk.
      (*sits in chair* L.C.)
                       If in any way you've loosened
The straps which hold in place our fairly workable
Wings of righteousness, and they say you have,
When my status in both this town and the after-life

Will be gone if either suspect me of having helped you
I have to be given a considerable reason
For risking that.

JENNET   I fondly hope I'm beginning
To misconstrue you.

HUMPHREY   (*rises and crosses in front of her to kneel on her* R.)
                 Later on tonight
When they've all gone small into their beauty sleep
I'll procure the key and come to your cell. Is that
Agreeable?

JENNET   Is it so to you?
Aren't you building your castles in foul air?

HUMPHREY   Foul? No; it's give and take, the basis
Of all understanding.

JENNET   You mean you give me a choice:
To sleep with you, or tomorrow to sleep with my fathers.
       (HUMPHREY *shrugs.*)
And if I value the gift of life,
Which, dear heaven, I do, I can scarcely refuse.

HUMPHREY   (*laughs*)
Isn't that sense?

JENNET   Admirable sense.
Oh, why, why am I not sensible?
Oddly enough, I hesitate. Can I
So dislike being cornered by a young lecher
That I would rather die? That would be
The maniac pitch of pride. Indeed it might
Even be sin. Can I believe my ears?
I seem to be considering heaven. And heaven,
From this angle, seems considerable.

HUMPHREY   (*rises and leans over* JENNET's *chair*)
Now, please, we're not going to confuse the soul and the body.
This, speaking bodily, is merely an exchange
Of compliments.

JENNET   And surely throwing away
My life for the sake of pride would seem to heaven
A bodily blasphemy, a suicide?

HUMPHREY   Even if heaven were interested. Or even
If you cared for heaven.
       (HUMPHREY *tries to kiss* JENNET, *she rises and*
       moves to below chair L.)
               Am I unattractive to you?

JENNET   Except that you have the manners of a sparrowhawk,

With less reason, no, you are not.
>   (HUMPHREY *takes a step toward her, she crosses*
>   *to* R.C.)
                                        But even so
I'd no more run to your arms than I wish to run
To death. I ask myself why. Surely I'm not
Mesmerised by some snake of chastity?
HUMPHREY   This isn't the time . . .
JENNET   Don't speak, contemptible boy,
>   I'll tell you: I am not. We have
>   To look elsewhere . . . for instance, into my heart
>   Where recently I heard begin a
>   Bell of longing which calls no one to church.
>   But need that, ringing away in vain,
>   Drown the milkmaid singing in my blood
>   And freeze into the tolling of my knell?
>   That would be pretty, indeed, but unproductive.
>   No, it's not that.
HUMPHREY   (*to above chair* C.)
>   Jennet, before they come
>   And interrupt us . . .
JENNET   (*crosses to above fire*)
>   I am interested
>   In my feelings, I seem to wish to have some importance
>   In the play of time. If not,
>   Then sad was my mother's pain, sad my breath,
>   Sad the articulation of my bones,
>   Sad, sad my alacritous web of nerves,
>   Woefully, woefully sad my wondering brain,
>   To be shaped and sharpened into such tendrils
>   Of anticipation, to feed the swamp of space.
>   What is deep as love is deep, I'll have
>   Deeply. What is good as love is good
>   I'll have well. Then if time and space
>   Have any purpose, I shall belong to it.
>   If not, if all is a pretty fiction
>   To distract the cherubim and seraphim
>   Who so continually do cry, the least
>   I can do is to fill the curled shell of the world
>   With human deep-sea sound, and hold it to
>   The ear of God, until he has appetite
>   To taste our salt sorrow on his lips.
>   (*sits stool*)

And so you see it might be better to die.
    (HUMPHREY *goes to her, kneels* R. *of her.*)
Though on the other hand, I admit it might
Be immensely foolish.
    (*a thundering noise from understage* D.L.)
                    Listen! What
Can all the thundering from the cellars be?

    [HUMPHREY *moves* C. JENNET *goes quickly to
    study door, then back to buttress, when caught
    by* HUMPHREY.]

HUMPHREY   I don't know at all.
    (*goes to her*)
                   You're simply playing for time.
    (*seizes her*)
Why can't you answer me before I'm thrown
By the bucking of my pulse, before Nicholas
Interrupts us? Will it be all right?
JENNET   Doesn't my plight seem pitiable to you?
HUMPHREY   (*leaning over her*)
Pitiable, yes. It makes me long for you
Intolerably. Now, be a saint, and tell me
I may come to your cell.

                .   .   .

                I wish I could believe
My freedom was not in the flames. Oh God, I wish
The ground would open.

Further Reading on Fry and *The Lady's Not for Burning*

Donoghue, Denis. *The Third Voice: Modern British and American Verse Drama.* Princeton: University Press, 1959, pp. 180–92.

Fry, Christopher. "The Author Explains." *World Review* (June, 1949), pp. 18–21.

Stanford, Derek. *Christopher Fry: An Appreciation.* London: Peter Nevill, 1951.

Recorded Performances

Slightly abridged performance: original Broadway cast, including Sir John Gielgud and Pamela Brown, Decca DX–110, two records.

Mary of Scotland

MAXWELL ANDERSON (1933)

From Act III

SCENE: For two women

CHARACTERS: Mary Stuart
Elizabeth Tudor

SETTING: A prison room in Carlisle Castle, in England. There are two windows, both barred.

TIME: An evening in the mid-sixteenth century.

SITUATION: *Mary of Scotland* is Maxwell Anderson's version of the historic conflict between the two queens Mary and Elizabeth. This conflict, both political and personal, was based in part on religion. Mary had been raised in France as a Catholic, and Elizabeth, daughter of Henry VIII, was raised as a Protestant. Through her own errors and through the political machinations of Elizabeth and her supporters, Mary has become Elizabeth's prisoner. Elizabeth offers Mary freedom if she will abdicate her throne. The alternative Mary faces is remaining for the rest of her life in prison, "darkened from news and from the sun." Mary's proud spirit, however, does not break, and she wins a moral victory in this, the final scene from the play. This scene is the first and only meeting between the two characters.

The actress will find it of interest to compare the portrait Anderson paints of Elizabeth in this play and the Elizabeth in his earlier play, *Elizabeth the Queen* (see p. 270).

ELIZABETH   You came here by your own road.
MARY   I see how I came.
　　Back, back, each step the wrong way, and each sign followed
　　As you'd have me go, till the skein picks up and we stand
　　Face to face here. It was you forced Bothwell from me—

You there, and always. Oh, I'm to blame in this, too!
I should have seen your hand!
ELIZABETH   It has not been my use
To speak much or spend my time—
MARY   How could I have been
Mistaken in you for an instant?
ELIZABETH   You were not mistaken.
I am all women I must be. One's a young girl,
Young and harrowed as you are—one who could weep
To see you here—and one's a bitterness
At what I have lost and can never have, and one's
The basilisk you saw. This last stands guard
And I obey it. Lady, you came to Scotland
A fixed and subtle enemy, more dangerous
To me than you've ever known. This could not be borne,
And I set myself to cull you out and down,
And down you are.
MARY   When was I your enemy?
ELIZABETH   Your life was a threat to mine, your throne to my throne,
Your policy a threat.
MARY   How? Why?
ELIZABETH   It was you
Or I. Do you know that? The one of us must win
And I must always win. Suppose one lad
With a knife in his hand, a Romish lad who planted
That knife between my shoulders—my kingdom was yours.
It was too easy. You might not have wished it.
But you'd take it if it came.
MARY   And you'd take my life
And love to avoid this threat?
ELIZABETH   Nay, keep your life.
And your love, too. The lords have brought a parchment
For you to sign. Sign it and live.
MARY   If I sign it
Do I live where I please? Go free?
ELIZABETH   Nay, I would you might,
But you'd go to Bothwell, and between you two
You might be too much for Moray. You'll live with me
In London. There are other loves, my dear.
You'll find amusement there in the court. I assure you
It's better than a cell.
MARY   And if I will not sign
This abdication?

ELIZABETH You've tasted prison. Try
  A diet of it.
MARY And so I will.
ELIZABETH I can wait.
MARY And I can wait. I can better wait than you.
  Bothwell will fight free again. Kirkaldy
  Will fight beside him, and others will spring up
  From these dragon's teeth you've sown. Each week that passes
  I'll be stronger, and Moray weaker.
ELIZABETH And do you fancy
  They'll rescue you from an English prison? Why,
  Let them try it.
MARY Even that they may do. I wait for Bothwell—
  And wait for him here.
ELIZABETH Where you will wait, bear in mind,
  Is for me to say. Give up Bothwell, give up your throne
  If you'd have a life worth living.
MARY I will not.
ELIZABETH I can wait.
MARY And will not because you play to lose. This trespass
  Against God's right will be known. The nations will know it,
  Mine and yours. They will see you as I see you
  And pull you down.
ELIZABETH Child, child, I've studied this gambit
  Before I play it. I will send each year
  This paper to you. Not signing, you will step
  From one cell to another, step lower always,
  Till you reach the last, forgotten, forgotten of men,
  Forgotten among causes, a wraith that cries
  To fallen gods in another generation
  That's lost your name. Wait then for Bothwell's rescue.
  It will never come.
MARY I may never see him?
ELIZABETH Never.
  It would not be wise.
MARY And suppose indeed you won
  Within our life-time, still looking down from the heavens
  And up from men around us, God's spies that watch
  The fall of great and little, they will find you out—
  I will wait for that, wait longer than a life,
  Till men and the times unscroll you, study the tricks
  You play, and laugh, as I shall laugh, being known
  Your better, haunted by your demon, driven

To death, or exile by you, unjustly. Why,
When all's done, it's my name I care for, my name and heart,
To keep them clean. Win now, take your triumph now,
For I'll win men's hearts in the end—though the sifting takes
This hundred years—or a thousand.

ELIZABETH   Child, child, are you gulled
By what men write in histories, this or that,
And never true? I am careful of my name
As you are, for this day and longer. It's not what happens
That matters, no, not even what happens that's true,
But what men believe to have happened. They will believe
The worst of you, the best of me, and that
Will be true of you and me. I have seen to this.
What will be said about us in after-years
By men to come, I control that, being who I am.
It will be said of me that I governed well,
And wisely, but of you, cousin, that your life,
Shot through with ill-loves, battened on lechery, made you
An ensign of evil, that men tore down and trampled.
Shall I call for the lord's parchment?

MARY   This will be said—?
But who will say it? It's a lie—will be known as a lie!

ELIZABETH   You lived with Bothwell before Darnley died,
You and Bothwell murdered Darnley.

MARY   And that's a lie!

ELIZABETH   Your letters, my dear. Your letters to Bothwell prove it.
We have those letters.

MARY   Then they're forged and false!
For I never wrote them!

ELIZABETH   It may be they were forged.
But will that matter, Mary, if they're believed?
All history is forged.

MARY   You would do this?

ELIZABETH   It is already done.

MARY   And still I win.
A demon has no children, and you have none,
Will have none, can have none, perhaps. This crooked track
You've drawn me on, cover it, let it not be believed
That a woman was a fiend. Yes, cover it deep,
And heap my infamy over it, lest men peer
And catch sight of you as you were and are. In myself
I know you to be an eater of dust. Leave me here

And set me lower this year by year, as you promise,
Till the last is an oubliette, and my name inscribed
On the four winds. Still, STILL I win! I have been
A woman, and I have loved as a woman loves,
Lost as a woman loses. I have borne a son,
And he will rule Scotland—and England. You have no heir!
A devil has no children.

ELIZABETH   By God, you shall suffer
For this, but slowly.

MARY   And that I can do. A woman
Can do that. Come, turn the key. I have a hell
For you in mind, where you will burn and feel it,
Live where you like, and softly.

ELIZABETH   Once more I ask you,
And patiently. Give up your throne.

MARY   No, devil.
My pride is stronger than yours, and my heart beats blood
Such as yours has never known. And in this dungeon,
I win here, alone.

ELIZABETH   (*turning*)
Goodnight, then.

MARY   Aye, goodnight.

> (ELIZABETH *goes to the door, which opens before
> her. She goes out slowly. As the door begins to
> close upon her* MARY *calls*)

Beaton.

ELIZABETH   (*turning*)
You will not see your maids again,
I think. It's said they bring you news from the north.

MARY   I thank you for all kindness.

> [ELIZABETH *goes out.* MARY *stands for a moment
> in thought, then walks to the wall and lays her
> hand against the stone, pushing outward. The
> stone is cold, and she shudders. Going to the win-
> dow she sits again in her old place and looks
> out into the darkness.*]

Reference Key to Plays in Anthologies

A copy of the complete play may be found in the following volume:
Number 71.

An abridged version of the play may be found in

Mantle, Burns. *The Best Plays of 1933–1934.* New York: Dodd, Mead, 1934.

Further Reading on Anderson and *Mary of Scotland*

Bailey, Mabel Driscoll. *Maxwell Anderson: The Playwright as Prophet.* London:
Abelard-Schuman, 1957.
Carmer, Carl. "Maxwell Anderson: Poet and Champion." *Theatre Arts Monthly,*
Vol. 17, No. 6 (June, 1933), pp. 437–46.
Foster, Edward. "Core of Belief: An Interpretation of the Plays of Maxwell
Anderson." *Sewanee Review,* Vol. 50, No. 1 (January, 1942), pp. 87–100.

Winterset

MAXWELL ANDERSON (1935)

From Act III

SCENE: For one man, one woman

CHARACTERS: Mio, aged seventeen
Miriamne, aged fifteen

SETTING: Near the East River by a tenement area in New York City, in the shadow of an enormous bridge.

TIME: An evening in the 1930's.

SITUATION: The plot of *Winterset* is based on the Sacco-Vanzetti murder case of the 1920's. Mio, a seventeen-year-old boy, is determined to avenge the death of his father, who was unjustly executed for murder. While tracing a key witness to the original crime, Mio meets and falls in love with Miriamne, but discovers that he cannot take revenge for his father's death without injuring Miriamne and her brother, who was the witness to the murder. As the real murderers learn of Mio's investigations, they prepare to kill him. Unable to clear his father without destroying his relationship with Miriamne, Mio sees no alternative to death. Mio says farewell to Miriamne, knowing that the murderers are waiting for him in the next street.

MIO *(looking up)*
Now all you silent powers
that make the sleet and dark, and never yet
have spoken, give us a sign, let the throw be ours
this once, on this longest night, when the winter sets
his foot on the threshold leading up to spring
and enters with remembered cold—let fall
some mercy with the rain. We are two lovers
here in your night, and we wish to live.

MIRIAMNE   Oh, Mio—
    if you pray that way, nothing good will come!
    You're bitter, Mio.
MIO   How many floors has this building?
MIRIAMNE   Five or six. It's not as high as the bridge.
MIO   No, I thought not. How many pomegranate seeds
    did you eat, Persephone?
MIRIAMNE   Oh, darling, darling,
    if you die, don't die alone.
MIO   I'm afraid I'm damned
    to hell, and you're not damned at all. Good God,
    how long he takes to climb![1]
MIRIAMNE   The stairs are steep.

        [*a slight pause*]

MIO   I'll follow him.
MIRAMNE   He's there—at the window—now.
    He waves you to go back, not to go in.
    Mio, see, that path between the rocks—
    they're not watching that—they're out at the river—
    I can see them there—they can't watch both—
    it leads to a street above.
MIO   I'll try it, then.
    Kiss me. You'll hear. But if you never hear—
    then I'm the king of hell, Persephone,
    and I'll expect you.
MIRIAMNE   Oh, lover, keep safe.
MIO   Good-bye.
        (*He slips out quickly between the rocks. There is
        a quick machine gun rat-tat. . . .* MIRIAMNE *runs
        toward the path.* MIO *comes back slowly, a hand
        pressed under his heart.*)
    It seems you were mistaken.
MIRIAMNE   Oh, God, forgive me!
        (*She puts an arm round him. He sinks to his
        knees.*)
    Where is it, Mio? Let me help you in! Quick, quick,
    let me help you!
MIO   I hadn't thought to choose—this—ground—
    but it will do.

        [*He slips down.*]

MIRIAMNE   Oh, God, forgive me!

1 Miriamne's reference is to her father, Esdras, who is in an adjacent building.

MIO Yes?
    The king of hell was not forgiven then,
    Dis is his name, and Hades is his home—
    and he goes alone—
MIRIAMNE Why does he bleed so? Mio, if you go
    I shall go with you.
MIO It's better to stay alive.
    I wanted to stay alive—because of you—
    I leave you that—and what he said to me dying:
    I love you, and will love you after I die.
    Tomorrow, I shall still love you, as I've loved
    the stars I'll never see, and all the mornings
    that might have been yours and mine. Oh, Miriamne,
    you taught me this.
MIRIAMNE If only I'd never seen you
    then you could live—
MIO That's blasphemy—Oh, God,
    there might have been some easier way of it.
    You didn't want me to die, did you, Miriamne—?
    You didn't send me away—?
MIRIAMNE Oh, never, never—
MIO Forgive me—kiss me—I've got blood on your lips—
    I'm sorry—it doesn't matter—I'm sorry—

                        .   .   .

MIRIAMNE Mio—
    I'd have gone to die myself—you must hear this, Mio,
    I'd have died to help you—you must listen, sweet,
    you must hear it—(*She rises.*)
        I can die, too, see! You! There!
    You in the shadows—You killed him to silence him!
        (*She walks toward the path.*)
    But I'm not silenced! All that he knew I know,
    and I'll tell it tonight! Tonight—
    tell it and scream it
    through all the streets—that Trock's a murderer
    and he hired you for this murder!   .
    Your work's not done—
    and you won't live long! Do you hear?
    You're murderers, and I know who you are!
        (*The machine gun speaks again. She sinks to her
        knees.*)

                        .   .   .

    (*She crawls toward* MIO.)

Look, Mio! They killed me, too. Oh, you can believe me
now, Mio. You can believe I wouldn't hurt you,
because I'm dying! Why doesn't he answer me?
Oh, now he'll never know!

[*She sinks down, her hand over her mouth, choking.*]

Reference Key to Plays in Anthologies

Copies of the complete play may be found in the following selected volumes:
Numbers 42, 69, 80, 82.

Further Reading on Anderson and *Winterset*

Adler, Jacob H. "Shakespeare in *Winterset*." *Educational Theatre Journal*, Vol.
6, No. 3 (October, 1954), pp. 241–8.
Bailey, Mabel Driscoll. *Maxwell Anderson: The Playwright as Prophet*. London:
Abelard-Schuman, 1957.
Wall, Vincent. "Maxwell Anderson: The Last Anarchist." *Sewanee Review*, Vol.
49, No. 3 (July, 1941), pp. 339–69.

Cyrano de Bergerac _____

EDMOND ROSTAND (1897)

translated by BRIAN HOOKER

From Act V

SCENE:	For one man, one woman
CHARACTERS:	Cyrano de Bergerac Roxane
SETTING:	The park of the convent occupied by the Ladies of the Cross, Paris.
TIME:	An afternoon in late October, 1665.
SITUATION:	In almost every respect Cyrano is the perfect hero. He is a great swordsman and soldier, philosopher and poet. His prodigious feats are matched only by his nose, likewise prodigious. Ashamed because of his ugliness to profess his love for his cousin Roxane, he helped his rival to woo her, even speaking himself the words that eventually won her for Christian. All this was unknown to Roxane, who always believed that the beautiful words she heard in the dark from beneath her balcony were spoken by Christian.

Fifteen years before this scene, Christian was killed in battle. In order to preserve her husband's memory, Roxane entered a convent. Cyrano has come to the convent every week since, bringing Roxane the court news. In all this time he has never told her the truth. This day is different, however, for Cyrano has been mortally wounded in an "accident." Despite the gaping wound in his head, Cyrano keeps his weekly appointment.

(This translation of *Cyrano* is the famous Brian Hooker version, made especially for the highly successful production which starred Walter Hampden in the 1920's.)

CYRANO (*returns to* ROXANE, *who is bending over her work*)
                              Now, may the devil
    Admire me, if I ever hope to see
    The end of that embroidery!
ROXANE (*smiling*)
                              I thought
    It was time you said that.

    [*A breath of wind causes a few leaves to fall.*]

CYRANO   The leaves—
ROXANE (*raises her head and looks away through the trees*)
                              What color—
    Perfect Venetian red! Look at them fall.
CYRANO Yes—they know how to die. A little way
    From the branch to the earth, a little fear
    Of mingling with the common dust—and yet
    They go down gracefully—a fall that seems
    Like flying!
ROXANE   Melancholy—you?
CYRANO   Why, no,
    Roxane!
ROXANE Then let the leaves fall. Tell me now
    The Court news—my gazette!
CYRANO   Let me see—
ROXANE   Ah!
CYRANO (*more and more pale, struggling against pain*)
    Saturday, the nineteenth: The King fell ill,
    After eight helpings of grape marmalade.
    His malady was brought before the court,
    Found guilty of high treason; whereupon
    His Majesty revived. The royal pulse
    Is now normal. Sunday, the twentieth:
    The Queen gave a grand ball, at which they burned
    Seven hundred and sixty-three wax candles. Note:
    They say our troops have been victorious
    In Austria. Later: Three sorcerers
    Have been hung. Special post: The little dog
    Of Madame d'Athis was obliged to take
    Four pills before—
ROXANE   Monsieur de Bergerac,
    Will you kindly be quiet!
CYRANO   Monday . . . nothing.
    Lygdamire has a new lover.

ROXANE　　　　　　　　　　　　Oh!

CYRANO　(*his face more and more altered*)
　　　　　　　　　　　　　　　Tuesday,
The twenty-second: All the court has gone
To Fontainebleau. Wednesday: The Comte de Fiesque
Spoke to Madame de Montglat; she said No.
Thursday: Mancini was the Queen of France
Or—very nearly! Friday: La Montglat
Said Yes. Saturday, twenty-sixth. . . .

　　[*His eyes close; his head sinks back; silence.*]

ROXANE　(*surprised at not hearing any more, turns, looks at him, and
　　rises, frightened*)
He has fainted—
　　(*She runs to him, crying out.*)
Cyrano!

CYRANO　(*opens his eyes*)
　　　　　What . . . What is it? . . .
　　(*He sees* ROXANE *leaning over him, and quickly
　　pulls his hat down over his head and leans back
　　away from her in the chair.*)
　　　　　　　　　　　　No—oh no—
It is nothing—truly!

ROXANE　　　　　　　　But—

CYRANO　　　　　　　　　　My old wound—
At Arras—sometimes—you know. . . .

ROXANE　　　　　　　　　　　　My poor friend!

CYRANO　Oh it is nothing; it will soon be gone. . . .
　　(*forcing a smile*)
There! It is gone!

ROXANE　(*standing close to him*)
　　　　　　　　　　We all have our old wounds—
I have mine—here . . .
　　(*her hand at her breast*)
　　　　　　　　　　under this faded scrap
Of writing. . . . It is hard to read now—all
But the blood—and the tears. . . .

　　[*Twilight begins to fall.*]

CYRANO　　　　　　　　　　His letter! . . . Did you Not promise me that some day . . . that some day. . . .
You would let me read it?

ROXANE　　　　　　　　His letter?—You . . .
You wish—

CYRANO   I do wish it—to-day.

ROXANE   (*gives him the little silken bag from around her neck*)

Here. . . .

CYRANO   May I . . . open it?

ROXANE   Open it, and read.

> [*She goes back to her work, folds it again, rear-*
> *ranges her silks.*]

CYRANO   (*unfolds the letter; reads*)

"Farewell Roxane, because to-day I die—"

ROXANE   (*looks up, surprised*)

Aloud?

CYRANO   (*reads*)

"I know that it will be to-day
My own dearly beloved—and my heart
Still so heavy with love I have not told,
And I die without telling you! No more
Shall my eyes drink the sight of you like wine,
Never more, with a look that is a kiss,
Follow the sweet grace of you—"

ROXANE   How you read it—

His letter!

CYRANO   (*continues*)

"I remember now the way
You have, of pushing back a lock of hair
With one hand, from your forehead—and my heart
Cries out—"

ROXANE   His letter . . . and you read it so . . .

> [*The darkness increases imperceptibly.*]

CYRANO   "Cries out and keeps crying: 'Farewell, my dear,
My dearest—'"

ROXANE   In a voice. . . .

CYRANO   "—My own heart's own,
My own treasure—"

ROXANE   (*dreamily*)

In such a voice. . . .

CYRANO   "—My love—"

ROXANE   —As I remember hearing . . .

(*She trembles.*)

                      —long ago. . . .

> [*She comes near him, softly, without his seeing*
> *her; passes the chair, leans over silently, look-*
> *ing at the letter. The darkness increases.*]

CYRANO "—I am never away from you. Even now,
I shall not leave you. In another world,
I shall be still that one who loves you, loves you
Beyond measure, beyond—"
ROXANE (*lays her hand on his shoulder*)
                              How can you read
Now? It is dark. . . .
        (*He starts, turns, and sees her there close to him.
        A little movement of surprise, almost of fear;
        then he bows his head. A long pause; then in the
        twilight now completely fallen, she says very
        softly, clasping her hands*)
                              And all these fourteen years,
He has been the old friend, who came to me
To be amusing.
CYRANO   Roxane!—
ROXANE   It was you.
CYRANO No, no, Roxane, no!
ROXANE   And I might have known,
Every time that I heard you speak my name! . . .
CYRANO No— It was not I—
ROXANE   It was . . . you!
CYRANO   I swear—
ROXANE I understand everything now: The letters—
That was you. . . .
CYRANO   No!
ROXANE   And the dear, foolish words—
That was you. . . .
CYRANO   No!
ROXANE   And the voice . . . in the dark. . . .
That was . . . you!
CYRANO   On my honor—
ROXANE   And . . . the Soul!—
That was all you.
CYRANO   I never loved you—
ROXANE   Yes,
You loved me.
CYRANO (*desperately*)
                No— He loved you—
ROXANE   Even now,
You love me!
CYRANO (*His voice weakens.*)
                No!

ROXANE (*smiling*)
                    And why . . . so great a "No"?
CYRANO No, no, my own dear love, I love you not! . . .

    [*pause*]

ROXANE How many things have died . . . and are newborn! . . .
    Why were you silent for so many years,
    All the while, every night and every day,
    He gave me nothing—you knew that— You knew
    Here, in this letter lying on my breast,
    Your tears— You knew they were your tears—
CYRANO (*holds the letter out to her*)
                                    The blood

    Was his.

Reference Key to Plays in Anthologies

Copies of the complete play may be found in the following selected volumes:
    Numbers 10, 14, 20, 42.

Alternate translations may also be found in the following volumes:
    Numbers 74, 82.

Further Reading on Rostand and *Cyrano de Bergerac*

Butler, Mildred Allen. "The Historical Cyrano de Bergerac as a Basis for
    Rostand's Play." *Educational Theatre Journal*, Vol. 6, No. 3 (October, 1954),
    pp. 231–40.
Gassner, John. *A Treasury of the Theatre*. Pt. 2, *From Ibsen to Ionesco*. 3rd
    ed. New York: Holt, Rinehart and Winston, 1960, pp. 274–5.
Smith, Hugh Allison. *Main Currents of Modern French Drama*. New York:
    Henry Holt, 1925, pp. 76–107. (An interesting analysis of Rostand and
    Cyrano written at the time of the play's famous revival in New York with
    Walter Hampden as Cyrano.)

Recorded Performances

Complete performance:
Sir Ralph Richardson as Cyrano, Caedmon 306 (stereo S–306), three records.

Abridged performance:
José Ferrer as Cyrano, Capitol W–283, one record.

Scenes in French:
Period 1526, one record.

Elizabeth the Queen ————————————

Maxwell Anderson (1930)
From Act II, Scene 3

SCENE: For one man, one woman

CHARACTERS: Queen Elizabeth of England
Lord Essex

SETTING: The council chamber in the palace at Whitehall, London.

TIME: The late sixteenth century.

SITUATION: The relationship between Queen Elizabeth and Lord Essex is more than that of queen and subject; they are deeply in love despite the fact that Elizabeth is many years older than Essex. In order to quell the Irish rebellion, Elizabeth sends Essex to Ireland with a military force. Essex returns to England at the head of a rebellion to unseat Elizabeth. His army is in London awaiting his orders. This confrontation between Essex and Elizabeth follows immediately Essex's arrival in London. Both Elizabeth and Essex here face a choice between love and power.

ELIZABETH   What did you write me?
ESSEX   I wrote you my love—for I thought you loved me then—
And then I pled with you not to bring me home
In the midst of my mission—and then at last angrily—
For I had not heard—but always to say I loved you—
Always.
ELIZABETH   But is this true?
ESSEX   Would I lie?
ELIZABETH   Some one
Has lied and will pay with his life if this is true!—
Before God and hell—some one will pay for this.
ESSEX   What did you write me?

FROM *Elizabeth the Queen* by Maxwell Anderson. Copyright 1930 by Longmans, Green & Co. Copyright renewed 1957 by Maxwell Anderson. All rights reserved. Reprinted by permission of Anderson House.

270 MODERN VERSE DRAMA

ELIZABETH   I wrote—my love—
   God keep you safe—I know not—and then, not hearing,
   I wrote God knows what madness—as to a rebel—
   Thinking you no longer mine—faithless!
   Thinking—
ESSEX   I would I had known—I was in torment—
   I—forgive me—
ELIZABETH   You should never have gone away.
   God, how I've hated you!—
ESSEX   No!
ELIZABETH   Planned to put you to torture!
ESSEX   I have been in torture!
   (*He steps toward her.*)
ELIZABETH   Not yet—I can't breathe yet—I can't breathe—
   Or think or believe—
ESSEX   Nor I.
ELIZABETH   Can we ever—
   Believe again? Can it be as it used to be?
ESSEX   We can make it so.
ELIZABETH   Come, kill me if you will. Put your arms round me—
   If you love me. Do you still love me?
ESSEX   Yes.
ELIZABETH   Yes, yes—
   If this were false, then, then truly—then I should die.
   I thought because I was older—you see—someone else—
ESSEX   No one—never a breath—
ELIZABETH   Is it all, all as before?
ESSEX   We have not changed.
ELIZABETH   No. Yes, a little, perhaps. They have changed us a little.
ESSEX   Not I. I have not changed.
ELIZABETH   Can I trust you now?
ESSEX   Sweet, think back, all those months,
   All those hideous months! No word, no love.
   And then word did come, it was to make me prisoner!
   Christ, I have pride!
   And though I came here in defiance, I came truly to find you
   Who have been lost from me.
ELIZABETH   Do you ask forgiveness?
   It is all forgiven.
ESSEX   Then, why then, hell's vanished—
   And here's heaven risen out of it, a heaven of years
   In the midst of desolate centuries.
ELIZABETH   We have so few years.

Let us make them doubly sweet, these years we have,
Be gracious with each other, sway a little
To left or right if we must to stay together—
Never distrust each other—nay, distrust
All others, when they whisper. Let us make this our pact
Now, for the fates are desperate to part us
And the very gods envy this happiness
We pluck out of loss and death.

ESSEX If two stand shoulder to shoulder against the gods,
Happy together, the gods themselves are helpless
Against them, while they stand so.

ELIZABETH Love, I will be
Your servant. Command me. What would you have?

ESSEX Why nothing—

ELIZABETH Take this my world, my present in your hands!
You shall stand back of my chair and together we
Shall build an England to make the old world wonder
And the new world worship!—What is this doubt in your brow?

ESSEX I am troubled to be dishonest. I have brought my army
Here to the palace—and though it's all true that we've said—
No letters—utter agony over long months—
It is something in myself that has made me do this,
Not Cecil—nor anyone. No one but myself.
The rest is all excuse.

ELIZABETH Speak what you will.

ESSEX If you had but shown anger I could have spoken
Easily. It's not easy now, but speak I must!
Oh, I've thought much about this
On lonely marches and in distant tents,
Thinking of you and me. I say this now
Without rancor—in all friendliness and love—
The throne is yours by right of descent and by
Possession—but if this were a freer time,
And there were election, I should carry the country before me,
And this being true, and we being equal in love,
Should we not be equal in power as well?

ELIZABETH We are equal.
I have made you so.

ESSEX Yes, but still it's all yours—
Yours to grant me now or take away.

ELIZABETH How could this well be otherwise?

ESSEX Am I not—and I say this too in all love—
As worthy to be king as you to be queen?

Must you be sovereign alone?

ELIZABETH You are young in policy,
My Essex, if you do not see that if I
Should grant high place to you now it would show ill to the kingdom—
It would be believed that you had forced this on me,
Would be called a revolution. It would undermine
All confidence. What is built up for years
In people's minds blows away like thistledown
When such things get abroad.

ESSEX But is this your reason
Or have you another? Would you trust me as King?

ELIZABETH No.

ESSEX And are you still reluctant to give up
Your prerogatives?

ELIZABETH Yes.

ESSEX Then now, when the country is mine, the court in my hands,
You my prisoner, I must send my men away,
Disband my army, give back your kingdom to you,
And know I have been king for a moment only
And never will be again?

ELIZABETH I am your prisoner?

ESSEX The palace and the city are in my hands.
This England is mine now for the taking—

ELIZABETH This is your friendship! This is your love!

ESSEX As water finds its level, so power goes
To him who can use it, and soon or late the name
Of king follows where power is.

ELIZABETH Oh, my Essex,
You are a child in war as you are in council.
Why all this talk of power? No army opposed you
When your troops came the road from Ireland.
    No guard was set
To stop your entrance with your thousand halberds.
Shall I tell you why? Because I wished to keep
A semblance of peace between us. And for that,
I am your prisoner!

ESSEX Yes. My dear prisoner.

ELIZABETH Now I do know at least
What it was you wanted. You wanted my kingdom.
    You have it.
Make the best of it. And so shall I.
What are your plans?

ESSEX I have none.

ELIZABETH   The Tower, the block—
  You could hardly take a queen prisoner and have no thought
  Of her destiny. I am my mother's daughter,
  I too can walk the path my mother walked.
ESSEX   These are heroics. You know you are free as air.
ELIZABETH   If I do as you ask.
ESSEX   Is it so hard to share your power with your love?
  I could have all—and I offer to share with you.
ELIZABETH   Let's have no more pretending.
  I'd have given all—but you came with an army, demanding—
  In short, you don't love—nor trust me—no—nor want me—
ESSEX   God knows I have wanted you. I have wanted power—
  Believed myself fitted to hold it—but not without you.
ELIZABETH   If you had wanted me would you rise and strike
  At me with an army? Never, never! You'd have come
  To me quietly, and we'd have talked of it together
  As lovers should—and we'd both have our way—
  And no one the wiser. But now, to take the palace,
  Hold me prisoner—no—what you wanted you've taken—
  And that is all you shall have. This is your kingdom—
  But I—I am not yours.
ESSEX   But I am yours
  And have been.
ELIZABETH   Who will believe that? Not the world,
  No, and not I. I'd rather go to the Tower
  Than share my place on terms like these.
      Put me where I
  Will do least harm.
ESSEX   I cannot, could not, will not.
ELIZABETH   If I could have given freely—
  But not now. Not surrendering. Not to a victor.
ESSEX   I am no victor if I lose you. The only gift
  That I could take from you is that we are equals.
ELIZABETH   Yes, but not now.
ESSEX   I ask one word from you.
  Give me this word—this one word—and these soldiers
  Shall leave, and you shall be free.
ELIZABETH   I'll believe that
  When it happens.
ESSEX   I'll believe you when you promise.
ELIZABETH   Then you have my promise.
  You shall share the realm with me. As I am queen,
  I promise it.

ESSEX   Then this is my answer.
    (*He kisses her, then calls*)
    Marvel!—Marvel!
        (MARVEL *enters.*)
    Carry out the order of release. Dismiss my guard—
    Return the palace into the queen's hands.
    Retire with all our forces to the Strand.
    Release all prisoners. Release the queen's guard
    And send them to their stations.
        (MARVEL *goes out.*)
    The palace will be
    Returned as quickly as taken. This is our last quarrel.
ELIZABETH   Yes—our last.

Reference Key to Plays in Anthologies

Copies of the complete play may be found in the following selected volumes:
    Numbers 42, 69, 72, 80, 82.

Further Reading on Anderson and *Elizabeth the Queen*

Bailey, Mabel Driscoll. *Maxwell Anderson: The Playwright as Prophet.* London:
    Abelard-Schuman, 1957.
Carmer, Carl. "Maxwell Anderson: Poet and Champion." *Theatre Arts Monthly,*
    Vol. 17, No. 6 (June, 1933), pp. 437–46.
Foster, Edward. "Core of Belief: An Interpretation of the Plays of Maxwell
    Anderson." *Sewanee Review,* Vol. 50, No. 1 (January, 1942), pp. 87–100.

four _____

SCENES FROM SHAKESPEARE

THE following scenes from the plays of Shakespeare provide a small
sample of the rich variety of dramatic situations and characters
available in the works of England's greatest dramatist. The diversity of
characters and the frequent nobility of language will challenge the actor
accustomed to contemporary realistic theatre.

The exercises have been chosen in order to provide a balanced mixture
of scenes for two men, for two women, and for one man and one woman.
Unlike the earlier exercises in this book, the Shakespeare exercises do not
include lists of anthologies or recommended readings. Complete editions
of the works of Shakespeare are readily available. Critical studies of the
plays are so numerous that to give a brief representative listing would be
impossible. At the end of this chapter, however, is a short list of works that
deal with problems in performing Shakespeare.

The list of recorded performances following each scene does not attempt to be comprehensive, but rather to suggest modern performances
that the actor may find helpful. The performances by the Marlowe Society
are complete; most of the others have been cut to conform to modern stage
productions.

Othello

WILLIAM SHAKESPEARE (c. 1604)

From Act IV, Scene 3

SCENE: For two women

CHARACTERS: Desdemona, wife of Othello
Emilia, friend and attendant of Desdemona

SETTING: Desdemona's bedchamber in a castle on the island of Cyprus.

TIME: An evening in the sixteenth century.

SITUATION: Othello, the Moor, commander of the Venetian military forces, has married Desdemona despite the violent protests of her father, Brabantio, a Venetian senator. Placed in charge of the forces on Cyprus, Othello is reunited there with Desdemona after the defeat of the Turkish fleet. He entrusts Desdemona to Iago and his wife, Emilia, unaware that Iago hates him because Othello promoted Cassio rather than Iago to the rank of lieutenant. Through a series of carefully planned incidents and suggestive remarks, Iago causes Othello to doubt Desdemona's honesty and virtue.

Desdemona becomes more and more distraught over Othello's behavior toward her. In this scene Emilia, innocent of her husband's plans to destroy Desdemona and Othello, tries to comfort Desdemona as she helps her prepare for bed.

See also the following scene from *Othello* (p. 282), which occurs later in the play.

EMILIA How goes it now? he looks gentler than he did.
DESDEMONA He says he will return incontinent:
  He hath commanded me to go to bed,
  And bade me to dismiss you.
EMILIA   Dismiss me!
DESDEMONA It was his bidding; therefore, good Emilia,
  Give me my nightly wearing, and adieu:
  We must not now displease him.
EMILIA I would you had never seen him!

DESDEMONA So would not I: my love doth so approve him,
That even his stubbornness, his checks, his frowns,—
Prithee, unpin me,—have grace and favour in them.

EMILIA I have laid those sheets you bade me on the bed.

DESDEMONA All's one. Good faith, how foolish are our minds!
If I do die before thee, prithee, shroud me
In one of those same sheets.

EMILIA   Come, come, you talk.

DESDEMONA My mother had a maid call'd Barbara:
She was in love, and he she loved proved mad
And did forsake her: she had a song of "willow";
An old thing 'twas, but it express'd her fortune,
And she died singing it: that song to-night
Will not go from my mind; I have much to do,
But to go hang my head all at one side,
And sing it like poor Barbara. Prithee, dispatch.

EMILIA Shall I go fetch your night-gown?

DESDEMONA   No, unpin me here.
This Lodovico is a proper man.

EMILIA A very handsome man.

DESDEMONA He speaks well.

EMILIA I know a lady in Venice would have walked barefoot to Pales-
tine for a touch of his nether lip.

DESDEMONA (singing)
"The poor soul sat sighing by a sycamore tree,
    Sing all a green willow;
Her hand on her bosom, her head on her knee,
    Sing willow, willow, willow:
The fresh streams ran by her, and murmur'd her moans;
    Sing willow, willow, willow;
Her salt tears fell from her, and soften'd the stones;—"
Lay by these:—
    (singing)
"Sing willow, willow, willow";
Prithee, hie thee; he'll come anon:—
    (singing)
"Sing all a green willow must be my garland.
Let nobody blame him; his scorn I approve,—"
Nay, that's not next.—Hark! who is 't that knocks?

EMILIA It's the wind.

DESDEMONA (singing)
"I call'd my love false love; but what said he then?
    Sing willow, willow, willow:

If I court moe women, you'll couch with moe men."—
So, get thee gone; good night. Mine eyes do itch;
Doth that bode weeping?

EMILIA   'Tis neither here nor there.

DESDEMONA   I have heard it said so. O, these men, these men!
Dost thou in conscience think,—tell me, Emilia,—
That there be women do abuse their husbands
In such gross kind?

EMILIA   There be some such, no question.

DESDEMONA   Wouldst thou do such a deed for all the world?

EMILIA   Why, would not you?

DESDEMONA   No, by this heavenly light!

EMILIA   Nor I neither by this heavenly light;
I might do 't as well i' the dark.

DESDEMONA   Wouldst thou do such a deed for all the world?

EMILIA   The world's a huge thing: it is a great price
For a small vice.

DESDEMONA   In troth, I think thou wouldst not.

EMILIA   In troth, I think I should; and undo 't when I had done. Marry, I
would not do such a thing for a joint-ring, nor for measures of lawn,
nor for gowns, petticoats, nor caps, nor any petty exhibition; but, for
the whole world,—why, who would not make her husband a cuckold to
make him a monarch? I should venture purgatory for 't.

DESDEMONA   Beshrew me, if I would do such a wrong
For the whole world.

EMILIA   Why, the wrong is but a wrong i' the world; and having the
world for your labour, 'tis a wrong in your own world, and you might
quickly make it right.

DESDEMONA   I do not think there is any such woman.

EMILIA   Yes, a dozen; and as many to the vantage as would store the
world they played for.
But I do think it is their husbands' faults
If wives do fall: say that they slack their duties,
And pour our treasures into foreign laps,
Or else break out in peevish jealousies,
Throwing restraint upon us; or say they strike us,
Or scant our former having in despite;
Why, we have galls, and though we have some grace,
Yet have we some revenge. Let husbands know
Their wives have sense like them: they see and smell
And have their palates both for sweet and sour,
As husbands have. What is it that they do
When they change us for others? Is it sport?

I think it is: and doth affection breed it?
I think it doth: is 't frailty that thus errs?
It is so too: and have not we affections,
Desires for sport, and frailty, as men have?
Then let them use us well: else let them know,
The ills we do, their ills instruct us so.

DESDEMONA   Good night, good night: heaven me such uses send,
Not to pick bad from bad, but by bad mend!

Recorded Performances

Complete performances:

Frank Silvera as Othello, Cyril Cusack as Iago, Anna Massey as Desdemona, and Celia Johnson as Emilia, Caedmon SRS 225 (stereo S–225), three records.

Paul Robeson as Othello, José Ferrer as Iago, and Uta Hagen as Desdemona, Columbia SL–153, three records.

Marlowe Society, London 4414, four records.

Sir Laurence Olivier as Othello, RCA Victor VDM–1000 (stereo VDS–1000), four records.

Excerpts:

William Marshall as Othello and Jay Robinson as Iago, Folkways 9618, two records.

Dublin Gate Theatre, Spoken Arts 783, one record.

Othello

WILLIAM SHAKESPEARE (c. 1604)
From Act V, Scene 2

SCENE:	For one man, two women
CHARACTERS:	Othello, a Moor in the service of the Venetian State Desdemona, wife of Othello Emilia, friend to Desdemona and wife of Iago
SETTING:	Desdemona's bedchamber in a castle on the island of Cyprus.
TIME:	An evening in the sixteenth century.
SITUATION:	See the preceding scene from *Othello* (p. 278), which occurs earlier in the play.
	Othello has fallen prey to Iago's scheme to convince him that Desdemona has been unfaithful. Although Desdemona is well aware of Othello's recent distraught behavior, she does not know that Iago has told Othello that she has been having an illicit affair with Othello's lieutenant, Cassio. An exceptionally jealous man, Othello is enraged by Iago's news and decides he must kill the wife he loves in order to defend his honor.

[A *bedchamber in the castle:* DESDEMONA *in bed asleep; a light burning. Enter* OTHELLO.]

OTHELLO   It is the cause, it is the cause, my soul,—
Let me not name it to you, you chaste stars!—
It is the cause. Yet I'll not shed her blood;
Nor scar that whiter skin of hers than snow,
And smooth as monumental alabaster.
Yet she must die, else she'll betray more men.
Put out the light, and then put out the light.
If I quench thee, thou flaming minister,
I can again thy former light restore,
Should I repent me: but once put out thy light,
Thou cunning'st pattern of excelling nature,
I know not where is that Promethean heat

That can thy light relume. When I have pluck'd the rose,
I cannot give it vital growth again,
It needs must wither: I'll smell it on the tree.
   (*kissing her*)
Ah, balmy breath, that doth almost persuade
Justice to break her sword! One more, one more.
Be thus when thou art dead, and I will kill thee,
And love thee after. One more, and this the last:
So sweet was ne'er so fatal. I must weep,
But they are cruel tears: this sorrow's heavenly;
It strikes where it doth love. She wakes.

DESDEMONA   Who's there? Othello?

OTHELLO   Aye, Desdemona.

DESDEMONA   Will you come to bed, my lord?

OTHELLO   Have you pray'd to-night, Desdemona?

DESDEMONA   Aye, my lord.

OTHELLO   If you bethink yourself of any crime
   Unreconciled as yet to heaven and grace,
   Solicit for it straight.

DESDEMONA   Alas, my lord, what do you mean by that?

OTHELLO   Well, do it, and be brief; I will walk by:
   I would not kill thy unprepared spirit;
   No; heaven forfend! I would not kill thy soul.

DESDEMONA   Talk you of killing?

OTHELLO   Aye, I do.

DESDEMONA   Then heaven
   Have mercy on me!

OTHELLO   Amen, with all my heart!

DESDEMONA   If you say so, I hope you will not kill me.

OTHELLO   Hum!

DESDEMONA   And yet I fear you; for you are fatal then
   When your eyes roll so: why I should fear I know not,
   Since guiltiness I know not; but yet I feel I fear.

OTHELLO   Think on thy sins.

DESDEMONA   They are loves I bear to you.

OTHELLO   Aye, and for that thou diest.

DESDEMONA   That death's unnatural that kills for loving.
   Alas, why gnaw you so your nether lip?
   Some bloody passion shakes your very frame:
   These are portents; but yet I hope, I hope,
   They do not point on me.

OTHELLO   Peace, and be still!

DESDEMONA   I will so. What's the matter?

OTHELLO   That handkerchief which I so loved and gave thee
   Thou gavest to Cassio.
DESDEMONA   No, by my life and soul!
   Send for the man, and ask him.
OTHELLO   Sweet soul, take heed,
   Take heed of perjury; thou art on thy deathbed.
DESDEMONA   Aye, but not yet to die.
OTHELLO   Yes, presently:
   Therefore confess thee freely of thy sin;
   For to deny each article with oath
   Cannot remove nor choke the strong conception
   That I do groan withal. Thou art to die.
DESDEMONA   Then Lord have mercy on me!
OTHELLO   I say, amen.
DESDEMONA   And have you mercy too! I never did
   Offend you in my life; never loved Cassio
   But with such general warranty of heaven
   As I might love; I never gave him token.
OTHELLO   By heaven, I saw my handkerchief in's hand.
   O perjured woman! thou dost stone my heart,
   And makest me call what I intend to do
   A murder, which I thought a sacrifice:
   I saw the handkerchief.
DESDEMONA   He found it then;
   I never gave it him: send for him hither;
   Let him confess a truth.
OTHELLO   He hath confess'd.
DESDEMONA   What, my lord?
OTHELLO   That he hath used thee.
DESDEMONA   How? unlawfully?
OTHELLO   Aye.
DESDEMONA   He will not say so.
OTHELLO   No, his mouth is stopp'd;
   Honest Iago hath ta'en order for 't.
DESDEMONA   O! my fear interprets: what, is he dead?
OTHELLO   Had all his hairs been lives, my great revenge
   Had stomach for them all.
DESDEMONA   Alas! he is betray'd and I undone.
OTHELLO   Out, strumpet! weep'st thou for him to my face?
DESDEMONA   O, banish me, my lord, but kill me not!
OTHELLO   Down, strumpet!
DESDEMONA   Kill me to-morrow: let me live to-night!
OTHELLO   Nay, if you strive,—

DESDEMONA   But half an hour!

OTHELLO   Being done, there is no pause.

DESDEMONA   But while I say one prayer!

OTHELLO   It is too late.

    [He stifles her.]

EMILIA   (*within*)

   My lord, my lord! what, ho! my lord, my lord!

OTHELLO   What noise is this? Not dead? not yet quite dead?

   I that am cruel am yet merciful;

   I would not have thee linger in thy pain:

   So, so.

EMILIA   (*within*)

     What, ho! my lord, my lord!

OTHELLO   Who's there?

EMILIA   (*within*)

   O, good my lord, I would speak a word with you!

OTHELLO   Yes: 'tis Emilia. By and by. She's dead.

   'Tis like she comes to speak of Cassio's death.—

   The noise was here. Ha! no more moving?

   Still as the grave. Shall she come in? were 't good?—

   I think she stirs again:—no. What's best to do?

   If she come in, she'll sure speak to my wife:

   My wife! my wife! what wife? I have no wife.

   O, insupportable! O heavy hour!

   Methinks it should be now a huge eclipse

   Of sun and moon, and that the affrighted globe

   Should yawn at alteration.

EMILIA   (*within*)

           I do beseech you

   That I may speak with you, O, good my lord!

OTHELLO   I had forgot thee: O, come in, Emilia:

   Soft; by and by. Let me the curtains draw.

   Where art thou?

     (*unlocks the door. Enter* EMILIA.)

          What's the matter with thee now?

EMILIA   O, my good lord, yonder's foul murders done!

OTHELLO   What, now?

EMILIA   But now, my lord.

OTHELLO   It is the very error of the moon;

   She comes more nearer earth than she was wont,

   And makes men mad.

EMILIA   Cassio, my lord, hath kill'd a young Venetian

   Call'd Roderigo.

OTHELLO   Roderigo kill'd!
   And Cassio kill'd!
EMILIA   No, Cassio is not kill'd.
OTHELLO   Not Cassio kill'd! then murder's out of tune,
   And sweet revenge grows harsh.
DESDEMONA   O, falsely, falsely murder'd!
EMILIA   Alas, what cry is that?
OTHELLO   That! what?
EMILIA   Out, and alas! that was my lady's voice.
   Help! help, ho! help! O lady, speak again!
   Sweet Desdemona! O sweet mistress, speak!
DESDEMONA   A guiltless death I die.
EMILIA   O, who hath done this deed?
DESDEMONA   Nobody; I myself. Farewell:
   Commend me to my kind lord: O, farewell!

      [*dies*]

OTHELLO   Why, how should she be murder'd?
EMILIA   Alas, who knows?
OTHELLO   You heard her say herself, it was not I.
EMILIA   She said so: I must needs report the truth.
OTHELLO   She's like a liar gone to burning hell:
   'Twas I that kill'd her.
EMILIA   O, the more angel she,
   And you the blacker devil!
OTHELLO   She turn'd to folly, and she was a whore.
EMILIA   Thou dost belie her, and thou art a devil.
OTHELLO   She was false as water.
EMILIA   Thou art rash as fire, to say
   That she was false: O, she was heavenly true!
OTHELLO   Cassio did top her; ask thy husband else.
   O, I were damn'd beneath all depth in hell,
   But that I did proceed upon just grounds
   To this extremity. Thy husband knew it all.
EMILIA   My husband!
OTHELLO   Thy husband.
EMILIA   That she was false to wedlock?
OTHELLO   Aye, with Cassio. Nay, had she been true,
   If heaven would make me such another world
   Of one entire and perfect chrysolite,
   I'd not have sold her for it.
EMILIA   My husband!
                  Aye, 'twas he that told me first:

An honest man he is, and hates the slime
That sticks on filthy deeds.

EMILIA My husband!

OTHELLO What needs this iteration, woman? I say thy husband.

EMILIA O mistress, villany hath made mocks with love!
My husband says that she was false!

OTHELLO He, woman;
I say thy husband: dost understand the word?
My friend, thy husband, honest, honest Iago.

EMILIA If he say so, may his pernicious soul
Rot half a grain a day! he lies to the heart:
She was too fond of her most filthy bargain.

OTHELLO Ha!

EMILIA Do thy worst:
This deed of thine is no more worthy heaven
Than thou wast worthy her.

OTHELLO Peace, you were best.

EMILIA Thou hast not half that power to do me harm
As I have to be hurt. O gull! O dolt!
As ignorant as dirt! thou hast done a deed—
I care not for thy sword: I'll make thee known,
Though I lost twenty lives.—Help! help, ho! help!
The Moor hath kill'd my mistress! Murder! murder!

For a list of recorded performances, see the preceding scene from *Othello* (p. 281).

Macbeth ————————————————————————————

WILLIAM SHAKESPEARE (c. 1606)
From Act II, Scene 2

SCENE: For one man, one woman

CHARACTERS: Macbeth, a Scottish nobleman, later King of Scotland
Lady Macbeth, his wife

SETTING: A courtyard of Macbeth's castle at Inverness, Scotland.

TIME: An evening in the eleventh century.

SITUATION: Macbeth, a Scottish nobleman, stands on the threshold of seizing the crown of Scotland. Earlier in the evening, King Duncan and his retinue paid a visit to Macbeth's castle. Duncan has now retired and is guarded by only two grooms. Macbeth and his wife have decided to take this opportunity to murder him. Lady Macbeth has drugged the drinks of Duncan's two guards so that Macbeth's path to Duncan's bedside will be clear. But despite their ambition and their preparations, the enormity of their deed weighs heavily on them. As the scene opens, Lady Macbeth enters the courtyard to wait for Macbeth who has just left for Duncan's bedchamber to commit the murder.

[*Enter* LADY MACBETH.]

LADY MACBETH   That which hath made them drunk hath made me bold;
What hath quench'd them hath given me fire. Hark! Peace!
It was the owl that shriek'd, the fatal bellman,
Which gives the stern'st good-night. He is about it:
The doors are open; and the surfeited grooms
Do mock their charge with snores: I have drugg'd their possets,
That death and nature do contend about them,
Whether they live or die.

MACBETH (*within*)

Who's there? what, ho!

LADY MACBETH   Alack, I am afraid they have awaked,
And 'tis not done. The attempt and not the deed
Confounds us. Hark! I laid their daggers ready;

He could not miss 'em. Had he not resembled
My father as he slept, I had done 't.

[*Enter* MACBETH.]

My husband!

MACBETH   I hav⌣ done the deed. Didst thou not hear a noise?

LADY MACBETH   I heard the owl scream and the crickets cry.
Did not you speak?

MACBETH   When?

LADY MACBETH   Now.

MACBETH   As I descended?

LADY MACBETH   Aye.

MACBETH   Hark!
Who lies i' the second chamber?

LADY MACBETH   Donalbain.

MACBETH   This is a sorry sight.
(*looking on his hands*)

LADY MACBETH   A foolish thought, to say a sorry sight.

MACBETH   There's one did laugh in's sleep, and one cried "Murder!"
That they did wake each other: I stood and heard them:
But they did say their prayers, and address'd them
Again to sleep.

LADY MACBETH   There are two lodged together.

MACBETH   One cried "God bless us!" and "Amen" the other;
As they had seen me with these hangman's hands.
Listening their fear, I could not say "Amen,"
When they did say "God bless us!"

LADY MACBETH   Consider it not so deeply.

MACBETH   But wherefore could not I pronounce "Amen"?
I had most need of blessing, and "Amen"
Stuck in my throat.

LADY MACBETH   These deeds must not be thought
After these ways; so, it will make us mad.

MACBETH   Methought I heard a voice cry "Sleep no more!
Macbeth does murder sleep," the innocent sleep,
Sleep that knits up the ravell'd sleave of care,
The death of each day's life, sore labour's bath,
Balm of hurt minds, great nature's second course,
Chief nourisher in life's feast—

LADY MACBETH   What do you mean?

MACBETH   Still it cried "Sleep no more!" to all the house:
"Glamis hath murder'd sleep, and therefore Cawdor
Shall sleep no more; Macbeth shall sleep no more."

LADY MACBETH   Who was it that thus cried? Why, worthy thane,
   You do unbend your noble strength, to think
   So brainsickly of things. Go get some water,
   And wash this filthy witness from your hand.
   Why did you bring these daggers from the place?
   They must lie there: go carry them; and smear
   The sleepy grooms with blood.
MACBETH   I'll go no more:
   I am afraid to think what I have done;
   Look on 't again I dare not.
LADY MACBETH   Infirm of purpose!
   Give me the daggers: the sleeping and the dead
   Are but as pictures: 'tis the eye of childhood
   That fears a painted devil. If he do bleed,
   I'll gild the faces of the grooms withal;
   For it must seem their guilt.
      [*Exit. Knocking within*]
MACBETH   Whence is that knocking?
   How is 't with me, when every noise appals me?
   What hands are here? Ha! they pluck out mine eyes.
   Will all great Neptune's ocean wash this blood
   Clean from my hand? No, this my hand will rather
   The multitudinous seas incarnadine,
   Making the green one red.
      [*Re-enter* LADY MACBETH.]
LADY MACBETH   My hands are of your colour; but I shame
   To wear a heart so white.
      (*knocking within*)
                     I hear a knocking
   At the south entry: retire we to our chamber:
   A little water clears us of this deed:
   How easy is it, then! Your constancy
   Hath left you unattended.
      (*knocking within*)
                     Hark! more knocking.
   Get on your nightgown, lest occasion call us,
   And show us to be watchers. Be not lost
   So poorly in your thoughts.
MACBETH   To know my deed, 'twere best not know myself.
      (*knocking within*)
   Wake Duncan with thy knocking! I would thou couldst!
      [*Exeunt.*]

Recorded Performances

Complete performances:

Anthony Quayle as Macbeth, Gwen ffrangcon-Davies as Lady Macbeth, and
Stanley Holloway as the Porter, Caedmon SRS 231 (stereo S–231), two
records.
Marlowe Society, London 4343 (stereo 1316), three records.
Sir Alec Guiness as Macbeth, RCA Victor LM–6010, two records.

Excerpts:

Anthony Quayle as Macbeth, Caedmon 1167, one record.
Dublin Gate Theatre, Spoken Arts 782, one record.

Measure for Measure

WILLIAM SHAKESPEARE (c. 1604)

From Act III, Scene 1

SCENE:	For one man, one woman
CHARACTERS:	Claudio, a young gentleman Isabella, his sister
SETTING:	A prison cell, Vienna.
TIME:	The sixteenth century.
SITUATION:	Angelo, appointed Lord Deputy of Vienna, has the power of life and death over its citizens. One of his first acts is to imprison Claudio who has gotten his betrothed Juliet with child. Under an old law that Angelo has revived, the offense is punishable by death. Claudio's sister Isabella goes to Angelo to plead for her brother's life, but Angelo, in a stern moral mood, at first rejects her plea. However, Isabella's beauty strikes the puritanical Angelo, and he begins to succumb to the very passion he is trying to punish in Claudio. In this scene, Isabella brings word of her interview to the imprisoned Claudio. Note particularly Claudio's change of attitude during the scene and Isabella's reaction when she realizes that her brother wants her to give up her chastity to Angelo in order to save him.

CLAUDIO   Now, sister, what's the comfort?
ISABELLA   Why,
　　As all comforts are; most good, most good indeed.
　　Lord Angelo, having affairs to heaven,
　　Intends you for his swift ambassador,
　　Where you shall be an everlasting leiger:
　　Therefore your best appointment make with speed;
　　To-morrow you set on.
CLAUDIO   Is there no remedy?
ISABELLA   None but such remedy as, to save a head,
　　To cleave a heart in twain.

CLAUDIO   But is there any?
ISABELLA   Yes, brother, you may live:
    There is a devilish mercy in the judge,
    If you'll implore it, that will free your life,
    But fetter you till death.
CLAUDIO   Perpetual durance?
ISABELLA   Aye, just; perpetual durance, a restraint,
    Though all the world's vastidity you had,
    To a determined scope.
CLAUDIO   But in what nature?
ISABELLA   In such a one as, you consenting to 't,
    Would bark your honour from that trunk you bear,
    And leave you naked.
CLAUDIO   Let me know the point.
ISABELLA   O, I do fear thee, Claudio; and I quake,
    Lest thou a feverous life shouldst entertain,
    And six or seven winters more respect
    Than a perpetual honour. Darest thou die?
    The sense of death is most in apprehension;
    And the poor beetle that we tread upon
    In corporal sufferance finds a pang as great
    As when a giant dies.
CLAUDIO   Why give you me this shame?
    Think you I can a resolution fetch
    From flowery tenderness? If I must die,
    I will encounter darkness as a bride,
    And hug it in mine arms.
ISABELLA   There spake my brother; there my father's grave
    Did utter forth a voice. Yes, thou must die:
    Thou art too noble to conserve a life
    In base appliances. This outward-sainted deputy,
    Whose settled visage and deliberate word
    Nips youth i' the head and follies doth emmew
    As falcon doth the fowl, is yet a devil;
    His filth within being cast, he would appear
    A pond as deep as hell.
CLAUDIO   The prenzie Angelo!
ISABELLA   O, 'tis the cunning livery of hell,
    The damned'st body to invest and cover
    In prenzie guards! Dost thou think, Claudio?
    If I would yield him my virginity,
    Thou mightst be freed.
CLAUDIO   O heavens! it cannot be.

ISABELLA   Yes, he would give 't thee, from this rank offence,
  So to offend him still. This night's the time
  That I should do what I abhor to name,
  Or else thou diest to-morrow.
CLAUDIO   Thou shalt not do 't.
ISABELLA   O, were it but my life,
  I'd throw it down for your deliverance
  As frankly as a pin.
CLAUDIO   Thanks, dear Isabel.
ISABELLA   Be ready, Claudio, for your death to-morrow.
CLAUDIO   Yes. Has he affections in him,
  That thus can make him bite the law by the nose,
  When he would force it? Sure, it is no sin;
  Or of the deadly seven it is the least.
ISABELLA   Which is the least?
CLAUDIO   If it were damnable, he being so wise,
  Why would he for the momentary trick
  Be perdurably fined? O Isabel!
ISABELLA   What says my brother?
CLAUDIO   Death is a fearful thing.
ISABELLA   And shamed life a hateful.
CLAUDIO   Aye, but to die, and go we know not where;
  To lie in cold obstruction and to rot;
  This sensible warm motion to become
  A kneaded clod; and the delighted spirit
  To bathe in fiery floods, or to reside
  In thrilling region of thick-ribbed ice;
  To be imprison'd in the viewless winds,
  And blown with restless violence round about
  The pendent world; or to be worse than worst
  Of those that lawless and incertain thought
  Imagine howling: 'tis too horrible!
  The weariest and most loathed worldly life
  That age, ache, penury and imprisonment
  Can lay on nature is a paradise
  To what we fear of death.
ISABELLA   Alas, alas!
CLAUDIO   Sweet sister, let me live:
  What sin you do to save a brother's life,
  Nature dispenses with the deed so far
  That it becomes a virtue.
ISABELLA   O you beast!
  O faithless coward! O dishonest wretch!

Wilt thou be made a man out of my vice?
Is 't not a kind of incest, to take life
From thine own sister's shame? What should I think?
Heaven shield my mother play'd my father fair!
For such a warped slip of wilderness
Ne'er issued from his blood. Take my defiance!
Die, perish! Might but my bending down
Reprieve thee from thy fate, it should proceed:
I'll pray a thousand prayers for thy death,
No word to save thee.

CLAUDIO   Nay, hear me, Isabel.

ISABELLA   O, fie, fie, fie!
Thy sin's not accidental, but a trade.
Mercy to thee would prove itself a bawd:
'Tis best that thou diest quickly.

CLAUDIO   O hear me, Isabella!

Recorded Performances

Complete performances:

Sir John Gielgud as Angelo, Sir Ralph Richardson as the Duke, and Margaret
    Leighton as Isabella, Caedmon SRS 204M (stereo S–204), three records.
Marlowe Society, London 4417, (stereo 1411), four records.

Julius Caesar

WILLIAM SHAKESPEARE (c. 1599)
From Act IV, Scene 3

SCENE: For two men

CHARACTERS: Marcus Brutus
              Caius Cassius

SETTING: The tent of Brutus, in an encampment near Sardis.

TIME: The Roman Empire, 42 B.C.

SITUATION: Following their assassination of Julius Caesar, Brutus and Cassius have joined forces in a military campaign against Antony and Octavius Caesar who seek to avenge Caesar's death. As the strain of the campaign increases, Brutus and Cassius grow more and more irritable. The dynamic and politically practical Cassius challenges Brutus' implication that he has been dishonest and involved in corruption. Unknown to Cassius, Brutus has recently received news of the death of his wife, Portia.

CASSIUS   That you have wrong'd me doth appear in this:
    You have condemn'd and noted Lucius Pella
    For taking bribes here of the Sardians;
    Wherein my letters, praying on his side,
    Because I knew the man, were slighted off.
BRUTUS   You wrong'd yourself to write in such a case.
CASSIUS   In such a time as this it is not meet
    That every nice offence should bear his comment.
BRUTUS   Let me tell you, Cassius, you yourself
    Are much condemn'd to have an itching palm;
    To sell and mart your offices for gold
    To undeservers.
CASSIUS   I an itching palm!
    You know that you are Brutus that speak this,
    Or, by the gods, this speech were else your last.
BRUTUS   The name of Cassius honours this corruption,
    And chastisement doth therefore hide his head.

CASSIUS Chastisement!

BRUTUS Remember March, the ides of March remember:
    Did not great Julius bleed for justice' sake?
    What villain touch'd his body that did stab,
    And not for justice? What, shall one of us,
    That struck the foremost man of all this world
    But for supporting robbers, shall we now
    Contaminate our fingers with base bribes,
    And sell the mighty space of our large honours
    For so much trash as may be grasped thus?
    I had rather be a dog, and bay the moon,
    Than such a Roman.

CASSIUS   Brutus, bait not me;
    I'll not endure it: you forget yourself,
    To hedge me in; I am a soldier, I,
    Older in practice, abler than yourself
    To make conditions.

BRUTUS   Go to; you are not, Cassius.

CASSIUS I am.

BRUTUS I say you are not.

CASSIUS Urge me no more, I shall forget myself;
    Have mind upon your health, tempt me no farther.

BRUTUS Away, slight man!

CASSIUS Is 't possible?

BRUTUS   Hear me, for I will speak.
    Must I give way and room to your rash choler?
    Shall I be frighted when a madman stares?

CASSIUS O ye gods, ye gods! must I endure all this?

BRUTUS All this! aye, more: fret till your proud heart break;
    Go show your slaves how choleric you are,
    And make your bondmen tremble. Must I budge?
    Must I observe you? Must I stand and crouch
    Under your testy humour? By the gods,
    You shall digest the venom of your spleen,
    Though it do split you; for, from this day forth,
    I'll use you for my mirth, yea, for my laughter,
    When you are waspish.

CASSIUS   Is it come to this?

BRUTUS You say you are a better soldier:
    Let it appear so; make your vaunting true,
    And it shall please me well: for mine own part,
    I shall be glad to learn of noble men.

CASSIUS You wrong me every way; you wrong me, Brutus;
    I said, an elder soldier, not a better:
    Did I say better?
BRUTUS   If you did, I care not.
CASSIUS When Caesar lived, he durst not thus have moved me.
BRUTUS Peace, peace! you durst not so have tempted him.
CASSIUS I durst not!
BRUTUS No.
CASSIUS What, durst not tempt him!
BRUTUS   For your life you durst not.
CASSIUS Do not presume too much upon my love;
    I may do that I shall be sorry for.
BRUTUS You have done that you should be sorry for.
    There is no terror, Cassius, in your threats,
    For I am arm'd so strong in honesty
    That they pass by me as the idle wind,
    Which I respect not. I did send to you
    For certain sums of gold, which you denied me:
    For I can raise no money by vile means:
    By heaven, I had rather coin my heart,
    And drop my blood for drachmas, than to wring
    From the hard hands of peasants their vile trash
    By any indirection: I did send
    To you for gold to pay my legions,
    Which you denied me: was that done like Cassius?
    Should I have answer'd Caius Cassius so?
    When Marcus Brutus grows so covetous,
    To lock such rascal counters from his friends,
    Be ready, gods, with all your thunderbolts;
    Dash him to pieces!
CASSIUS   I denied you not.
BRUTUS You did.
CASSIUS I did not: he was but a fool that brought
    My answer back. Brutus hath rived my heart:
    A friend should bear his friend's infirmities,
    But Brutus makes mine greater than they are.
BRUTUS I do not, till you practise them on me.
CASSIUS You love me not.
BRUTUS   I do not like your faults.
CASSIUS A friendly eye could never see such faults.
BRUTUS A flatterer's would not, though they do appear
    As huge as high Olympus.

CASSIUS Come, Antony, and young Octavius, come,
Revenge yourselves alone on Cassius,
For Cassius is aweary of the world;
Hated by one he loves; braved by his brother;
Check'd like a bondman; all his faults observed,
Set in a note-book, learn'd, and conn'd by rote,
To cast into my teeth. O, I could weep
My spirit from mine eyes! There is my dagger,
And here my naked breast; within, a heart
Dearer than Plutus' mine, richer than gold:
If that thou be'st a Roman, take it forth;
I, that denied thee gold, will give my heart:
Strike, as thou didst at Caesar; for, I know,
When thou didst hate him worst, thou lovedst him better
Than ever thou lovedst Cassius.
BRUTUS   Sheathe your dagger:
Be angry when you will, it shall have scope;
Do what you will, dishonour shall be humour.
O Cassius, you are yoked with a lamb
That carries anger as the flint bears fire;
Who, much enforced, shows a hasty spark,
And straight is cold again.
CASSIUS   Hath Cassius lived
To be but mirth and laughter to his Brutus,
When grief, and blood ill-temper'd, vexeth him?
BRUTUS When I spoke that, I was ill-temper'd too.
CASSIUS Do you confess so much? Give me your hand.
BRUTUS And my heart too.
CASSIUS   O Brutus!
BRUTUS   What's the matter?
CASSIUS Have not you love enough to bear with me,
When that rash humour which my mother gave me
Makes me forgetful?
BRUTUS   Yes, Cassius; and, from henceforth,
When you are over-earnest with your Brutus,
He'll think your mother chides, and leave you so.

Recorded Performances

Complete performances:

Sir Ralph Richardson as Julius Caesar, Anthony Quayle as Brutus, John Mills as Cassius, Alan Bates as Antony, and Michael Gwynn as Casca, Caedmon SRS 230 (stereo S–230), three records.
Marlowe Society, London 4334, three records.
Dublin Gate Theatre, Spoken Word A–15, three records.

Excerpts:

Dublin Gate Theatre, Spoken Arts 809, one record.

The Taming of the Shrew

WILLIAM SHAKESPEARE (c. 1593)
From Act II, Scene 1

SCENE:	For one man, one woman
CHARACTERS:	Petruchio, a rich gentleman from Verona Katharina, a shrewish young woman, daughter of Baptista
SETTING:	A room in Baptista's house in Padua, Italy.
TIME:	The sixteenth century.
SITUATION:	Baptista, an elderly gentleman of Padua, has two daughters of marriageable age. The older of the two, Katharina, is a shrew, and no suitor has been able to tame her. More than one suitor has felt the sharpness of her tongue and nails. A young gentleman from Verona, Petruchio, has arrived in Padua in order "haply to wive and thrive as best I may." After settling financial arrangements with Baptista, Petruchio sets out to win Katharina for his wife. He finds it no easy task, but he turns out to be a bit more than the shrewish young woman bargained for. This is a lusty scene, both verbally *and* physically, as each tries to get the upper hand.

PETRUCHIO I will attend her here,
And woo her with some spirit when she comes.
Say that she rail; why then I'll tell her plain
She sings as sweetly as a nightingale:
Say that she frown; I'll say she looks as clear
As morning roses newly wash'd with dew:
Say she be mute and will not speak a word;
Then I'll commend her volubility,
And say she uttereth piercing eloquence:
If she do bid me pack, I'll give her thanks,
As though she bid me stay by her a week:
If she deny to wed, I'll crave the day
When I shall ask the banns and when be married.
But here she comes; and now, Petruchio, speak.
   (*Enter* KATHARINA.)

Good morrow, Kate; for that's your name, I hear.

KATHARINA Well have you heard, but something hard of hearing:
They call me Katharine that do talk of me.

PETRUCHIO You lie, in faith; for you are call'd plain Kate,
And bonny Kate and sometimes Kate the curst;
But Kate, the prettiest Kate in Christendom,
Kate of Kate Hall, my super-dainty Kate,
For daintiest are all Kates, and therefore, Kate.
Take this of me, Kate of my consolation;
Hearing thy mildness praised in every town,
Thy virtues spoke of, and thy beauty sounded,
Yet not so deeply as to thee belongs,
Myself am moved to woo thee for my wife.

KATHARINA Moved! in good time: let him that moved you hither
Remove you hence: I knew you at the first
You were a moveable.

PETRUCHIO   Why, what's a moveable?

KATHARINA A join'd-stool.

PETRUCHIO   Thou hast hit it: come, sit on me.

KATHARINA Asses are made to bear, and so are you.

PETRUCHIO Women are made to bear, and so are you.

KATHARINA No such jade as you, if me you mean.

PETRUCHIO Alas! good Kate, I will not burden thee;
For, knowing thee to be but young and light—

KATHARINA Too light for such a swain as you to catch;
And yet as heavy as my weight should be.

PETRUCHIO Should be! should—buzz!

KATHARINA   Well ta'en, and like a buzzard.

PETRUCHIO O slow-wing'd turtle! shall a buzzard take thee?

KATHARINA Aye, for a turtle, as he takes a buzzard.

PETRUCHIO Come, come, you wasp; i' faith, you are too angry.

KATHARINA If I be waspish, best beware my sting.

PETRUCHIO My remedy is then, to pluck it out.

KATHARINA Aye, if the fool could find it where it lies.

PETRUCHIO Who knows not where a wasp does wear his sting?
In his tail.

KATHARINA In his tongue.

PETRUCHIO Whose tongue?

KATHARINA Yours, if you talk of tails: and so farewell.

PETRUCHIO What, with my tongue in your tail? Nay, come again,
Good Kate; I am a gentleman.

KATHARINA   That I'll try.

[*She strikes him.*]

PETRUCHIO   I swear I'll cuff you, if you strike again.
KATHARINA   So may you lose your arms:
  If you strike me, you are no gentleman;
  And if no gentleman, why then no arms.
PETRUCHIO   A herald, Kate? O, put me in thy books.
KATHARINA   What is your crest? a coxcomb?
PETRUCHIO   A combless cock, so Kate will be my hen.
KATHARINA   No cock of mine; you crow too like a craven.
PETRUCHIO   Nay, come, Kate, come; you must not look so sour.
KATHARINA   It is my fashion, when I see a crab.
PETRUCHIO   Why, here's no crab; and therefore look not sour.
KATHARINA   There is, there is.
PETRUCHIO   Then show it me.
KATHARINA   Had I a glass, I would.
PETRUCHIO   What, you mean my face?
KATHARINA   Well aim'd of such a young one.
PETRUCHIO   Now, by Saint George, I am too young for you.
KATHARINA   Yet you are wither'd.
PETRUCHIO   'Tis with cares.
KATHARINA   I care not.
PETRUCHIO   Nay, hear you, Kate: in sooth you scape not so.
KATHARINA   I chafe you, if I tarry: let me go.
PETRUCHIO   No, not a whit: I find you passing gentle.
  'Twas told me you were rough and coy and sullen,
  And now I find report a very liar;
  For thou art pleasant, gamesome, passing courteous,
  But slow in speech, yet sweet as spring-time flowers:
  Thou canst not frown, thou canst not look askance,
  Nor bite the lip, as angry wenches will,
  Nor hast thou pleasure to be cross in talk,
  But thou with mildness entertain'st thy wooers,
  With gentle conference, soft and affable.
  Why does the world report that Kate doth limp?
  O slanderous world! Kate like the hazel-twig
  Is straight and slender and as brown in hue
  As hazel nuts and sweeter than the kernels.
  O, let me see thee walk: thou dost not halt.
KATHARINA   Go, fool, and whom thou keep'st command.
PETRUCHIO   Did ever Dian so become a grove
  As Kate this chamber with her princely gait?
  O, be thou Dian, and let her be Kate;
  And then let Kate be chaste and Dian sportful!
KATHARINA   Where did you study all this goodly speech?

PETRUCHIO It is extempore, from my mother-wit.

KATHARINA A witty mother! witless else her son.

PETRUCHIO Am I not wise?

KATHARINA Yes; keep you warm.

PETRUCHIO Marry, so I mean, sweet Katharine, in thy bed:
And therefore, setting all this chat aside,
Thus in plain terms: your father hath consented
That you shall be my wife; your dowry 'greed on;
And, will you, nill you, I will marry you.
Now, Kate, I am a husband for your turn;
For, by this light, whereby I see thy beauty,
Thy beauty, that doth make me like thee well,
Thou must be married to no man but me;
For I am he am born to tame you, Kate,
And bring you from a wild Kate to a Kate
Conformable as other household Kates.
Here comes your father: never make denial;
I must and will have Katharine to my wife.

Recorded Performances

Complete performances:

Trevor Howard as Petruchio and Margaret Leighton as Kate, Caedmon SRS
    211 (stereo S–211), two records.
Marlowe Society, London 4367 (stereo 1367), three records.
Dublin Gate Theatre, Spoken Word A–7, three records.

Excerpts:

Lewis Casson as Petruchio, Spoken Arts 884, one record.

King Lear

WILLIAM SHAKESPEARE (c. 1605)
From Act IV, Scene 6

SCENE: For two men

CHARACTERS: Earl of Gloucester
Edgar, his son

SETTING: The fields near Dover.

TIME: Ancient Britain.

SITUATION: One of the most overwhelming plays in world literature, *King Lear* deals with man's inhumanity to man, both in its main plot —the agony caused Lear by his daughters—and its subplot, which concerns the betrayal of the Earl of Gloucester by his illegitimate son Edmund. Exposed by Edmund, Gloucester is blinded as punishment for giving aid to the outcast Lear. Edmund makes Gloucester suspicious of his other son, Edgar, and Gloucester turns him away. Disguised as a beggar, Edgar wanders the countryside alone until he comes one day by chance upon his blind father. Gloucester asks the stranger to take him to a high cliff where with a leap he can end his misery. Edgar leads him instead to the fields near Dover.

[*Enter* GLOUCESTER, *and* EDGAR *dressed like a peasant.*]

GLOUCESTER When shall we come to the top of that same hill?
EDGAR You do climb up it now: look, how we labour.
GLOUCESTER Methinks the ground is even.
EDGAR   Horrible steep.
    Hark, do you hear the sea?
GLOUCESTER   No, truly.
EDGAR Why, then, your other senses grow imperfect
    By your eyes' anguish.
GLOUCESTER   So may it be, indeed:
    Methinks thy voice is alter'd; and thou speak'st
    In better phrase and matter than thou didst.

EDGAR You're much deceived: in nothing am I changed
   But in my garments.
GLOUCESTER   Methinks you're better spoken.
EDGAR Come on, sir; here's the place: stand still. How fearful
   And dizzy 'tis, to cast one's eyes so low!
   The crows and choughs that wing the midway air
   Show scarce so gross as beetles: half way down
   Hangs one that gathers samphire, dreadful trade!
   Methinks he seems no bigger than his head:
   The fisherman, that walk upon the beach,
   Appear like mice; and yond tall anchoring bark,
   Diminish'd to her cock; her cock, a buoy
   Almost too small for sight: the murmuring surge,
   That on the unnumber'd idle pebbles chafes,
   Cannot be heard so high. I'll look no more;
   Lest my brain turn, and the deficient sight
   Topple down headlong.
GLOUCESTER   Set me where you stand.
EDGAR Give me your hand: you are now within a foot
   Of the extreme verge: for all beneath the moon
   Would I not leap upright.
GLOUCESTER   Let go my hand.
   Here, friend, 's another purse; in it a jewel
   Well worth a poor man's taking: fairies and gods
   Prosper it with thee! Go thou farther off;
   Bid me farewell, and let me hear thee going.
EDGAR Now fare you well, good sir.
GLOUCESTER   With all my heart.
EDGAR Why I do trifle thus with his despair
   Is done to cure it.
GLOUCESTER (kneeling)
           O you mighty gods!
   This world I do renounce, and in your sights,
   Shake patiently my great affliction off:
   If I could bear it longer, and not fall
   To quarrel with your great opposeless wills,
   My snuff and loathed part of nature should
   Burn itself out. If Edgar live, O, bless him!
   Now, fellow, fare thee well.
      [He falls forward.]
EDGAR   Gone, sir: farewell.
   And yet I know not how conceit may rob

The treasury of life, when life itself
Yields to the theft: had he been where he thought,
By this, had thought been past. Alive or dead?
Ho, you sir! friend! Hear you, sir! speak!
Thus might he pass indeed: yet he revives.
What are you, sir?
GLOUCESTER   Away, and let me die.
EDGAR   Hadst thou been aught but gossamer, feathers, air,
So many fathom down precipitating,
Thou'dst shiver'd like an egg: but thou dost breathe;
Hast heavy substance; bleed'st not; speak'st; art sound.
Ten masts at each make not the altitude
Which thou hast perpendicularly fell:
Thy life's a miracle. Speak yet again.
GLOUCESTER   But have I fall'n, or no?
EDGAR   From the dread summit of this chalky bourn.
Look up a-height; the shrill-gorged lark so far
Cannot be seen or heard: do but look up.
GLOUCESTER   Alack, I have no eyes.
Is wretchedness deprived that benefit,
To end itself by death? 'Twas yet some comfort,
When misery could beguile the tyrant's rage,
And frustrate his proud will.
EDGAR   Give me your arm:
Up: so. How is 't? Feel you your legs? You stand.
GLOUCESTER   Too well, too well.
EDGAR   This is above all strangeness.
Upon the crown o' the cliff, what thing was that
Which parted from you?
GLOUCESTER   A poor unfortunate beggar.
EDGAR   As I stood here below, methought his eyes
Were two full moons; he had a thousand noses,
Horns whelk'd and waved like the enridge sea:
It was some fiend; therefore, thou happy father,
Think that the clearest gods, who make them honours
Of men's impossibilities, have preserved thee.
GLOUCESTER   I do remember now: henceforth I'll bear
Affliction till it do cry out itself
"Enough, enough," and die. That thing you speak of,
I took it for a man; often 'twould say
"The fiend, the fiend": he led me to that place.
EDGAR   Bear free and patient thoughts.

Recorded Performances

Complete performances:

Paul Scofield as King Lear, Cyril Cusack as the Earl of Gloucester, John Stride as Edmund, Pamela Brown as Goneril, Rachel Roberts as Regan, and Ann Gell as Cordelia, Caedmon SRS 233 (stereo S–233), four records.
Marlowe Society, London 4423 (stereo 1414), four records.
Dublin Gate Theatre, Spoken Word A–9, four records.

Excerpts:

Dublin Gate Theatre, Spoken Arts 784, one record.

Romeo and Juliet

WILLIAM SHAKESPEARE (c. 1595)
From Act III, Scene 2

SCENE: For two women

CHARACTERS: Juliet, daughter of the house of Capulet
Nurse to Juliet

SETTING: The Capulet orchard, Verona.

TIME: A morning in the fourteenth century.

SITUATION: This scene from *Romeo and Juliet* follows the duel in the public square of Verona, where, while avenging his friend Mercutio, Romeo killed Tybalt, kinsman to Juliet. At the opening of this scene, the ecstatic Juliet is waiting for evening when Romeo will secretly join her. Juliet has sent her nurse to find ropes so that Romeo can climb to her room. The Nurse enters with the ropes and with news of the duel. Her excitement, however, makes it difficult for Juliet to understand exactly what has happened.

[*Enter* NURSE, *with cords.*]

JULIET   Now, nurse, what news? What hast thou there? the cords
That Romeo did thee fetch?
NURSE   Aye, aye, the cords.

[*throws them down*]

JULIET   Aye me! what news? why dost thou wring thy hands?
NURSE   Ah, well-a-day! he's dead, he's dead, he's dead!
We are undone, lady, we are undone!
Alack the day! he's gone, he's kill'd, he's dead!
JULIET   Can heaven be so envious?
NURSE   Romeo can,
Though heaven cannot: O Romeo, Romeo!
Who ever would have thought it? Romeo!
JULIET   What devil art thou, that dost torment me thus?
This torture should be roar'd in dismal hell.

Hath Romeo slain himself? say thou but "I,"
And that bare vowel "I" shall poison more
Than the death-darting eye of cockatrice:
I am not I, if there be such an I;
Or those eyes shut, that make the answer "I."
If he be slain, say "I"; or if not, no:
Brief sounds determine of my weal or woe.

NURSE   I saw the wound, I saw it with mine eyes,—
God save the mark!—here on his manly breast:
A piteous corse, a bloody piteous corse;
Pale, pale as ashes, all bedaub'd in blood,
All in gore-blood; I swounded at the sight.

JULIET   O, break, my heart! poor bankrupt, break at once!
To prison, eyes, ne'er look on liberty!
Vile earth, to earth resign; and motion here;
And thou and Romeo press one heavy bier!

NURSE   O Tybalt, Tybalt, the best friend I had!
O courteous Tybalt! honest gentleman!
That ever I should live to see thee dead!

JULIET   What storm is this that blows so contrary?
Is Romeo slaughter'd, and is Tybalt dead?
My dear-loved cousin, and my dearer lord?
Then, dreadful trumpet, sound the general doom!
For who is living if those two are gone?

NURSE   Tybalt is gone, and Romeo banished;
Romeo that kill'd him, he is banished.

JULIET   O God! did Romeo's hand shed Tybalt's blood?

NURSE   It did, it did; alas the day, it did!

JULIET   O serpent heart, hid with a flowering face!
Did ever dragon keep so fair a cave?
Beautiful tyrant! fiend angelical!
Dove-feather'd raven! wolvish-ravening lamb!
Despised substance of divinest show!
Just opposite to what thou justly seem'st,
A damned saint, and honourable villain!
O nature, what hadst thou to do in hell,
When thou didst bower the spirit of fiend
In mortal paradise of such sweet flesh?
Was ever book containing such vile matter
So fairly bound?   O, that deceit should dwell
In such a gorgeous palace!

NURSE   There's no trust,
No faith, no honesty in men; all perjured,

All forsworn, all naught, all dissemblers.
Ah, where's my man? give me some aqua vitae:
These griefs, these woes, these sorrows make me old.
Shame come to Romeo!

JULIET   Blister'd be thy tongue
For such a wish! he was not born to shame:
Upon his brow shame is ashamed to sit;
For 'tis a throne where honour may be crown'd
Sole monarch of the universal earth.
O, what a beast was I to chide at him!

NURSE   Will you speak well of him that kill'd your cousin?

JULIET   Shall I speak ill of him that is my husband?
Ah, poor my lord, what tongue shall smooth thy name,
When I, thy three-hours wife, have mangled it?
But, wherefore, villain, didst thou kill my cousin?
That villain cousin would have kill'd my husband:
Back, foolish tears, back to your native spring;
Your tributary drops belong to woe,
Which you, mistaking, offer up to joy.
My husband lives, that Tybalt would have slain;
And Tybalt's dead, that would have slain my husband:
All this is comfort; wherefore weep I then?
Some word there was, worser than Tybalt's death,
That murder'd me: I would forget it fain;
But, O, it presses to my memory,
Like damned guilty deeds to sinners' minds:
"Tybalt is dead, and Romeo—banished";
That "banished," that one word "banished,"
Hath slain ten thousand Tybalts. Tybalt's death
Was woe enough, if it had ended there:
Or, if sour woe delights in fellowship
And needly will be rank'd with other griefs,
Why follow'd not, when she said "Tybalt's dead,"
Thy father, or thy mother, nay, or both,
Which modern lamentation might have moved?
But with a rearward following Tybalt's death,
"Romeo is banished," to speak that word,
Is father, mother, Tybalt, Romeo, Juliet,
All slain, all dead. "Romeo is banished!"
There is no end, no limit, measure, bound,
In that word's death; no words can that woe sound.
Where is my father, and my mother, nurse?

NURSE   Weeping and wailing over Tybalt's corse:

Will you go to them? I will bring you thither.

JULIET Wash they his wounds with tears: mine shall be spent,
When theirs are dry, for Romeo's banishment.
Take up those cords: poor ropes, you are beguiled,
Both you and I; for Romeo is exiled:
He made you for a highway to my bed;
But I, a maid, die maiden-widowed.
Come, cords, come nurse; I'll to my wedding bed;
And death, not Romeo, take my maidenhead!

NURSE Hie to your chamber: I'll find Romeo
To comfort you: I wot well where he is.
Hark ye, your Romeo will be here at night:
I'll to him; he is hid at Laurence' cell.

JULIET O, find him! give this ring to my true knight,
And bid him come to take his last farewell.

Recorded Performances

Complete performances:

Claire Bloom as Juliet, Albert Finney as Romeo, and Dame Edith Evans as the
Nurse, Caedmon SRS 228 (stereo S–228), three records.
Marlowe Society, London 4419 (stereo 1407), four records.
Dublin Gate Theatre, Spoken Word A–16, four records.

Excerpts:

London Swan Theatre Players, Spoken Arts 812, one record.

SHAKESPEARE AND THE ACTOR: A Selective Bibliography

Joseph, Bertram L. *Acting Shakespeare*. New York: Theatre Arts, 1960.

————. "A Style for Shakespeare." *Educational Theatre Journal*. Vol. 7, No. 3 (October, 1955), pp. 212–16.

Kernodle, George R. "Basic Problems in Reading Shakespeare." *Quarterly Journal of Speech*, Vol. 35, No. 1 (February, 1949), pp. 36–43.

Knight, G. Wilson. *Principles of Shakespearian Production*. Harmondsworth, England: Penguin, 1949.

LePage, R. B. "The Dramatic Delivery of Shakespeare's Verse." *English Studies*, Vol. 32, No. 2 (1951), pp. 63–68.

Watkins, Ronald. *On Producing Shakespeare*. New York: Norton, 1950.

Webster, Margaret. *Shakespeare Without Tears*. New York: Fawcett, 1957.

Reference Key

TO PLAYS IN ANTHOLOGIES

THE anthologies listed below contain the complete plays from which the exercise scenes in this book have been taken. The numbers preceding the anthology titles correspond to the reference numbers given at the end of each scene.

1   Allison, Alexander W., Arthur J. Carr, and Arthur M. Eastman, eds. *Masterpieces of the Drama.* New York: Macmillan, 1957.

2   Ashton, John William, ed. *Types of English Drama.* New York: Macmillan, 1940.

3   Barnet, Sylvan, Morton Berman, and William Burto, eds. *Eight Great Comedies.* New York: New American Library, 1958.

4   ———. *The Genius of the Later English Theater.* New York: New American Library, 1962.

5   Bentley, Eric, ed. *The Play: A Critical Anthology.* New York: Prentice-Hall, 1951.

6   Bentley, Gerald Eades, ed. *The Development of English Drama.* New York: Appleton-Century-Crofts, 1950.

7   Bierman, Judah, James Hart, and Stanley Johnson, eds. *The Dramatic Experience.* Englewood Cliffs, N.J.: Prentice-Hall, 1958.

8   Blair, Walter, and John Gerber, eds. *Repertory.* Chicago: Scott, Foresman, 1960.

9   Block, Haskell M., and Robert G. Shedd, eds. *Masters of Modern Drama.* New York: Random House, 1962.

10 Bloomfield, Morton W., and Robert C. Elliott, eds. *Ten Plays.* New York: Rinehart, 1951.

11 Brooks, Cleanth, and Robert B. Heilman. *Understanding Drama: Twelve Plays.* New York: Holt, 1948.

12 Brooks, Cleanth, John Thibaut Purser, and Robert Penn Warren, eds. *An Approach to Literature.* Rev. ed. New York: Crofts, 1939.

13 Buck, Philo M., Jr., and Hazel Alberson, eds. *An Anthology of World Literature.* Rev. ed. New York: Macmillan, 1940.

14 Carpenter, Bruce, ed. *A Book of Dramas.* Rev. ed. New York: Prentice-Hall, 1949.

15 Cartmell, Van H., and Bennett A. Cerf, eds. *Famous Plays of Crime and Detection.* Philadelphia: Blakiston, 1946.

16 Cassidy, Frederic G., ed. *Modern American Plays*. New York: Longmans, Green, 1949.

17 Cerf, Bennett A., ed. *Six American Plays for Today*. New York: Modern Library, 1961.

18 Cerf, Bennett A., and Van H. Cartmell, eds. *Sixteen Famous American Plays*. New York: Modern Library, 1941.

19 ———. *Sixteen Famous British Plays*. New York: Modern Library, 1942.

20 ———. *Sixteen Famous European Plays*. New York: Modern Library, 1943.

21 ———. *S.R.O.: The Most Successful Plays in the History of the American Stage*. New York: Doubleday, Doran, 1944.

22 Chandler, Frank Wadleigh, and Richard Albert Cordell, eds. *Twentieth Century Plays*. Rev. ed. New York: Nelson, 1939.

23 ———. *Twentieth Century Plays—British*. Rev. and enl. ed. New York: Nelson, 1941.

24 Clayes, Stanley A., and David G. Spencer, eds. *Contemporary Drama*. New York: Scribner's, 1962.

25 Clurman, Harold, ed. *Famous American Plays of the 1930's*. New York: Dell, 1959.

26 Cooper, Charles W. *Preface to Drama*. New York: Ronald Press, 1955.

27 Cordell, Richard Albert, ed. *Twentieth Century Plays—American*. 3rd ed. New York: Ronald Press, 1947.

28 Corrigan, Robert W. *The Modern Theatre*. New York: Macmillan, 1964.

29 *The Critics' Prize Plays*. Introduction by George Jean Nathan. Cleveland: World, 1945.

30 Cubeta, Paul M., ed. *Modern Drama for Analysis*. Rev. ed. New York: Dryden, 1955.

31 ———. *Modern Drama for Analysis*. 3rd ed. New York: Holt, Rinehart and Winston, 1962.

32 Durham, Willard Higley, and John W. Dodds, eds. *British and American Plays 1830–1945*. New York: Oxford University Press, 1947.

33 *Eighteenth-century Plays*. Introduction by Ricardo Quintana. New York: Modern Library, 1952.

34 *Four Great Comedies of the Restoration and Eighteenth Century*. Introduction by Brooks Atkinson. New York: Bantam, 1958.

35 *Four Modern French Comedies*. Introduction by Wallace Fowlie. New York: Capricorn, 1960.

36 Fulton, Albert Rondthaler, ed. *Drama and Theatre*. New York: Holt, 1946.

37   Gassner, John, ed. *Best American Plays: Second Series 1939–1946.* New York: Crown, 1947.

38   ———. *Best American Plays: Third Series 1945–1951.* New York: Crown, 1952.

39   ———. *Best American Plays: Fourth Series 1951–1957.* New York: Crown, 1958.

40   ———. *Best American Plays: Fifth Series 1958–1963.* New York: Crown, 1964.

41   ———. *Best American Plays: Supplementary Volume 1918–1958.* New York: Crown, 1961.

42   ———. *A Treasury of the Theatre.* Pt. 2, *From Ibsen to Ionesco.* 3rd ed. New York: Holt, Rinehart and Winston, 1960.

43   ———. *Twenty Best European Plays on the American Stage.* New York: Crown, 1957.

44   ———. *Twenty Best Plays of the Modern American Theatre.* New York: Crown, 1939.

45   Gassner, John, and Morris Sweetkind, eds. *Introducing the Drama.* New York: Holt, Rinehart and Winston, 1963.

46   Gaver, Jack, ed. *Critics' Choice; New York Drama Critics' Circle Prize Plays 1935–1955.* New York: Hawthorn, 1955.

47   Goodman, Randolph, ed. *Drama on Stage.* New York: Holt, Rinehart and Winston, 1961.

48   Gosse, Edmund William, ed. *Restoration Plays from Dryden to Farquhar.* London: Dent, 1932.

49   Hartley, Lodwick Charles, and Arthur Irish Ladu, eds. *Patterns in Modern Drama.* New York: Prentice-Hall, 1948.

50   Hatcher, Harlan Henthorne, ed. *Modern American Dramas.* New ed. New York: Harcourt, Brace & World, 1949.

51   ———. *Modern Continental Dramas.* New York: Harcourt, Brace & World, 1941.

52   ———. *A Modern Repertory.* New York: Harcourt, Brace & World, 1953.

53   Huberman, Edward, and Robert R. Raymo, eds. *Angles of Vision.* Boston: Houghton Mifflin, 1962.

54   Kronenberger, Louis, ed. *Cavalcade of Comedy.* New York: Simon and Schuster, 1953.

55   MacMillan, Dougald, and Howard Mumford Jones, eds. *Plays of the Restoration and Eighteenth Century.* 2nd ed. New York: Holt, 1938.

56   McNamee, Maurine B., James E. Cronin, and Joseph A. Rogers, eds. *Literary Types and Themes.* New York: Rinehart, 1960.

57   Mersand, Joseph E., ed. *Three Comedies of American Family Life.* New York: Washington Square Press, 1961.

58 Miller, Jordan Yale, ed. *American Dramatic Literature.* New York: McGraw-Hill, 1961.

59 Morgan, Arthur Eustace, ed. *English Plays 1660–1820.* New York: Harper, 1935.

60 Moses, Montrose Jonas, ed. *British Plays from the Restoration to 1820.* 2 vols. Boston: Little, Brown, 1929.

61 Nettleton, George Henry, and Arthur Ellicott Case, eds. *British Dramatists from Dryden to Sheridan.* Boston: Houghton Mifflin, 1939.

62 *New Voices in the American Theatre.* Forward by Brooks Atkinson. New York: Modern Library, 1955.

63 Reinert, Otto, ed. *Drama: An Introductory Anthology.* Boston: Little, Brown, 1961.

64 ———. *Modern Drama: Nine Plays.* Boston: Little, Brown, 1961.

65 *Restoration Plays.* Introduction by Brice Harris. New York: Modern Library, 1955.

66 *Six Great Modern Plays.* New York: Dell, 1956.

67 *Six Modern American Plays.* Introduction by Allan G. Halline. New York: Modern Library, 1951.

68 Sper, Felix, ed. *Favorite Modern Plays.* New York: Globe, 1953.

69 Steinberg, M. W., ed. *Aspects of Modern Drama.* New York: Henry Holt, 1960.

70 Strasberg, Lee, ed. *Famous American Plays of the 1950's.* New York: Dell, 1962.

71 *The Theatre Guild Anthology.* New York: Random House, 1936.

72 Thomas, Russell Brown, ed. *Plays and the Theatre.* Boston: Little, Brown, 1937.

73 Trewin, J. C., ed. *Plays of the Year.* London: Paul Elek, 1949.

74 Tucker, S. Marion, and Alan S. Downer, eds. *Twenty-five Modern Plays.* 3rd ed. New York: Harper, 1953.

75 Tupper, Frederick, and James Waddell Tupper, eds. *Representative English Dramas from Dryden to Sheridan.* New and enl. ed. New York: Oxford University Press, 1934.

76 *Twelve Famous Plays of the Restoration and Eighteenth Century.* New York: Modern Library, 1933.

77 Warnock, Robert, ed. *Representative Modern Plays: American.* Chicago: Scott, Foresman, 1952.

78 ———. *Representative Modern Plays: British.* Chicago: Scott, Foresman, 1953.

79 Watson, Ernest Bradlee, and Benfield Pressey, eds. *Contemporary Drama: Eleven Plays.* New York: Scribner's, 1956.

80 ———. *Contemporary Drama: European, English and Irish, American Plays.* New York: Scribner's, 1941.

81 ———. *Contemporary Drama: Fifteen Plays.* New York: Scribner's, 1959.

82 Whitman, Charles Huntington, ed. *Representative Modern Dramas.* New York: Macmillan, 1936.

83 Wilson, John Harold, ed. *Six Restoration Plays.* Boston: Houghton Mifflin, 1959.

C 9
D 0
E 1
F 2
G 3
H 4
I 5
J 6